ENGLISH ESTATES OF AMERICAN SETTLERS

American Wills and Administrations in the Prerogative Court of Canterbury, 1800-1858

By Peter Wilson Coldham

CLEARFIELD

ENGLISH ESTATES OF
AMERICAN SETTLERS: 1800-1858

INTRODUCTION

The appearance of this third volume of abstracts from the Probate and Administration Act Books of the Prerogative Court of Canterbury (PCC) marks the completion of a series which now embraces the period from the founding of the first American plantations to the eve of the Civil War.[1]

In February 1858 responsibility for administration of probate matters in England passed from ecclesiastical and private hands to the civil authority, and for the first time centralised records, adequately indexed, were instituted for all testators and intestates.[2] The preamble to the Act of Parliament which set up the machinery for the change reads: "It is expedient that all jurisdiction in relation to the grant and revocation of probates of wills and letters of administration should be exercised in the name of Her Majesty by one Court. . . . The jurisdiction and authority of all ecclesiastical, royal peculiar, peculiar, manorial, and other courts and persons in England . . . shall . . . absolutely cease." [3]

In order to prepare this volume, the following series of PCC Act Books over the relevant period were consulted[4]: Administrations (PROB 6), Limited Administrations (PROB 7), Probates (PROB 8), and Limited Probates (PROB 9). Grants in respect of persons dying abroad with estate or credits in England were recorded in the so-called *Register's* sections of the Act Books, and it is these sections only that have been examined. It should be noted, however, that occasional entries are to be found in other sections of the Act Books, whether by design or accident, recording the deaths abroad of English citizens. The introductory notes to the 1700-1799 volume should be read for a more detailed explanation of the sources used and of the supplementary sources available to which the abstracts provide a key.

Since publication of the two earlier volumes in this trilogy, a number of critics have suggested the need for a place index in addition to the name index already provided. An attempt has now been made to satisfy that demand. The second index is presented with some reservation, if only because the probate clerks' acquaintance with geography remained as sketchy during the nineteenth century as it had been throughout the eighteenth and seventeenth. Phonetic spelling or faulty copying produced such delicious cryptograms as *Kanion* for *Canyon, Milwankel* for *Milwaukee,* and *Sinoinattic* for *Cincinnati.*[5]

Peter Wilson Coldham
Purley, Surrey,   Lent 1981
England.   AMDG.

Abstracts from documents in Crown copyright are published by permission of Her Britannic Majesty's Stationery Office

NOTES

1. *English Estates of American Colonists, 1610-1699* and *English Estates of American Colonists, 1700-1799,* both published by Genealogical Publishing Co., Inc., 1980.

2. Records and indexes are housed and open to public inspection at Somerset House, Strand, London.

3. *Public General Acts:* Act to amend the law relating to Probates and Letters of Administration in England (Cap. 77, 1857).

4. Located at the Public Record Office, Chancery Lane, London.

5. In both name and place indexes an asterisk beside the page number indicates that the name or place is mentioned more than once on the page.

ENGLISH ESTATES
OF AMERICAN SETTLERS

TESTATORS AND INTESTATES

Abbott, William, formerly of St. James' Street, Middlesex,
late of New York City. Administration to relict Eliza
Abbott. (Aug. 1844).

Aborn, Anne, of Providence, Rhode Island. Administration to
Melvil Wilson, attorney for husband Peleg Aborn at Providence. (May 1828).

Aborn, William Wellington, of Cranston, Rhode Island, bachelor.
Administration to father Peleg Aborn. (June 1839).

Abrahams, Benjamin, formerly of Sheerness, Kent, late of New
Orleans, bachelor. Administration to brother Lawrence
Abrahams; mother Rachel Abrahams having died. (June 1857).

Adams, Henry, formerly of Loughton, Essex, bricklayer, late of
New York City, widower. Administration to son Charles Adams.
(July 1848).

Adams, Henry the younger, of New York City, bachelor. Administration to Charles Adams, son and executor of father Henry
Adams deceased. (July 1848).

Addison, Anthony, of Prince George's Co., Maryland. Probate
to nephew Henry Addison Callis. (Feb. 1838).

Agar formerly Hayward, Margaret, of New Orleans, widow. Administration to sister Ann, wife of John Saunderson. (Mar. 1827).

Albin, Catherine - see King.

Alderson, Robert, formerly of Stockton upon Tees, Durham, late
of Hopkins Creek, California, bachelor. Administration to
brother and sisters Daniel Forsick Alderson, Elizabeth Hill,
widow, and Martha Alderson. (May 1857).

Alexander, Isabella, formerly of Londonderry, Ireland, late of
Baltimore, U.S.A., spinster. Administration to nephew
James McClintock. (June 1839).

Alexander, James, formerly of Maidstone, Kent, late of New York.
Limited administration to Edward Wildes, attorney for George
Burr of Maidstone. (Dec. 1826). Revoked and granted to
James George Langham. (Dec. 1832). Revoked and granted to
Henry Atkinson Wildes; testator now described as late of
East Florida. (Oct. 1840).

Alexander, Robert, of Kentucky, U.S.A. Probate to son Robert
Alexander with similar powers reserved to Jacob Swigert,
Joseph Weisiger and John Hoard Slaughter. (June 1841).

Allen, Aaron, of Nether Providence, Delaware Co., Pennsylvania.
Administration with will to Nathaniel Mason, attorney for
son Thomas Bidmead Allen at Ridley, Delaware Co.; surviving
executor Henry Forrest renouncing. (July 1837).

Allen, Abijah, Daniel, Elizabeth, of Pennsylvania, bachelors
and spinster. Administration to Elizabeth, wife of James
Bottomley, administratrix with will to the mother Sarah
Allen, widow; brother Aaron Allen and sister Sarah, wife
of Peter Heacock, having also died. (Apr. 1836).

Allen, Samuel, of Saluda Mills, South Carolina, bachelor.
Administration to Joseph Jeffries Evans, attorney for father
Samuel Allen at Saluda Mills. (Apr. 1800).

Allen, Sarah, of Craven Co., North Carolina, widow. Administration to Malcolm Ross, attorney for son Whichcote White at
Craven Co. (Mar. 1805).

Allen, Sarah, of Ridley, Delaware Co., Pennsylvania, widow.
Administration with will to granddaughter Elizabeth, wife
of James Bottomley. (Apr. 1836).

Allenby, William Charles, of Baltimore, Maryland. Probate to
brother George Allenby. (June 1801).

Allison, John, formerly of Bradfield, Norfolk, miller, late of
Berry, Dane Co., (Wisconsin), widower. Administration to
father James Allison. (May 1855).

Allman, formerly Douglas, Susanna, of New York City, widow.
Limited administration with will to Howard Douglas, attorney
for only child Louisa Douglas during her minority. (Nov.
1807). Revoked and granted to John Philpot. (Feb. 1812).

Allwood, Hon. Robert, formerly of St. Catherine, Jamaica, late
of New York. Probate to son Rev. Robert Allwood with similar
powers reserved to John Gale Vidal and son James Allwood.
(Jan. 1839).

Alston, David, Captain on half pay of New Jersey Volunteers who
died at Staten Island, New York. Administration with will
to David Davies, attorney for sons Warren and Japhet Alston
at New York. (July 1806).

Ambrose, Isabella, of Newport, Rhode Island. Administration
to James Cockburn, attorney for husband Robert M. Ambrose
at Newport. (Feb. 1802).

Amphlett, William, Lieutenant of Royal Navy who died at St.
Louis, Missouri. Probate to brother Richard Paul Amphlett
with similar powers reserved to brother Samuel Holmden Amphlett.
(July 1852).

Anderson, James, of George Town District, South Carolina, planter.
Probate to son Richard Oswald Anderson. (Aug. 1821).

Anderson, James, of New York, merchant. Limited administration
with will to sons Andrew, Smith Weeks and Abel Tyler Anderson
with similar powers reserved to relict Hannah Anderson.
(Oct. 1832).

Anderson, Julia Ann, of Detroit, Wayne Co., Michigan, widow.
Limited administration with will to Henry Barkly and Henry
John Lias. (Feb. 1845).

Andrade alias Andrada, Abraham, of Ohio, bachelor. Administration to brother and only next of kin Moses Andrade. (Nov.
1826).

Andrews, Abraham, formerly of Hertford, Hertfordshire, late of
Baltimore, Virginia (sic). Probate to son Samuel Andrews.
(Oct. 1801).

Andrews, John, formerly of Diss, Norfolk, afterwards of Beulah
Cottages, Clifton Street, Wandsworth Road, Surrey, late of
New York, bachelor. Administration to sister Mary Andrews.
(Sept. 1852).

Antill, John, of New Burgh, Orange Co., New York, Major of 2nd
Batallion of late New Jersey Regiment of Volunteers. Admini-
stration with will to William Young, attorney for relict Jane
Antill at New York. (Apr. 1819).

Apthorp, William Rice, formerly of Boston, North America, who
died on Island of St. Thomas, West Indies. Probate to brother
Charles Ward Apthorp. (Feb. 1800).

Arnold, Henry, of New York City, Lieutenant in His Majesty's
Service. Administration with will to Pownal Phipps, attorney
for relict Hannah Arnold and daughter Sophia Matilda Arnold
at New York. (July 1827).

Arnold, Henry, formerly of Uttoxeter, Staffordshire, late of
Republic of Texas. Administration to father William Arnold
the elder. (Jan. 1843).

Arnold, Mary Anne, of Union Township, Bush Co., Indiana.
     Administration to Andrew Arnold, attorney for husband John
     Arnold at Union Township. (Aug. 1830).
Arthur, John, formerly of 42 North Street, Pentonville, Middle-
     sex, late of San Francisco, California, engraver. Probate
     to mother Mary Arthur, widow. (July 1856).
Ash, Francis, of Charleston, Philadelphia, cabinet maker.
     Administration to brother and sister and only next of kin
     James and Elizabeth Ash. (May 1839).
Ashlin, William, formerly of Boston, Lincolnshire, late of
     Philadelphia, bachelor. Administration to sister Mary Anne,
     wife of Valentine Mantz Close. (Sept. 1828).
Ashwood, Mary Ann, of Adams Co., Illinois. Administration to
     Nathaniel Hollingsworth, attorney for husband Joseph Ashwood
     in Illinois. (Jan. 1857).
Aslat, Edward, formerly of Vale Place, Hammersmith, Middlesex,
     late of Galveston, North America, bricklayer. Probate to
     sister Elizabeth Aslat. (June 1840).
Atherstone, William, formerly of Leicester late of U.S.A.
     Probate to Hannah Brown, spinster. (Feb. 1836).
Atkins, Samuel, of Warren Herkimer, New York. Administration
     to brother James Atkins; relict Margaret Atkins renouncing.
     (Dec. 1842).
Atkyns, Ringrose, formerly of Devonshire Street, Portland Place,
     Middlesex, late of Kanion, California, bachelor. Administra-
     tion to brother Rev. Walter Baker Atkyns; mother and next
     of kin Sarah Atkins, widow, having died. (July 1855).

Austin, John, of New York City, M.D. Administration with will
     to Charles Dean, attorney for relict Mary Austin, son John
     Austin, John Parkinson, John Singleton, Copley Greene and
     William Joseph Hubbard in U.S.A. (July 1839).
Axby, Thomas - see Haxby.

Babb, Thomas, of New York City. Administration to William Babb,
     uncle and guardian of children Julia and Thomas Sherry Babb
     during their minority. (Mar. 1800).
Baber, Charles, of Tazwell Co., Illinois. Administration to
     James Baber, attorney for relict Mary Ann Baber in Tazwell
     Co. (Aug. 1855).
Backman, Catherine, formerly of Easter, Northampton Co., Penn-
     sylvania, late of St. Louis, Missouri, widow. Administration
     to George Cox, attorney for son William Shurlock Backman at
     St. Louis. (Feb. 1857). New grant May 1879.
Bayley, Barnard, of New York City. Probate to Edward Dry with
     similar powers reserved to father Thomas Bayley, Robert
     Henderson and Joseph Jennings. (June 1833).
Bayley, James Augustus, of Dexter, New York, merchant. Admini-
     stration to relict Martha Washington Bayley. (Mar. 1855).
Baily, Robert Nalder, of New York City. Administration to
     George Dibley, attorney for only child Sarah, wife of George
     Henry Geib at New York; relict Sally Baily having died.
     (Nov. 1847).

Bailey, William Hyde, of Southfield, Richmond Co., New York.
Probate to relict Ann, now wife of John Taylor, with similar
powers reserved to Hyde Williams. (May 1850).
Baker, John, of New York. Administration to son Alfred Edward
Baker. (Feb. 1845).
Baker, Stephen, formerly of Dungarvon, Waterford Co., Ireland,
late of Oxford, Indiana, widower. Administration to credi-
tor John Sparkes Dalton; son Stephen Edward Baker renouncing
for himself and as guardian of only other children William
Robert, Roger and Samuel Baker. (June 1851).
Ballard, William, of Charleston, South Carolina, bachelor.
Administration to brother Samuel James Ballard. (Feb. 1812).
Balsley nee Jope, Priscilla, of Pittsburgh, Allegheny Co.,
Pennsylvania. Administration to George Cox, attorney for
husband John Balsley at Pittsburgh. (May 1837).
Bannister, William, formerly of Tutbury, Staffordshire, farmer,
late of U.S.A. Probate to Jenny Hall and son Luke Bannister
with similar powers reserved to William Riley. (Apr. 1832).
Barber, Mary, of Amonia, Duchess Co., New York, spinster.
Administration to father Henry Barber. (Sept. 1849).
Barclay, Thomas, HM Consul for Eastern States of America.
Limited administration with will to John Brodribb Bergne,
attorney for relict Susan Barclay and sons Thomas, George
and Anthony Barclay in U.S.A. (May 1831).
Barclay, William, formerly of Fenchurch Buildings, London, late
of Baltimore, U.S.A. Probate to Robert Barclay. (Aug. 1814).
Barling, Aaron, of Baltimore, North America. Probate to relict
Sarah Barling. (July 1810).
Barlow, Rev. John, formerly of Saxby, Leicestershire, late of
Rochester, Munroe Co., New York, widower. Administration
to daughter Charlotte Barlow. (Jan. 1841).
Barmby, Ellen, of Lee, Oneida Co., New York, spinster. Admini-
stration to Elizabeth Risque, administratrix of father Henry
Barmby deceased. (Feb. 1846).
Barnes, Charles, formerly of Carshalton, Surrey, late of Spring-
field, Washington Co., Kentucky. Administration with will
to Ann, wife of Robert Gumbrell, executrix to mother Ann
Barnes, widow. (Aug. 1809).
Barnes, Mary, of Trenton, North America, widc . Administration
with will to Daniel Coxe, attorney for Sarah Barnes Hooton
and Mary Barnes, spinster, at Trenton. (June 1808).
Barrell, Theodore, of Saugerties, Ulster Co., New York. Admini-
stration with will to Thomas Boosey, attorney for relict
Elizabeth Beckles Barrell, daughter Charlotte Bar ell and
Isaac Winslow at Saugerties. (Aug. 1847).
Barritt nee Scantlebury, Joanna, of Charlton, New York. Admini-
stration to husband William Barritt. (July 1854).
Barron, formerly Keith, Charlotte, wife of Thomas Barron of
Charles Town, South Carolina. Limited administration to John
Tunno, attorney for brother John Keith. (Aug. 1807).
Barry, Edward, of New York who died at sea, bachelor. Admini-
stration to brother and next of kin Timothy Barry. (Nov. 1841).
Barton, Henry Lane, of Sussex, New Jersey, Lieutenant of 1st
Batallion of New Jersey Volunteers. Administration to David
Thomas, attorney for relict Mary, now wife of Eben Owen, at
Sussex. (Oct. 1801).
Barton, Joshua Joseph, of New Orleans, bachelor. Administration
to brother Philip Henry Barton; mother Sarah Elizabeth Barton
having died. (Dec. 1849).
Barziza, Count Antonio and Countess Lucia Paradine, of Venice,
having property in Williamsburg, Virginia. Limited admini-
stration with wills to Count Giovanni Alvise Barziza. (Oct.
1815).

Batchelder, Rev. William, of Haverhill, Essex Co., Mass.
Administration to relict Huldah Batchelder. (Oct. 1819).
Batchelor, Elizabeth, of 233 Broadway, New York City. Admini-
stration to husband Charles Batchelor. (Dec. 1857).
Bates, James, formerly of Holbeach, Lincolnshire, late of
Cincinnati, bachelor. Administration to Edward Key,
attorney for brothers John and Richard Bates at Cincinnati;
mother Susanna Bates, widow, having died. (Nov. 1851).
Batley, John, formerly of Portland Street, Middlesex, late of
Norwalk, Connecticut, widower. Administration to son
William Batley. (Mar. 1851).
Baxter, Benjamin, formerly of Wapping, Middlesex, late of
Nantucket. Administration to Thomas Dickason, attorney
for relict Lydia Baxter at Nantucket. (June 1801).
Baxter, John Exall, of Petersburgh, Virginia, bachelor.
Administration to Rev. George Guildford Exall, attorney
for father Thomas Baxter at Petersburgh. (June 1846).
Bayley - see Bailey.
Bayzand, William Seddon, of Baltimore, North America, who died
at sea. Administration to son William Henry Bayzand; relict
Susanna Asquith Bayzand having died. (Oct. 1827).
Beasant, Richard, formerly of Wolverton, Buckinghamshire, late
of New York, merchant. Limited administration to Campbell
Hobson. (May 1833).
Beaucham, Joseph, formerly of High Street, Portland Town,
St. Marylebone, Middlesex, late of Fredericksburg, Virginia.
Administration to Richard Hewlett, attorney for relict
Rachel Beaucham at Fredericksburg. (Oct. 1849).
Beekman, Gerard, of Mount Pleasant, Westchester Co., New York.
Administration with will to Gabriel Shaw, attorney for
relict Cornelia Beekman, Pierre Van Cortlandt, son Stephen
D. Beekman and Robert G.S. De Freyster in U.S.A. (Nov. 1823).
Beekman, Gerard G., of Mount Pleasant, Westchester Co., New
York, widower. Administration to Gabriel Shaw, administra-
tor with will to only child Gerard Beekman and attorney for
his executors. (Nov. 1823).
Belin, Peter, formerly of Knightsbridge, St. George Hanover
Square, Middlesex, afterwards of Birmingham, Warwickshire,
but who died at sea on passage to South Carolina, widower.
Administration to Francis Cope, administrator to creditor
Thomas Salt the elder deceased. (June 1843).
Belisario, Henry Mendes, of Baltimore, North America. Probate
to uncle Charles Mendes Da Costa and Jacob Mendes Da Costa
with similar powers reserved to Benjamin Mendes Da Costa
and Isaac Pretto. (June 1855).
Bell nee Webb, Eliza alias Elizabeth, of Mobile, Alabama.
Administration to husband William Bell. (Sept. 1827).
Bell, John, of Vera Cruz, Mexico, who died at Charleston, U.S.A.,
bachelor. Administration to brother Robert Bell. (Aug. 1853).
Bell, John, of St. Louis, U.S.A., surgeon, bachelor. Admini-
stration to brother and sister and only next of kin William
Edward Bell and Catherine Meredith, widow. (Oct. 1853).
Bell, William, formerly of Princes Street, Edinburgh, late of
South Carolina. Probate to nephew Alexander Morton, James
Kilgour, Robert Saunders and William Young. (May 1827).
Bendelow, William, formerly of Putneyvill, Wayne Co., late of
Williamson, New York. Administration to Thomas Bendelow,
attorney for relict Jane Bendelow at Williamson. (July 1857).
Bengough, John Sowerby, formerly of Austin Friars, London,
afterwards of Mazatlin, Mexico, late of New York. Probate
to John Francis Bacon with similar powers reserved to Joseph
Javier de Lizardi. (June 1856).

Bennett, Ellen C. - see Green.

Bennett, John Morris, formerly of Brosely, Shropshire, late of Baltimore, North Britain (sic). Administration to son John Morris Bennett; relict Margaret Bennett cited but not appearing. (May 1831).

Bennett, Joseph, of New York who died at New Orleans, bachelor. Administration to brother John Morris Bennett. (Mar. 1834).

Bennett, Reuben, of Manlius, New York, widower. Administration to Ann Church, spinster, attorney for only children Albertus Reuben, James Azariah and Oscar Bennett at Manlius. (Dec. 1832).

Bennett, Robert, of Charleston, South Carolina. Probate to Benjamin Burton Johnson with similar powers reserved to Robert Downie, Henry Brimar, John Coburn, Edgar Corrie and Thomas Corrie. (May 1817).

Benskin, Thomas, of Bethlehem, Ohio, widower. Administration to son William Benskin. (Apr. 1854).

Benson, William George, of Perth Amboy, New Jersey, bachelor Administration to mother Elizabeth Benson, widow. (Feb.1811).

Benson, William John Chapman, of Quebec, Canada, who died at Whitehall, New York, merchant. Probate to brother Thomas Benson and William Robert Chapman with similar powers reserved to Christopher Richardson. (Jan. 1851).

Bentley, Susannah - see Rabbeth.

Berry, George Charles Bradbury, of New York, bachelor. Administration to father John Robert Berry. (Sept. 1850).

Berry, John, of New York City. Administration with will of estate unadministered by surviving executor Edward Cox now deceased to nephew John Berry. (June 1802).

Bertie, Hon. Peregrine, of Philadelphia, bachelor. Administration to brother and next of kin Hon. & Rev. Frederick Bertie. (Jan. 1850).

Best, Eliza, of Washington, Pennsylvania, spinster. Administration to George Cox, attorney for father John Best the elder at Washington. (July 1840).

Best, George, of Newark, New Jersey. Probate to relict Mary Best and Thomas Colpitts Granger. (May 1842). Further grant July 1872.

Best, Isabella, of Washington, Pennsylvania. Administration to George Cox, attorney for husband John Best the elder at Washington. (July 1840).

Besuchet, Francois, of New Orleans, Louisiana. Administration with will to Philip Walther and Auguste de Vos, attornies for relict Fredericke Besuchet nee Heinert at Pesnetz near Desan in Principality of Anhalt, Germany. (Sept. 1849).

Betty, Robert Bell, of Philadelphia, bachelor. Administration to James Watson, attorney for mother and next of kin Mary Betty, widow, at Ithaca, America. (Apr. 1840).

Bexfield, Joseph, formerly of Richmond Terrace, Dalston, Middlesex, late of Cabell Co., Virginia. Probate to son Stephen Bexfield with similar powers reserved to daughter Mariana Bexfield. (July 1850).

Bibby, formerly McEvers, Margaret Johnson, of New York City. Administration to Gabriel Shaw, attorney for husband Thomas Bibby at New York City. (May 1823).

Bibby, Thomas, of New York, Captain on half pay of 7th Regiment of Foot. Administration to James Tidbury, attorney for relict Rebecca Bibby at New York. (June 1830).

Bickerton, John, of New York City, bachelor. Administration to sister Mary, wife of Jonathan Watmough; mother and next of kin Martha Bickerton, widow, having died. (May 1854).

Bickerton, Martha, of Constantia, Oswego Co., New York, widow.
Administration to daughter Mary, wife of Jonathan Watmough.
(May 1854).
Bicknell, Dorcas, formerly of Coleman Street, London, late of
New York City, who died at Peckham, Surrey. Limited administration with will to husband David Bicknell. (Mar. 1856).
Bicknell, Mary, of Philadelphia. Administration to John Bain-
bridge the younger, attorney for daughter Elizabeth Bicknell
at Philadelphia; husband Peter Bicknell having died. (July
1812).
Bidmead, Samuel, of Bristol, Illinois, bachelor. Administration
to father James Bidmead. (Jan. 1847).
Billing, Eliza, of Williams Town, Oswego Co., New York. Admini-
stration to John Chalk, attorney for husband James Billing
at Williams Town. (May 1854).
Birch, Edward, of New York. Administration to relict Sarah
Birch. (Apr. 1826).
Bird - see Byrd.
Birkett, Henry, of Albion, Edwards Co., Illinois. Limited
administration with will to brother John Birkett; relict
Sarah Birkett renouncing. (Mar. 1826).
Bisdee, Edwin, of Lysander, Onandaga Co., New York, bachelor.
Administration to William Millett Beauchamp, attorney for
father John Bisdee at Waterloo, New York. (Dec. 1848).
Bishop, Richard, of Potz Ville, North America. Administration
to George Bishop, attorney for relict Eleanor Ann Bishop at
Potz Ville. (Feb. 1837).
Bize, Hercules Daniel, of Newark, New Jersey. Probate to Anthony
Bordenave with similar powers reserved to daughters Ursula
Elizabeth wife of ---- Roberti, Elizabeth wife of John Tavel,
and to John Woddrop, James Crawford, Thomas Bibby and Nicholas
Gouverneur. (May & June 1800).
Blaau, Eleanor, of New York City, widow. Administration to
Jonathan Poot the younger, attorney for daughter Cornelia
Blaau at New York. (July 1803).
Black, James, formerly of Philadelphia, afterwards of St. Cuth-
bert Street but late of East Claremont Street, Edinburgh,
merchant. Probate to Alexander Merton and Thomas Leburn
with similar powers reserved to George Morris, John McAllister
and Quinton Campbell. (Apr. 1843).
Blackwell, Monro, formerly of Somers Town Terrace, Middlesex,
late of New York City, surgeon on half pay of Royal Artillery,
bachelor. Administration to brother Alexander Blackwell.
(Mar. 1839).
Blagborne, Rev. William, formerly of Brooklyn, New York, late of
Bermondsey, Surrey, widower. Administration with will to
daughter Elizabeth Blagborne; surviving executors Rowles
Scudamore and Thomas Holy renouncing. Administration as of
intestate to said Elizabeth Blagborne of March 1816 revoked
on presentation of will. (Dec. 1817).
Blanchard, William, of Louisville, Kentucky, widower. Admini-
stration with will to son George Blanchard. (Aug. 1840).
Blane, Charles Collins, of Richmond, Virginia, unattached
Lieutenant-Colonel and Brevet Colonel of H.M. Army, bachelor.
Administration to brother and only next of kin Sir Hugh
Seymour Blane. (Apr. 1855).
Blennerhasset, James, of Virginia, bachelor. Administration to
mother and next of kin Ann Blennerhasset, widow. (Apr. 1848).
Bliss alias Hide, Jean, formerly of London, late of Philadelphia,
spinster. Administration to brother and only next of kin
James Bliss. (May 1820).

Blogg, Anna Maria, of Savannah, America, spinster. Admini-
stration to Charles Robert Simpson, attorney for mother
Mary Blogg, widow, at Savannah. (Jan. 1821).
Boddily, Benjamin Peach, of Newbury Port, Essex Co., Mass.
Limited administration to Petty Vaughan, attorney for Caleb
Cushing, guardian of only daughter Mary Cushing Boddily
and only son Benjamin Cushing Boddily in U.S.A. during their
minority; relict Ann Mary Boddily renouncing. (Mar. 1827).
Bonthron, John, of Capitol Hill, Washington, U.S.A., stone-
cutter. Administration to George Cox, attorney for relict
Grace Bonthron at Washington. (Aug. 1840).
Booth, Sarah, of Richmond, Virginia, widow. Administration to
James Dunlop, attorney for only child Sarah Bateman Boyce,
widow, in Virginia. (Nov. 1827).
Booth, William, formerly of Chatham, Kent, late of Philadelphia.
Administration to daughter Mary, wife of William Belk;
relict Elizabeth Booth cited but not appearing. (Jan. 1817).
Bordman, Amos, of Reading, Mass., bachelor. Administration to
Asbury Dickins, attorney for father Amos Bordman in Mass.
(May 1812).
Bordwine, Charles, formerly of Naval Yard, New York, afterwards
of St. Martin in Fields, Middlesex, late of Montreal, Canada.
Limited administration with will to Joseph Bordwine; relict
Hannah Bordwine having died. (Aug. 1826).
Botson, Mary, of Pringo, North Carolina, spinster. Administra-
tion to John Smith Davis, son and administrator of sister
Elizabeth, wife of David Davis; mother Mary Botson having
died. (Dec. 1818).
Bourdillon, Rev. Peter, Minister of church at Charleston, South
Carolina. Administration to relict Helena Bourdillon. (Feb.
1801).
Bourne, Thomas, of Fredonia, New York. Probate to relict Huldah
Ann Bourne. (Jan. 1841).
Boustead, James, of Philadelphia, tanner and currier. Probate
to son John Boustead with similar powers reserved to Joseph
Snowdon. (Mar. 1852).
Bowdoin, Hon. James, of Boston, New England. Limited admini-
stration with will to George Lee, George Ewing and Thomas
Latham. (May 1803).
Bowen, Thomas, formerly of Bristol, late of Charles Town, America,
bachelor. Administration to brother Henry Edward Bowen;
mother Ann Bowen, widow, having died. (Feb. 1813).
Bowerbank, Edward, formerly of Lothbury, London, late of New
York, merchant. Administration to brother John Bowerbank.
(Oct. 1844). Revoked on his death and granted to brother
William Bowerbank. (Oct. 1854).
Bowles, Tobias, of St. Philip's parish, South Carolina. Admini-
stration with will to John Stevens, attorney for Rebecca
Drayton, widow, and Thomas Winstanley at St. Philip's.
(Oct. 1811).
Bown, Robert Tytherleigh, of Mobile, Alabama, journeyman baker,
acting steward on steam vessel *Palmyra*, bachelor. Admini-
stration to father Robert Bown. (Dec. 1848).
Bown, Samuel Hasel, of Chicago, U.S.A., bachelor. Administration
to sister Susanna Elizabeth, wife of Robert William Smith;
mother Mary Bown, wife of Robert Bown, formerly Bown, widow,
having died. (Aug. 1856).
Bowring, Mary Kelsey, of North Carolina who died at sea. Admini-
stration to husband James Bowring. (Jan. 1824).
Boyd, Alexander, formerly of South Leith, Edinburgh, late of
Savannah, Georgia, bachelor. Administration to father
William Boyd. (Dec. 1804).

Boyd, George, formerly of Portsmouth, New Hampshire, late of
Low Layton, Essex, who died passenger on merchant ship
Kitty. Double probate of will registered in 1787 to John
Lane and son William Boyd with similar powers reserved to
Joseph Champney. (Mar. 1804).
Boyd, William, of Charleston, North America. Administration to
Edward Boyd, uncle and guardian of only child Maitland Boyd
during his minority; relict Isabel Susan Boyd having died.
(July 1817).
Boyle, Catherine, of New York City. Administration to Joseph
Boyle, attorney for husband John Thomas Boyle at New York
City. (Oct. 1851). Revoked on death of Joseph Boyle and
granted to Alexander Boyle as attorney. (July 1855).
Boylston, Ward Nicholas, of Princeton, Worcester and late of
Roxbury, Mass. Limited administration with will to Petty
Vaughan, attorney for John Quincy Adams, President of U.S.A.,
Nathaniel Custis and his wife Alicia Broughton in U.S.A.
(July 1828).
Bradley, Anna alias Ann, of Wilmington, North Carolina, spinster.
Administration to brother John Bradley; grant of November
1789 revoked on death of mother Elizabeth Bradley. (Aug. 1802).
Bradshaw, Robert, formerly of Hungerford, Berkshire, late of
U.S.A. Administration to relict Elizabeth Bradshaw. (Aug.
1825).
Bradshaw, Thomas the younger, formerly of Coventry Street,
Haymarket, Middlesex, late of Somerset, Maryland, bachelor.
Administration to father Thomas Bradshaw. (Aug. 1814).
Brailsford, Samuel, of New York City. Administration to relict,
now Mary Evans. (May 1819). Further grant September 1861.
Bratt, Esther, of Lost Creek, Terra Hanto, Vigo Co., Indiana,
widow. Probate to Enoch Pearson with similar powers reserved
to William Hartill Bayliss. (Oct. 1842).
Brazier, John, of New York City. Administration to William
Vaughan, attorney for relict Rebecca Brazier at New York.
(Jan. 1810).
Brentnall, Catherine, of Newark, New Jersey, widow. Administra-
tion to son Amos Brentnall. (Feb. 1856).
Brett née Jenkins, Elizabeth, formerly of Rotherhithe, Surrey,
late of Savannah, North America. Administration to husband
John Brett. (June 1832).
Bridgen, Thomas Bridgen, of Sussex Co., New Jersey. Administra-
tion with will to Edward Winwood, attorney for son Thomas
Bridgen at Albany, North America; executors Sanders Lausing
and John Vander Spegle cited but not appearing. (May 1817).
Broadbent, Edward, of New Orleans, widower. Administration to
daughter Sarah Broadbent. (Feb. 1851).
Broadhurst, Dorothy, formerly of Philadelphia, late of Charleston,
North America, spinster. Administration to mother Dorothy
Broadhurst, widow. (Nov. 1806).
Bromfield, Thomas, of Boston, New England. Administration with
will to Henry Bromfield the younger, attorney for Henry Brom-
field, son of cousin Edward Bromfield, at Harvard, Mass;
grant of September 1787 revoked on death of William Phillips.
(Sept. 1804).
Broughton, Edmund, formerly of Crewkerne, Somerset, late of
Charles Town, South Carolina, currier, widower. Administra-
tion to sister and next of kin Margaret Broughton. (May 1813).
Brown, Isabel, of Cincinnati, U.S.A., widow. Administration
with will to children Eliza Liddell Brown, Jane Spears Brown
and Isabella Livingstone Brown. (June 1851).

9

Brown, William, of Lyonsburg and Richmond, Virginia. Limited
administration with will to father and mother James and
Margaret Brown. (Feb. 1815).
Brown, William, of 24 East Lane, Bermondsey, Surrey, mariner,
who died passenger on ship *Charles Bartlett* (bound to New
York). Administration to relict Susan Brown. (Aug. 1849).
Brown, William Hugh, of Sportsman's Hall Estate, Trelawney,
Cornwall Co., Jamaica, who died at New York. Probate to
William Dawson with similar powers reserved to John Brown.
(Apr. 1835).
Brownrigg, Henry, of New Orleans, bachelor without parent.
Administration to sister Ann Brownrigg. (May 1828).
Bruce, Charles Key, formerly of Calcutta, East Indies, late of
Richmond, New York. Probate to James MacKillop and Joseph
Boulderson with similar powers reserved to John Shoolbred,
M.D. (Apr. 1827).
Bruce, Frances, of New York City, widow. Administration with
will to John Chambers White and John Scott, attornies for
Peter Jay Munro in New York. (Sept. 1821).
Bryant, Alexander Drake, of Cincinnati. Administration to John
Gribble, attorney for relict Frances Ann Drake Bryant at
Louisville, Kentucky. (Nov. 1836).
Bryant, Samuel Drake the younger, of Cincinnati, Ohio. Admini-
stration to John Gribble, attorney for father Samuel Drake
Bryant at Cincinnati; relict Ann Drake having died. (May
1837).
Bubb, Arthur and Mary Jane, formerly of Bourton on the Water,
Gloucestershire, late of New York. Administration to father
Charles Bubb the younger. (Aug. 1854).
Buckland, David, of New York, soap boiler. Administration to
relict Sarah Buckland. (July 1837).
Buckley, Michael, of New York City. Probate to Jeremiah Shine
with similar powers reserved to Very Rev. John Power and
John Williams. (Aug. 1840).
Buckmaster, Christopher, of Ohio City. Administration to
Richard Price, attorney for relict Louisa, now wife of James
Bradley, at Ohio City. (Aug. 1853).
Buckoll, William, of New York City, bachelor. Administration
to brother Henry Buckoll; mother Sarah Buckoll having died.
(July 1829).
Bulfinch, Hannah, of Boston, Mass. Administration to husband
Charles Bulfinch. (Aug. 1842). Further grant December 1874.
Burchett, Arthur Tertius Nicholas, of Hubbard Street, Chicago,
Illinois, bachelor. Administration to brother George Martin-
dale Burchett. (Dec. 1855).
Burchett, Frances Anne, of Clark Street, Chicago, Illinois,
spinster. Administration to brother George Martindale
Burchett. (Dec. 1855).
Burke, Redmond, of Philadelphia, bachelor. Administration to
brother and next of kin Myles Burke. (Sept. 1814).
Burling, Samuel, of Shelburne, Nova Scotia, bachelor. Admini-
stration by decree to John Fry, attorney for sister Hannah
Smith, formerly Burling, at Burlington, New Jersey. Grant
of September 1799 revoked as having been made under false
suggestion. (Apr. 1803).
Burn, James, formerly of Upper Berkeley Street, Norton Street
and Upper Norton Street, Middlesex, late of Frankford,
Pennsylvania. Probate to Joel Roberts Poinsett with similar
powers reserved to Richard Willing. (Aug. 1831).
Burnell, Robert, formerly of Newton Nottage, Glamorgan, late of
South Carolina. Probate to one of six children surviving at
date of will Mary Davies, widow, with similar powers reserved

to relict Elizabeth Burnell and children Ann wife of David
Thomas and Margaret wife of Rees Rees. (Apr. 1856).
Burnell, Thomas, formerly of Whitehaven, Cumberland, mariner,
afterwards of Montego Bay, Jamaica, late of New York.
Limited probate to Richard Gordon and Henry Sands with
similar powers reserved to John Wallas and Christian Archer.
(June 1833).
Burnett, Charlotte, of New York, widow. Administration to
Arthur Edward Francis, attorney for only child Ward Benjamin
Burnett at New York. (July 1856).
Burnett, Thomas, of New York, bachelor. Administration to
Arthur Edward Francis, attorney for brother Ward Benjamin
Burnett at New York; mother Charlotte Burnett having died.
(July 1856).
Burnside, James, of Calcutta, East Indies, who died at Norfolk,
U.S.A.. Administration of estate unadministered by brother
Anthony Austin Burnside deceased to brother Richard Henry
Burnside. (Feb. 1829).
Burt, George, of New Barbadoes, Bergen Co., New Jersey. Probate
to relict Harriet Burt and John Andrew Zobriskie. (Mar. 1849).
Burton, John, formerly of Birmingham, Warwickshire, late of
Port Caddo, Texas. Administration to relict Eliza Burton.
(Apr. 1851). Revoked on her death and granted to Thomas
Smith James, attorney for Anne Burton, widow, in Texas,
guardian of only children George, Eliza, Hannah Sarah,
Caroline Ruth and Louisa Burton. (July 1852 & Nov. 1853).
Bushe, Elizabeth - see Noel.
Bussa, Alexander Placide, of Richmond, Virginia, professor of
music, bachelor. Administration to William Frederick Collard,
attorney for brother Henry Placide Bussa at New York. (Apr.
1837).
Butler, Elizabeth, of Cincinnati, Hamilton Co., Ohio, wife of
Edmund Butler. Limited administration with will to Edmund
Butler the younger, attorney for Francis Miller at Cincinnati.
(June 1847).
Butlin, Ann and Martha, of Amherst Plato, Lorraine, Ohio, spin-
sters. Administration to sister Mary, wife of Nathaniel
Buswell; mother and next of kin Martha Butlin having died.
(Feb. 1854).
Butt, John, of New York. Administration to creditor Amos Butt;
relict Alice Butt and only children George Amos, Mary Anne,
Isabella wife of ----- Lord, Matilda Diana, Frederick and
John Felix Butt having been cited but not appearing. (Mar.
1829).
Butt, John Yenn, of Cincinnati, U.S.A. Administration to relict
Cynthia Butt. (Apr. 1852).
Buxton, Cornelia, of New York City. Administration to husband
Charles Buxton, Doctor of Physic. (June 1819).
Bird, John, of Allen Town, Northampton Co., Pennsylvania.
Limited probate to sister Mary Shrigley, widow. (Mar. 1802).
Byrd, Mary, of Westover, Virginia, widow. Administration with
will to Walter Stirling, attorney for surviving executor
William Byrd Page in Frederick Co., Virginia. (Sept. 1819).
Bird, Thomas, formerly of Finsbury Terrace, London, late of New
York City, who died at sea. Administration with will to
father William Bird; relict Anne Bird renouncing. (Oct.1808).
Byrd, William, of Westover, Charles City Co., Virginia. Probate
to relict Mary Byrd. (Oct. 1806).

Cadwallader, Thomas, of Martinsbury, Bedford Co., Pennsylvania.
Probate to Isaac Ironside. (Oct. 1842).

Cahill, Bryan, died passenger on American steam vessel *Panama*,
bachelor. Administration to sister Mary Foran, widow.
(Nov. 1850).

Callaghan, David, of Philadelphia. Administration to William
Farquhar, attorney for relict Elizabeth Callaghan at (*blank*).
(Jan. 1807).

Callanan, Michael, of Philadelphia. Administration with will
to Robert Barclay, attorney for Benjamin Wilson and Thomas
Park at Philadelphia. (Oct. 1807).

Callaway, Thomas, formerly of Maidstone, Kent, late of New York
City. Administration to creditor John Durrant; relict
Elizabeth Callaway and only children Elizabeth wife of
William Leaycraft, Thomas Christopher and George Callaway
cited but not appearing. (May 1846).

Cameron, Abigail, of New York City, widow of Alexander Cameron,
Lieutenant of Royal Navy. Administration to Leonard Streate
Coxe, attorney for son William H. Cameron at New York. (Jan.
1808).

Cameron, Alexander, Lieutenant of H.M.S. *Roebuck*. Administration to Daniel Coxe, attorney for relict Abigail Cameron at
New York City. (Jan. 1802).

Cameron, Mary Ann, formerly of Philadelphia, late of Everton
near Liverpool, Lancashire, widow. Limited probate to
Samuel Moon and William Cameron Moore. (Aug. 1848).

Campbell, Duncan, of Louisville, Kentucky, bachelor. Administration to sister Elizabeth Campbell. (Dec. 1841).

Campbell, Edward, formerly of Charing Cross, St. Martin in Fields,
Middlesex, late of New York City, M.D. Probate to Alexander
Campbell with similar powers reserved to Henry Remsen and
John B. Yates. (Dec. 1822).

Campbell, William, formerly Master of brig *Helen* of Pontaferry,
Ireland, late of New York, bachelor. Administration to
mother and next of kin Grace Campbell, widow. (Feb. 1845).

Cantell, Isaac, formerly of Ensham, Oxfordshire, late of Texas.
Probate to brother John Cantell; executor John Brend renouncing. (Aug. 1847).

Carnes, Burrell, formerly of Boston, North America, late of
Essequibo, South America. Probate to brother Joseph Carnes.
(Nov. 1805).

Carpenter, Bushrod, formerly of Launceston, Cornwall, late of
Virginia, bachelor, who died in 1794. Limited administration
to Samuel Steward. (Nov. 1840).

Carpenter, Thomas, of Lamingburgh, U.S.A., adjutant of De Lancey's
Regiment on half pay. Administration with will to James
Tidbury, attorney for John Taylor and Andrew Thompson in
America. (May 1832).

Carr, Simeon, formerly of Chesterfield, Derbyshire, miller,
late of Beardstown, Morgan Co., Illinois. Probate to brother
Robert Carr with similar powers reserved to John Roebuck.
(Mar. 1839).

Carson, Patrick, of Baltimore, U.S.A., bachelor. Administration
to sister and next of kin Rosanna wife of William Corbett.
(Sept. 1822).

Carter, John James, formerly of Liverpool, Lancashire, late of
Fearing, Washington Co., Ohio, who died at Cincinnati.
Administration to relict Margaret, now wife of Edward William
Jones. (May 1839).

Casey, Michael alias Mick, private soldier in U.S. Army of
Florida, bachelor. Administration to brother Timothy Casey.
(Feb. 1843).

Cass, Jane - see Truefitt.
Chadwick, Richard, of Nantucket, Mass. Administration to Paul
    Pease, attorney for relict Mary Chadwick at Nantucket.
    (June 1811).
Chalk, John Self, of Buffalo, U.S.A., widower. Administration
    to only child George Henry Chalk. (Aug. 1851).
Chamberlayne, Esther, formerly of Bath, Somerset, late of
    Charlestowne, North America. Probate to sister Patience,
    wife of Joseph Cook. (Aug. 1808).
Chamberlin, William, of General Hospital, Boston, U.S.A.,
    bachelor. Administration to brother Charles Chamberlin;
    mother Ann Chamberlin, widow, having died. (July 1846).
Chambers, Joseph, of Lucas Co., Ohio, widower. Administration
    to James Percival, attorney for son Joseph Chambers at
    Toledo, Lucas Co., Ohio. (Dec. 1843).
Champion, Richard, formerly of Bristol, late of Rocky Branch,
    South Carolina, widower. Administration to son George Lloyd
    Champion. (Dec. 1800).
Chandler, Charlotte, formerly of Russell Place, Fitzroy Square,
    Middlesex, late of New York City, spinster. Administration
    to sister Mary Ann, wife of Richard Money. (Mar. 1853).
Chandler, Henry Whateley, of New Orleans. Administration to
    relict Mary Caroline Chandler. (Apr. 1854).
Chandler, Nathaniel, of Worcester, Mass. Administration with
    will to Samuel Paine, attorney for brother Thomas Greene
    Chandler. (Aug. 1801).
Chandler, Robert, of New London, Connecticut, seaman of H.M.S.
    Penelope. Administration with will to William Compton,
    attorney for relict Lucy Chandler at New London. (Mar. 1801).
Chapline, formerly Nourse, Elizabeth, formerly of Brook, Vir-
    ginia, late of Clark Co., Missouri, widow. Probate to Jesse
    Sisson. (July 1847).
Chaplin, Harriet - see Newens.
Chapman, Mary, of Philadelphia, widow. Administration to son
    James Chapman. (July 1839).
Chappell, Christopher, of Williamsburgh, U.S.A., bachelor.
    Administration to Rev. Thomas Westlake Blackmore, executor
    to father William Chappell deceased. (May 1855).
Charlton, formerly Walters, Emily, of Savannah, Georgia.
    Administration to John Grierson, attorney for husband Thomas
    Usker Palaskie Charlton in Savannah. (Sept. 1821).
Charlton, Robert, of Liverpool, Lancashire, Master of American-
    owned ship *The Sisters*. Limited administration pending suit
    Lees v. Goodrich. (Jan. 1804).
Cheltnam, John, of Norfolk, Virginia. Administration to relict
    Sarah Cheltnam. (Apr. 1800).
Chiene, Margaret, of Philadelphia, widow. Probate to Peter A.
    Browne with similar powers reserved to Charles G. Paleske.
    (Nov. 1834).
Cheyne, William, of New York, M.D. Administration to relict
    Laura Matilda Cheyne. (Oct. 1842).
Chichester, John, of Virginia. Administration with will of
    estate unadministered by Richard Chicnester deceased to
    his administrator with will William Murdoch, attorney for his
    relict Sarah Chichester at Fairfax. (June 1803).
Chichester, Richard, of Fairfax, Virginia. Administration with
    will to William Murdoch, attorney for relict Sarah Chichester
    at Fairfax. (June 1803).
Chichester, Richard, of Virginia. Administration with will of
    estate unadministered by grandson Richard Chichester deceased
    executor of son John Chichester deceased to William Murdoch
    administrator with will to said John Chichester and attorney
    for Sarah Chichester, relict of the said Richard, now at

Fairfax, Virginia; Ellen Chichester renouncing and administration of March 1746 revoked. (June 1803).

Chiene - see Cheyne.

Child, Mary - see Morse.

Child, Richard, formerly of Lambeth, Surrey, late in America, bachelor. Administration to Henry Hughes, father of nephews and niece Richard, Henry and Mary Hughes during their minority. (June 1822).

Child, Richard, formerly of Castle Street, Piccadilly, Middlesex, currier, late of Newhaven, Connecticut. Limited administration to Robert Hume and Joseph Abbott. (Dec. 1824).

Child, Sarah, of Cincinnati, Ohio, widow. Administration to John Collins, attorney for son John Abbott Child at Medicine, Indiana. (July 1857).

Chollet, Abraham Louis, of Charleston, U.S.A., bachelor. Administration to Henry Chollet, attorney for brother Isaac Henry Chollet at Maudon, Switzerland. (Mar. 1821).

Chrisolme, John, of Carolina, bachelor. Administration to John Ord, attorney for brother and next of kin Kenneth Chrisolme at Balintrade, Scotland. (Mar. 1801).

Christie, William, of Charleston, South Carolina. Administration to children William and Maxwell Christie; relict Ann Christie having died. (Jan. 1838).

Chubb, Lydia, of New York, spinster. Administration to William Phillips Parker, attorney for father William Chubb at New York. (Jan. 1851).

Churton, Sarah, of Vernon, Oneida Co., New York. Administration to husband Thomas Churton. (Apr. 1843).

Clancy alias Clansie, William, formerly of Bache's Row, Hoxton, Middlesex, late of New York, who died at sea, bachelor. Administration to niece and nephews and next of kin Mary wife of Thomas Clancy, Patrick Curran and John Curran. (Apr. 1828).

Clare, Alfred, formerly Principal Clerk of Will Office of Bank of England and of Pittsburg but late of Philadelphia. Probate to nephew George Thatcher. (May 1835).

Clare, Charlotte S. - see Warren.

Clarke, Elizabeth, of Allet's Cove, Long Island, New York. Administration to husband Richard Clarke. (July 1845).

Clark, George, of Brandy Wine Hundred, Newcastle Co., Delaware, Captain on half pay of New Jersey Volunteers. Administration with will to Thomas Courtney, attorney for relict Ann Clark and John Tally in America. (Oct. 1812).

Clarke, George, of Springfield, New York, and of Hyde, Cheshire. Probate to son George Rochfort Clarke. (Aug. 1838).

Clark, James, formerly of Great Hermitage Street, Wapping, Middlesex, late of Peoria Co., Illinois. Probate to James Balfour with similar powers reserved to relict Isabella Clark. (Feb. 1842).

Clark, James Alderson, of Savannah, Georgia. Administration to relict Elizabeth Ann Clark. (Mar. 1829).

Clarke, James Henry, of New Orleans. Probate to sister Mary Clarke. (Oct. 1831).

Clarke, John, of Albion, Edwards Co., Illinois. Administration to relict Lucy Clarke. (Dec. 1842).

Clark, John, of Delaware, Pennsylvania. Administration to relict Mary Clark. (Feb. 1846).

Clarke, Joseph, formerly of Leicester, late of Brooklyn, King's Co., U.S.A. Probate to brother John Pretty Clarke. (June 1844).

Clark, Joseph George, formerly of Adam Street, Adelphi, Middle-
sex, late of Thompson, New York, widower. Administration to
Alexander Massey, attorney for children Ann wife of Josiah
Henderson Watts and Mary Williams wife of Joseph Plummer at
New York City. (Oct. 1845).

Clark, Sarah, of Clark's Mills, Leeds, Fauquier Co., Virginia,
widow. Administration with will to John Birkett, attorney
for Peter Adams in Fauquier Co. (Feb. 1835).

Clark, William, of Burnt Prairie, Edwards Co., Illinois. Limited
administration with will to Charles Clark, attorney for sons
David and Joseph Clark at Edwards Co. (Oct. 1842).

Cleghorn, John, of Frederick Co., Maryland. Administration with
will to John Rothery, attorney for brother Alexander Cleghorn
in Jamaica; sole executor John Creagh having been cited but
not appearing. (May 1824).

Clements, James, of New York City. Limited administration with
will to John Baring, attorney for relict Harriet Clements,
William Giffing, Timothy Hutton and William Mandeville at New
York. (Jan. 1831).

Clendinen, formerly Stewart, Elizabeth Ann, formerly of Blizzard
Street, Greenwich, Kent, late of Baltimore, U.S.A. Admini-
stration to Thomas Aspinwall, attorney for husband Alexander
Clendinen at Baltimore. (Aug. 1836).

Coates, Alfred, of Whuling, Virginia, bachelor. Administration
to father William Coates. (Nov. 1841).

Coates, formerly Dean, Fanny, of Boston, U.S.A. Administration
to sister Elizabeth, wife of William Withers; husband Joshua
Coates having died. (Aug. 1830).

Cogswell, Nathaniel, of New York City. Probate to brother
Jonathan Cogswell and sister Lois Cogswell. (May 1834).

Cohen, Jacob Aron, formerly of Jermyn Street, St. James, Westminster, Middlesex, late of South Carolina. Probate to John
Bulow. (June 1813).

Coleman, Bailey, formerly of Lakenheath, Suffolk, late of Mass-
illon, Stark Co., Ohio. Administration to William Bailey
Coleman, attorney for husband William Coleman at Massillon.
(Jan. 1854).

Coleman, Christopher, formerly of Woolwich, Kent, late of U.S.A.
Administration to only child John Christopher Coleman; relict
Sarah Coleman having died. (Apr. 1823).

Coleman, Obed Mitchell, of Saratoga Springs, Saratoga Co., New
York, bachelor. Administration to Ezra Coleman, attorney for
father John Coleman at Saratoga Springs. (Feb. 1846).

Coleman, Peter, of Marblehead, Mass., seaman of H.M.S. *Worcester*.
Administration to John Traill, attorney for relict Ann Coleman.
(June 1800).

Coleman, formerly Stickney, Sarah, of Newbury, Mass. Administration to son John Stickney; husband Benjamin Coleman having
died. (Dec. 1801).

Coles, John, of New London, U.S.A. Administration to daughter
Lydia, wife of Richard Langslow; relict Ann Coles having
died. (Sept. 1827).

Collet, John, of Washington Co., D.C., U.S.A. Limited administration with will to Thomas Wilson, attorney for relict
Anne Collet and son Thomas Collet in America. (July 1822).

Collyer, James, of Coolspring, Mercer Co., Pennsylvania. Admini-
stration with will to John Goodman, attorney for daughter
Jane Collyer at Coolspring; relict Mary Collyer having died.
(July 1844).

Collyer, Samuel Charles, formerly of Kendall Place, Vassall Road,
Brixton, Surrey, late of Market Street, New York. Administration to relict Margaret Eliza Collyer. (Mar. 1837).

Colston, Rawleigh, of Berkeley Co., Virginia. Limited administration with will to John Dunlop, attorney for son Edward Colston in Berkeley Co. (Mar. 1827).

Comerford, John Francis, formerly of Corunna, Spain, who died in America in 1794, bachelor. Limited special probate to sister Frances Jane Frances Comerford. (Feb. 1805). Revoked on her death and granted to her husband Francis, Count de Bryas; sole executor Diego Joseph Borrers having died. (Aug. 1816).

Conquest, George, of New York City. Administration with will to brother John Fricker Conquest, M.D.; executors John Staple and Richard Spaw and mother Ruth Conquest, widow, having died. (Aug. 1835).

Cook, Ellis, of Chatham, Morris Co., New Jersey, widower. Administration to Charles James Partington, attorney for son James Cook at Brandon, Vermont. (July 1855).

Cook, Isabel, of Hanover, Morris Co., New Jersey. Administration to Charles James Partington, administrator to husband Ellis Cook, attorney for son James Cook in Vermont. (July 1855).

Cook, William, seaman of merchant ship *Greenock* who died at Wilmington, U.S.A., bachelor. Administration to mother Ann Cook, widow. (Mar. 1824).

Cook, William, formerly of Folkestone, Kent, late of New York, baker, widower. Administration to Robert Cook, son and surviving executor of father Thomas Cook deceased. (Aug. 1838).

Coombes, Nathaniel, Ensign on half pay of New Jersey Volunteers who died at Allentown, New Jersey. Administration to James Tidbury, attorney for relict Alice Coombes at Allentown. (Dec. 1822).

Cooper, Edward, of Boston, Mass. Probate to brother George Cooper. (Aug. 1809).

Cooper, Elizabeth S. - see Lewer.

Cooper, Thomas, formerly of Canterbury, Kent, late of Philadelphia, bachelor. Administration to brother James Cooper. (Aug. 1806).

Corfield, Richard, of Charleston, South Carolina, bachelor. Administration to sister Elizabeth, wife of George Williams. (Jan. 1807).

Cornish, Henry, of Athol, Warren Co., New York. Administration to James Charles Calver, attorney for relict Mary Ann Cornish at Athol. (Apr. 1847).

Corran, James, of New York, Master of American ship *Factor* who died at sea. Probate to John Younger. (Feb. 1821).

Corre, Helene Florentine, of Charleston, South Carolina, spinster. Administration to sister Carolina Renata Corre. (Oct. 1805).

Cosgrave, John Mahon, of Columbia, Texas, who died at sea on steamer *Sarah Barnes*. Administration to relict Eliza Cosgrave. (Oct. 1844).

Couch, Charles, formerly of Cow Lane, St. Sepulchre, London, late of Baltimore, Maryland, bachelor. Administration to Sophia Couch, relict and administratrix of cousin german Christopher Couch; cousin german Elizabeth wife of John Parlby having died. (Aug. 1802).

Courtenay, Charles Edward Foster, of Pleasant Retreat, Lumpkin Co., Georgia. Administration to relict Nancey Carey, now wife of John Archibald Moodey, M.D. (June 1854).

Cowan, Joseph, formerly of New York, late of Prosperous near Dublin, Ireland. Administration with will of estate unadministered by relict Jane, wife of Thomas Davies, now

deceased to her administrator Samuel Stephenson; grant of
November 1791 revoked. (Feb. 1814).
Cowman, John, of New York City. Probate to James Hay and
Daniel Lord the younger with similar powers reserved to
David Rogers. (May 1833).
Cowper, Mary, of Savannah, Georgia, widow. Limited admini-
stration and limited administration with will to Charles
Shaw, attorney for daughters and only next of kin Mary
Anne Cowper and Margaret wife of John McQueen at Savannah.
(Aug. 1822).
Cox, Henry, formerly of Sheffield, Yorkshire, late of New York.
Administration to Thomas Champion, attorney for relict
Caroline Cox at Boston, North America. (Nov. 1818).
Craig, Archibald Cummings, of Philadelphia who died at Bed-
minster, Somerset Co., New Jersey. Administration with
will to Rev. Joseph Anderson; no executor having been
named and half brother and only next of kin William Currie
cited but not appearing. (Nov. 1802).
Craig, Eleanor, formerly of Donegal, Ireland, who died at sea
passenger on merchant steam ship *Arctic*. Administration
to William Patterson, attorney for only child Eliza Jane
Patterson at Penn Township, Butler Co., Pennsylvania.
(Aug. 1855).
Craig, John, of Philadelphia. Administration with will to
James Mackenzie, attorney for relict Margaret Craig, son
James Craig, and Robert Oliver, John Oliver, David Lenox
and William Miller, all in North America. (Jan. 1810).
Craig, John, of Albany, North America, bachelor. Administra-
tion to mother and next of kin Hellen Craig, widow. (Apr.
1833).
Cram, Dorothy, of Philadelphia, widow. Administration to son
John Cram. (Apr. 1837).
Crate, Joseph Henshaw, of Middleton, Carroll Co., Mississippi.
Probate to Sarah Micoll, spinster, and Charles James Abbott.
(June 1856).
Craufurd, James, formerly of Park Lane, Middlesex, late of New
York City. Administration to brother John Craufurd; relict
Alice Craufurd cited but not appearing. (May 1812).
Craven, Sarah, of New York City. Administration to husband
Joseph Craven. (July 1851).
Crawley, Jacob, formerly of Fulham, Middlesex, mariner, late of
New York City, bachelor. Administration to brother and
sister John Crawley and Rebekah Jones, widow. (Feb. 1837).
Crawley, John, formerly of Bristol, late of New Jersey, widower.
Administration with will to Peter Barlow, attorney for son
John Crawley in New Jersey; executors Thomas Griffith, M.D.
having died, wife Catherine Crawley having died in her
husband's lifetime, and Elisha Boudinet renouncing. (Nov.
1800).
Crawley, Mary - see Morrell.
Crease, Alfred, formerly of Canal side, Camberwell, Surrey,
late of Northern Liberties of Philadelphia, manufacturing
chemist. Administration with will to Orlando Crease, attorney
for relict Ann Constant Crease at Philadelphia. (Jan. 1836).
Creighton, John, formerly of Dudley, Worcestershire, late of
Poor House, Oswego, New York. Probate to Jesse Wright with
similar powers reserved to Edward Crockett. (Dec. 1846).
Cressey, John, formerly of Christ Church, Surrey, late of North
America, bachelor. Administration to brother William Henry
Cressey. (May 1812).

17

Cresswell, Estcourt, of Camden, New Jersey, bachelor. Administration to brother Joseph Cresswell; mother and next of kin Sarah Cresswell renouncing. (Nov. 1843).

Creswell, Frederick, of Baltimore, U.S.A., bachelor. Administration to half sister and only next of kin Mary Ninde Columbia, wife of John Savadge Davenhill. (Mar. 1857).

Creswell, George, formerly of New York, afterwards of Barnsley Hall, Bromsgrove, Worcestershire, late seaman of merchant ship *Nottingham* who died at sea. Administration with will to half sister Mary Nind Columbia, wife of John Savadge Davenhill; executors Joseph Creswell having died and John Creswell renouncing. (Jan. 1854).

Cresswell, Joseph, formerly of Box, Wiltshire, late of Holmesbury near Philadelphia. Probate to surviving executor John Gibbs. (Mar. 1856). Further grant January 1868.

Crispe, Jemimà Humphreys, of Buffalo, New York, spinster. Administration to William Baxter the younger, administrator with will to father John Crispe deceased and attorney for his executor John Bowles at Hamilton Co., Ohio. (Jan. 1840).

Crispe, John, of Buffalo, New York. Administration with will to William Baxter the younger, attorney for John Bowles at Hamilton Co., Ohio. (Jan. 1840).

Critchell, Michael, of Perry Co., Ohio. Probate to Charles Carter with similar powers reserved to relict Ann, now wife of Mathias D. Stotlar. (Dec. 1851).

Cronen, Eleanor, formerly of Bristol, late of Philadelphia, spinster. Administration with will to George Haslewood, attorney for Mary Foulke, widow, at Philadelphia. (Aug. 1816).

Crook, Edward, formerly of Heddington, Wiltshire, late of South Carolina. Probate to George Lockey. (Oct. 1803).

Croskey, Alfred, of Philadelphia. Administration to relict Elizabeth Croskey. (Aug. 1842).

Cross, Margaret, formerly of Bradford Township, afterwards of Huntingdon Co., late of Clearfield Co., Pennsylvania, spinster. Administration to Richard Smith, attorney for father Henry Cross at Clearfield Co. (Mar. 1836).

Crozier, Samuel, of Staten Island, New York, master mariner who died at Petersburgh, Virginia, bachelor. Administration to mother Margaret Robinson, formerly Crozier, widow. (Feb. 1801).

Cruger, Catharine, of New York City, wife of Bertram Peter Cruger. Limited probate to son John Church Cruger. (Apr. 1840).

Cruger, John, of New York. Probate to relict Martha Cruger. (Mar. 1825).

Cruger, Nicholas, of New York City. Probate to relict Ann, now wife of William Rogers, with similar powers reserved to Robert Watts, John Watts, Cornelius Stevenson and William Henry Krause. (Jan. 1805).

Cudlipp, Jonathan, of New York. Administration to relict Lucy Cudlipp. (June 1849).

Cummings, Elizabeth Peach, of Newbury Port, Mass., widow. Limited administration to Petty Vaughan, attorney for only children Elizabeth Maria and Sarah Ann Cummings. (Mar. 1827).

Cundy, William, formerly of Queen Anne Street, Cavendish Square, Middlesex, late of Kent Settlement, Kimbles Bend, Texas, civil engineer. Administration to relict Mary Charlotte Cundy. (Nov. 1852).

Cunningham, Charles, formerly of New Providence, late of Jefferson Co., U.S.A. Limited administration to Robert Eve Cunningham, attorney for relict Ann Pritchard Cunningham in U.S.A. (Sept. 1826).

18

Curran, Lucy alias Lucinda Marcella, of Buffalo, North America.
Administration to husband Michael Curran. (Jan. 1851).
Curson, Richard, of Baltimore, North America. Administration
to relict Elizabeth Curson. (June 1809).
Curtis, Betsey, of Halifax, Nova Scotia. Administration to
Thomas Aspinwall, attorney for husband Henry Curtis at
Roxburgh, Norfolk Co., Mass. (Feb. 1851).
Curwen, Edward, formerly of London, late of Dubuque City, Iowa.
Administration with will to relict Eliza Susannah Curwen.
(Mar. 1857).
Cutmore nee Reddicliffe, Ann Cole, formerly of South Brent,
Devon, late of Laselle, Illinois. Administration to John
Thomas Savery, attorney for husband George Cutmore at Laselle.
(July 1853).
Cuyler, Abraham, Mayor of Albany, U.S.A. who died at Montreal,
Canada. Probate to relict Jane Cuyler with similar powers
reserved to son Jacob Cuyler. (Dec. 1816). Revoked and
granted to Archibald Campbell, attorney for son and surviving
executor Jacob Glen (in will written as Jacob Cuyler) at
Uitehage, Cape of Good Hope. (Apr. 1829).
Cuyler, Henry, of Greenbush, Rensselaer Co., New York, commissary
on half pay of Staff of Martinico. Administration with will
to John Thompson, attorney for relict Catherine Cuyler,
William Howe Cuyler and Ralph Barton Cuyler at Greenbush.
(July 1806).

Dagley, Elizabeth, of Charleston, U.S.A., spinster. Administra-
tion to brother William Thomas Dagley. (June 1856).
Dallett, Judith, of Philadelphia, widow. Probate to son Gillies
Dallett with similar powers reserved to son Elijah Dallett.
(July 1854).
Dalton, Henry, formerly of Sligo, Ireland, late of New York City.
Probate to Rev. Patrick Burke. (May 1825).
Daniel, Henry, formerly of St. Botolph Bishopsgate, London,
late of New York, widower. Administration to brother Alexan-
der Daniel. (June 1800).
Darch, Thomas, formerly of Taunton, Somerset, late of Pinchill,
Kentucky. Administration to son Thomas Darch; relict Joan
Darch cited but not appearing. (Apr. 1801).
Dash, John Balthazar, of New York City, widower. Administra-
tion to son Daniel Bowie Dash. (May 1830).
Daulby, William, formerly of Liverpool, Lancashire, late of New
York City. Probate to Ambrose Lace with similar powers
reserved to Henry Roscoe. (Dec. 1827).
Davenport, Thomas Donald, formerly of Marlborough Cottages,
College Street, Chelsea, Middlesex, late of Cincinnati.
Probate to relict Sophia Donald Davenport alias Danby,
daughter Margaret Donald Davenport and Henry Rance with
powers reserved to John Holland and William Stevenson Fitch.
(Sept. 1852).
Davey, Thomas Henry, formerly of Montpellier Farm, Bristol,
farmer, late of Memphis, U.S.A. Administration to relict
Ellen Davey. (Apr. 1855).

Davis, formerly Botson, Elizabeth, wife of David Davis, of
Pringo, North Carolina. Administration to son John Smith
Davis. (Dec. 1818).

Davis, George, of Philadelphia. Probate to John Wood Nelson
and Benjamin Adam with similar powers reserved to Ebenezer
Duncan, doctor of physic, and Philip McKenna. (Sept. 1822).

Davis, John, of Nantucket, Mass. Administration to Thomas
Banner, attorney for children Obed, William and James Davis
at Boston, America; relict Susanna Davis having died.
(Mar. 1843).

Davis alias Davies, Richard, of St. Louis, Missouri. Administration with will to John Bryan the elder, grandfather and
guardian of son Richard Davis during his minority;   sole
executor James Nolan cited but not having appeared. (Feb.
1853). Revoked on death of John Bryan and granted to Lemuel
Davies, uncle and guardian of son Richard Davis. (May 1854).

Davies, Richard, formerly Lieutenant in 44th Regiment of Foot
who died at New Orleans. Administration to Hickman Rose,
attorney for father Simon Davies at Cork, Ireland. (Aug.
1818).

Davies, William, formerly of Newport, Monmouth, who died in
America, bachelor. Administration to brother and next of
kin Thomas Davies. (Jan. 1802).

Davis, William, of New Orleans, planter. Administration to
Mary Davis, daughter and executrix of creditrix Mary Davis,
widow;   relict, now Maria Holliday, widow, and only surviving children Eliza and Maria Davis, being next of kin of
William Beaumont Davis, a minor, deceased, cited but not
having appeared. (July 1828).

Dawson, Eleanor, of Baltimore, U.S.A., who died at Brighton,
Sussex, widow. Administration to son William Dawson.
(Aug. 1834).

Dawson, William, formerly of Wakefield, Yorkshire, late H.M.
Consul for Maryland. Probate to relict Eleanor Dawson.
(June 1822).

Dawson, William, formerly of Wakefield, Yorkshire, late of
Baltimore, North America, M.D. Limited administration to
Henry Willoughby Rooke. (Jan. 1828).

Day, Benjamin, of Norwich, Norfolk, but late of York Town,
Pennsylvania, widower. Administration to son Jeremiah Ives
Day. (Oct. 1805).

Day, John, of New York and of Liverpool, Lancashire, merchant,
bachelor. Administration to sister Sarah, wife of William
Stewart Lodington. (Dec. 1852).

Dayrell, Paul, of Brooklyn, New York. Administration with will
to Robert Miller, attorney for relict Mary Dayrell and Caleb
Shrive at Brooklyn. (June 1805).

Dean, Fanny - see Coates.

de Begnis, Giuseppe, of New York, professor of music. Administration to relict Josephine Ronzi de Begnis. (Nov. 1849).
Revoked on her death and granted to Robert Wynne Williams,
attorney for daughter Clotilde, wife of Gaetano Fraschini,
at Naples. (Sept. 1854).

De Butts, Mary, formerly of Prince George's Co., Maryland, late
of Alexandria Co., D.C., widow. Probate to John Peyton
Dulany with similar powers reserved to son John Henry De
Butts. (June 1831).

De Butts, Samuel, of Prince George's Co., America. Probate to
Richard Earl Welby with similar powers reserved to relict
Mary De Butts. (Apr. 1816).

De Cevallos alias Ceballos, Don Ciracio, of New Orleans, Louisiana. Probate to Pedro Marin Argote and Thomas Urquhart. (Aug. 1819).

De Conty, Esther, of New York, widow. Administration to nephew Rev. William Dupre, attorney for only sister Elizabeth Harrison, an idiot incapable of taking administration upon herself, during her idiotry. (Aug. 1819).

Degen, Elizabeth, of New Orleans, widow. Administration to James Graves Russell, attorney for son Charles Russell Degen at Mobile, North America. (Sept. 1825).

De Gerstner, Francis Anthony Chevalier, formerly of Prague in Austria, late of Philadelphia. Administration to relict Clara Elisabetha Louisa De Gerstner. (June 1840).

Delafield, Charles, of Milwaukee, Wisconsin, merchant. Administration to John Teesdale, attorney for relict Louisa Maria Delafield at Milwaukee. (Jan. 1844). Revoked on death of Teesdale and granted to Horatio Nelson Fisher as attorney. (Mar. 1854).

De Lancey, Oliver, formerly of New York, late of Beverley, Yorkshire. Probate to son Oliver De Lancey with similar powers reserved to relict Phila De Lancey, Ann wife of John Cruger, and Lady Charlotte Dundas (formerly De Lancey) wife of Sir David Dundas. Grant of December 1785 revoked. (Nov. 1809).

Del Castillo, Dom Manuel Samaniego, of New Orleans, Lieutenant on half pay in Mexican service. Limited administration with will to Anselmo de Arrogave, attorney for Dom Andres Antonio de la Leata at Soto de la Marina, Mexico. (Dec. 1833).

Del Corral, Atanasio Gutienez, of New Orleans, Louisiana. Administration to relict Maria Josefe Arrieta. (Jan. 1834).

de Mazas, Francisco, formerly of Tampico, late of Philadelphia. Administration to Robert Grant, attorney for relict Mary Ann de Mazas at Philadelphia. (Nov. 1831).

Dendy, Samuel, formerly of Theobalds Road, Red Lion Square, Middlesex, late of North America. Administration to father John Dendy; relict Sarah Dendy having died. (Apr. 1808).

De Neufville, John, formerly of Amsterdam, late of Cambridge, Mass. Administration with will to Samuel Williams, attorney for relict Anna Margaret, now wife of John Stoughton, at Boston, Mass. (Apr. 1801).

Denoon, David, of Charleston, South Carolina. Administration with will to Thomas Crokate, attorney for relict Margaret Denoon at Charleston. (July 1823).

Densley, Edith, formerly of St. James, Westminster, late of Alexandria, Virginia. Administration to Joseph Hume, attorney for husband John Bogue (sic). (Mar. 1800).

Dent, Elizabeth, of Manchester Square, Middlesex, widow, (sister-in-law Anna Travers of Philadelphia, widow). Administration with will to Sir William Gibbons, uncle and guardian of great nephews and nieces Frederick, Emily, Robert and Barton Gibbons. (Mar. 1809). Revoked and granted to great niece Caroline Gibbons. (Jan. 1816).

De Olazabal, Jose Javier, of New Orleans. Limited administration with will to Pedro de la Quintana, attorney for relict Maria Nicolasa Migoni de Olazabal at New York. (Dec. 1833).

De Peyster, Frederick, of New York City, Captain on half pay of New York Regiment of Volunteers. Administration to Charles Downes, attorney for son Frederic De Peyster at New York; relict Ann De Peyster renouncing. (Sept. 1836).

Derkheim, Moses Myer, of Norfolk, Virginia. Probate to relict Elizabeth Derkheim, John Busher and Richard Adams. (Feb. 1817).

Des Bouttels, Claude Francois Jean Bellanger, formerly of Paris
late of New Orleans, widower, native subject of France.
Limited administration to Henry Trappes, attorney for Jean
Emmanuel Albert Gustave de Bellanger, only child of nephew
Alexander Marie Odillon de Bellanger, and Daniel Ferdinand
Osterwald, now in Paris. (May 1837).

Desbrosses, James, of New York City, widow. Limited administration to Henry Waddington, attorney for daughters and only
next of kin Charlotte Magdalene Overing, wife of Henry
Overing, and Elizabeth, wife of John Hunter, at New York
City. (June 1808).

Desombrages, Marie Joseph Adine Vezien, of New Orleans, widow.
Administration to daughter Marie Augustine Elisabeth Sophie
Richard, wife of Jean Baptiste Louis Augustine Cauderon.
(June 1833).

D'Espinose, Jerome Francois, of Savannah, Georgia. Administra-
tiob to relict Claire Adelaide Armaignac D'Espinose. (Oct.
1830).

Deveaux, Andrew, of Red Hook Township, Duchess Co., New York.
Administration to Daniel Davies, attorney for relict Anne
Maria Deveaux at New York. (June 1813).

Devereux, Olivia Camilla, of Port Augusta, America, spinster.
Administration to mother Sarah Devereux. (Dec. 1804).

Dickson, William, of Norfolk, Virginia. Probate to relict
Angeline Mallory Dickson, brother Thomas Southgate and John
Southgate. (July 1823).

Dittrich, Rudolph Moritz, of Tampico, Mexico, and New Orleans,
merchant. Administration to relict Jane Louisa Dittrich.
(Mar. 1851).

Dobridge, Robert, of Orange, New Jersey, widower. Administration to James Hoppe, attorney for daughter Sarah Ann Dobridge
at Orange. (June 1846).

Docker, nee Shakespear, Elizabeth Smith, formerly of Filloughley,
Warwickshire, afterward of Birmingham, Warwickshire, late of
Commerce, Scott Co., Missouri. Limited administration with
will to William Wilmot, attorney for husband William Docker
at Missouri. (Dec. 1855).

Docker, Timothy Strickland, formerly of Birmingham, Warwickshire,
late of New Orleans, bachelor. Administration to brother
William Docker. (Apr. 1839).

Docker, William, of Commerce, Scott Co., Missouri, widower.
Administration to nephew William Alcock. (Nov. 1857).

Dodsworth, Sarah Mary, of Marietta, Washington Co., U.S.A.
Administration to husband Thomas Dodsworth. (Oct. 1854).

Dolbeare, Grizzle, of Boston, Mass., spinster. Administration
to niece Hannah Rebecca Dolbeare. (Sept. 1828).

Douglass, John, formerly of St. Augustine, East Florida, late
of Crooked Island, Bahamas. Administration with will to
John Malleson, attorney for brother Benjamin Douglass at
Providence Island; brother David Douglass, sisters Ann
Douglass and Kathrine Smith, widow, and John Graham having
died. (June 1820).

Douglass, Samuel, formerly of Savannah, Georgia, late of Jamaica.
Limited probate to William Douglass, Samuel McClymont and
Hugh McClymont with similar powers reserved to Samuel Douglass,
James Gordon and Alexander Gordon. (Dec. 1800). Revoked and
granted to Rev. James Black, Minister of Penningham, Wigtown-
shire, Rev. John Sibbald, Minister of Kirkmabreck, Kirkud-
bright, and William McCullock. (Apr. 1823).

Douglas, Susanna - see Allman.

Downey, Margaret and Mary, spinsters, formerly of 6 Torr's
Terrace, Rotherhithe, Surrey, who died passengers on
American ship *Charles Bartlett* on passage to New York.
Limited administration to cousin german once removed Justin
McCartley. (Sept. 1849).

Dowsing, Ann, formerly of New Broad Street, London, late of
New York, spinster. Administration to niece and next of
kin Elizabeth Kirby, spinster. (Feb. 1825).

Drew, James, of New York City, Captain in Royal Navy. Administration with will to Rev. Lucius Coglan and Benjamin Samuel
Judah, attornies for Lydia Beckman alias Drew, wife of James
Beckman at New York City; executors Charles Watkins having
died and Samuel Watkins renouncing, and grant of August 1802
to creditor Stephen Drew revoked by decree. (June 1803).

Drexhagen, formerly Medland widow, Jane, formerly of Holsworthy,
Devon, late of New York City. Administration with will to
Henry Henrichsen, attorney for husband Arend alias Aaron
Drexhagen at New York City. (Aug. 1856).

Driver, Thomas, of Salem, Mass., seaman of H.M.S. *Goliath*.
Administration to George Bainbridge, attorney for relict
Rebecca Driver at Salem. (Oct. 1800).

Ducheman, Francis Christopher Ambrose, of Baltimore Co., Maryland. Probate to relict Margaret Moujent Ducheman and
daughter Frances Susanna, wife of Jacob Crawford. (July
1826).

Dudley, Mary Ann Sarah, of 398 Pearl Street, New York City.
Administration to husband Ellis William Dudley. (June 1854).

Duffy, Francis Thomas, of New York City, bachelor. Administration to Peter Franklin Duffy, son and administrator of father
Peter Duffy. (Sept. 1841).

Duffy, Peter, of New York City, widower. Administration to son
Peter Franklin Duffy. (Sept. 1841).

Dulany, Rebecca, of Newport, Rhode Island, widow. Administration
with will to Ann Dulany, executrix to son Daniel Dulany
deceased. (May 1826).

Du Moulin, James, of Baltimore, Maryland. Limited probate to
brother Andrew Joseph Aloysius Du Moulin. (Dec. 1821).

Dunant, George John, of New York, bachelor. Administration to
creditor Charles Robert Sparrow; father James Dunant renouncing. (Dec. 1821).

Dunbar, George, of Queen's Co., New York, Captain on half pay of
1st Batallion of Brigadier-General De Lancey's Provincials.
Administration to David Davies, attorney for relict Elizabeth
Dunbar at Queen's Co. (Dec. 1807).

Dunbar, Tryphene - see Morel.

Dunkin, Anthony Parker and Henry, formerly of Bermondsey, Surrey,
afterwards of Morganfield, Kentucky, late of Philadelphia,
bachelors. Administration to brother Zebedee Dunkin. (June
1826).

Dunkin, John, formerly of Aldersgate Street, London, late of New
York and Philadelphia. Administration to son John Dunkin;
relict Mary Dunkin having died. (Nov. 1840).

Dunkley, Carleton, of Charlestown, America, bachelor. Administration to sister Mary, wife of John Rudd. (Oct. 1817).

Dunn, Nathan, of Philadelphia and of Mount Holly, New Jersey,
who died at Vevay, Switzerland. Limited probate to Samuel
Gurney the younger. (May 1845).

Dunn, Walter, of Middlesex, Virginia. Limited administration
with will to father William Dunn. (Apr. 1820).

Dunn, William, formerly of Bristol, mason, late of New York.
Probate to sister Jane, wife of William Muggleworth, formerly
Jane Locoak, widow. (Apr. 1842).
Durston, Elizabeth, formerly of Catcott, Somerset, late of
Palmyra, Jefferson Co., Wisconsin. Administration to Joseph
Ruscombe Poole, attorney for husband Edmund Durston at Pal-
myra. (Dec. 1856).

Easton, Peter, of Nantucket, Mass. Probate to relict Janice
Easton. (Sept. 1819).
Eaves, Thomas, of Philadelphia, widow. Administration to
daughter Ann, wife of Henry Smith. (Aug. 1809).
Eddy, Caspar Wistar, of New York. Limited administration with
will to Joseph Jackson Lister, attorney for relict Cornelia
Eddy, Benjamin Roosevelt Kissam and Richard Vanck Kissam at
New York. (Nov. 1838).
Eilbeck, John, partner in Eilbeck, Chambre, Ross & Co. at White-
haven, Cumberland, with personal estate in America. Limited
administration with will to only surviving child Mary Eilbeck.
(July 1821).
Eilbeck, Jonathan, formerly partner in Eilbeck, Chambre, Ross
& Co. of Whitehaven, Cumberland, late of Norfolk, Virginia.
Limited probate to Peter Hodgson with similar powers reser-
ved to nephew Rev. Jonathan Benson. (July 1821).
Eisdell, Thomas, formerly of Cornawall Road, Lambeth, Surrey,
late of Lasalle, Illinois, bachelor. Administration to
brother Robert Eisdell. (Aug. 1842).
Elam, Samuel, formerly of Leeds, Yorkshire, merchant, late of
Rhode Island. Administration with will to brothers Gervas
and Robert Elam. (Feb. 1815).
Ellaway, Edward, formerly of Surinam, late of New York. Admini-
stration with will to sister Philly Maria, wife of John McCall;
executor Jonathan Rudge having died. (Jan. 1816).
Ellens, Sarah Elizabeth, of Pass Christian, Louisiana, widow.
Administration to sister and only next of kin Emm, wife of
John Hester. (June 1845).
Ellison, Ellen, formerly of New York City, late of Williamsburgh,
New York. Administration with will to John Frederick Isaac-
son, attorney for nephew Joseph Ellison Palmer at Williams-
burgh. (Nov. 1852).
Elston, David, formerly of Carshalton, Surrey, late of Morris,
New Jersey. Probate to son David Elston with similar powers
reserved to William Britton and James Wood. (Oct. 1857).
Elwyn, Thomas Langdon, of Portsmouth, New Hampshire. Probate
to brother William Brame Elwyn with similar powers reserved
to Samuel Pickering Gardner and relict Elizabeth Langdon
Elwyn. (Mar. 1818).
Emery, Ann, of Wappelow, Louisa Co., Iowa, spinster. Administration to brother John Emery. (Feb. 1856).
English, William Molesworth, formerly of Boston, North America,
late of Manchester, Lancashire, merchant. Limited administration with will to Richard Foster Breed with similar powers
reserved to Aaron Stone. (Oct. 1816).

Evans, Joseph, of Salina, Onandaga Co., New York, bachelor.
Administration to nephew John Evans. (Feb. 1839).
Evans, William, formerly of London, Canada, late of Springfield,
Ohio, widower. Administration to John Wickham Flower,
attorney for son Robert Evans at Paris, Canada. (*Administra-
tion of wife Mary Evans granted same date to son Robert Evans*).
(June 1853).
Evans, William Henry, of Charleston, South Carolina, steam
engineer. Administration to relict Eliza Ann Evans. (June
1833).
Evelyn, Martha B. - see Vincent.
Evill, Luke, formerly of Bath, Somerset, late of Wilmington
Dearborn, North America. Limited administration to Henry
Nethersole. (Jan. 1849).
Ewart, John, formerly of Berwick on Tweed late of Albany, North
America, bachelor. Administration to sister Elizabeth, wife
of Bartholomew Mitchelson; mother Isabella Lanford, formerly
Ewart, widow, having died. (May 1825).
Ewens, Edwin Erastus, of New York City, bachelor. Administra-
tion to brother John Samuel Ewens; father Daniel Ewens
renouncing. (Mar. 1846).
Exter, John and Julia Margaret, bachelor and spinster, of New
York City. Administration to mother and next of kin Dolores
Soto de Beales, wife of John Charles de Beales, formerly
Exter, widow. (Aug. 1852).

Faber, Conrad William, of New York. Probate to Thomas Achelis
with similar powers reserved to relict Emilia Faber and
Christian H. Sands. (Aug. 1855).
Fagg, Francis, of Philadelphia. Administration with will to
relict Martha Fagg; sole executor James Sibborn having died.
(Dec. 1829).
Falcon, Thomas, of Roxbury, Mass. Limited administration with
will to George Frazar with consent of relict Bridget Falcon.
(Sept. 1856).
Farley, Sarah, formerly of Edinburgh, late of Savannah, Georgia,
spinster. Administration with will to Robert Cooper, attor-
ney for aunts Sarah Drysdale, widow, Elizabeth Irvine, widow,
and Rachel Johnston, spinster, at Savannah. (Oct. 1814).
Farmar, Susan Ravand, of New York City, widow. Administration
with will to Francis Martin, attorney for John Warren and
Edward Martin at New York City. (Oct. 1841).
Farmer, Jasper, formerly of New Jersey, afterwards of Barbados,
and late of New York, Captain of 21st Regiment of Foot.
Administration to Effingham Lawrence, attorney for relict
Susan Farmer at New Jersey. (Mar. 1801).
Farr, Robert, of New Orleans, merchant, widower. Administration
to only child Augustus Farr. (Jan. 1857).
Farr, Sarah - see Scott.
Farrant, Charlotte Caroline, of Belleville, New Jersey. Admini-
stration to husband Thomas Farrant. (May 1837).
Farrant, Thomas, of Skaneateles, Onodaga Co., New Yotk. Probate
to brother William Farrant with similar powers reserved to
relict Mary Farrant. (Oct. 1855).

Farrington, Charles, formerly of 8 Union Street, Kingsland
Road, Middlesex, late belonging to American brig *Herald*
who died at Isle of France in 1817, bachelor. Limited
administration to John Farrington, attorney for Joseph
Farrington at 24 Rue de Villiers, Neuilly, France. (Mar.
1844).

Fay, Julia Margaret, of New York City, spinster. Probate to
Arthur Tracy Jones. (Apr. 1843).

Fearnley, Anthony, of Grenville's Camp, Ottoway River, U.S.A.,
bachelor. Administration to brother and only next of kin
John Fearnley. (Mar. 1848).

Fennell, James, formerly of New York, late of Philadelphia,
comedian. Administration to relict Barbara Harriet Fennell.
(Nov. 1817). Revoked on her death and granted to daughter
Caroline Maria Fennell. (Oct. 1826).

Fenner, nee Reeve, Ann, of Baltimore, U.S.A. Administration to
Alexander Cavell, attorney for husband Richard Sankey Fenner
at Baltimore. (Aug. 1848).

Fenner, Margaret, of Rochester, U.S.A. Administration to
husband John Fenner. (May 1854).

Ferguson, Adam, of Newport, Rhode Island. Administration with
will to James Cockburn, administrator to daughter Isabella,
wife of Robert M. Ambrose, and attorney for said Ambrose
at Newport. (Feb. 1802).

Ferrers, John, of New York City, merchant. Administration with
will to James Strachan Glennie, attorney for Cadwallader D.
Colden, Charles Wilkes and relict Jane Anne Ferrers at New
York. (Apr. 1815).

Ferris, Samuel the younger, formerly of St. Thomas the Apostle,
Devon, late of Yazoo Valley, Mississippi, surgeon and apothe-
cary. Probate to John Stogdon with similar powers reserved
to William Cann and James Cook Cann. (Aug. 1841).

Field, Elizabeth Truelock, of New York City, widow. Administration to son John Field. (Oct. 1851).

Field, Tabitha, of Petersburg, Virginia. Administration to
husband Thomas Field. (Oct. 1806).

Fielding, John, formerly of Butterworth, Rochdale, Lancashire,
woollen carder, late of Cass Co., Illinois. Probate to
Isaac Platt & Robert Brearley. (Aug. 1845).

Finch, Hon. John, formerly of Grosvenor Square, Middlesex, late
of New York, bachelor. Administration to brothers Hon. Charles
and Edward Finch. (Apr. 1810).

Fisher, Giles, formerly of Corn Street, St. James, Bath, late
of Savannah, North America, bachelor. Administration to
brother Henry Fisher. (Dec. 1845).

Fisher, James, seaman of schooner *Revenue* in service of U.S.A.,
bachelor. Administration to sister Sarah Fisher. (Mar. 1847).

Fisher, Joseph, formerly of Holborn Hill, London, late of ----,
North America. Limited administration to Timothy Fisher.
(July 1839).

Fisher, Miers the younger, of Philadelphia who died at city of
Petersburgh. Administration with will to John Bainbridge
the younger, attorney for brother Redwood Fisher at Philadelphia. (Feb. 1815).

Fleming, Rev. John, formerly of Higley, Shropshire, late chaplain
of H.M.S. *Ajax*, who died at New York, widower. Administration
to only child Mary, wife of Zachariah Slaney. (Feb. 1829).

Fletcher, Reuben, formerly of Doctors Commons, London, late of
Napoleon, Ripley Co., Indiana. Limited probate to George
Fletcher Walker. (Nov. 1856).

Flower, Elizabeth, of Edwards Co., Illinois. Administration
    with will to Edward Fordham Flower, attorney for son George
    Flower and Hugh Ronalds the elder at Illinois. (July 1847).
Flower, Richard, formerly of Marden, Hertfordshire, late of
    Park House near Albion, Edwards Co., Illinois. Administra-
    tion with will to Edward Fordham Flower, attorney for relict
    Elizabeth Flower at Albion. (May 1830).
Forbes, Ann K. - see Issit.
Ford, Arthur Perroneau, of Charlestown, South Carolina, bachelor.
    Administration to brother and next of kin Frederick Augustus
    Ford. (Nov. 1849).
Foster, James Montague, of Richmond, Virginia, bachelor. Admini-
    stration to John Henry Foster, executor to father John Foster
    deceased. (Dec. 1826).
Foster, John, of Richmond, Virginia. Limited probate to son
    John Henry Foster. (Dec. 1826).
Foster, John, of Leonard Street, New York City, widower.
    Administration to George Cox, attorney for daughter Charlotte,
    wife of Nicholas Spaulding at New York City. (Feb. 1844).
Foster, John, of St. Sacramento, California, bachelor. Admini-
    stration to brother Henry Foster; mother Sarah Foster,
    widow, having died. (Apr. 1850).
Foster, Martha, of 184 Franklin Streeet, New York City, spinster.
    Administration to George Cox, attorney for sister Charlotte,
    wife of Nicholas Spaulding, at New York City. (Feb. 1844)
Fothergill, Anthony, formerly of Bath, Somerset, afterwards of
    Philadelphia, late of St. George's Place, Blackfriars Road,
    Surrey, M.D. Limited administration with will to Thomas
    Bainbridge and, by solemn affirmation, to John Coakley.
    (Dec. 1813).
Fountain, Thomas, of Sugar Castle, Walworth Co., Wisconsin.
    Probate to relict Sarah Fountain. (Aug. 1857).
Fowler, Samuel, of New York, bachelor. Administration to
    brother William Fowler. (Apr. 1828).
Fox, Gilbert, of Charleston, South Carolina, widower. Admini-
    stration to John Somerville, attorney for only child Eliza-
    beth, wife of Edward Veazey, at Lancaster Co., Pennsylvania.
    (Aug. 1829).
Fox, Henry Stephen, formerly British Envoy to U.S.A., late of
    Washington, U.S.A. Administration to sister Caroline, wife
    of William Francis Patrick Napier. (Dec. 1846).
Fox, James, of Liverpool, Lancashire, who died at Savinilla,
    America. Idministration to relict Mary Fox. (Jan. 1843).
Fox, Phillips, formerly of Totnes, Devon, late of North America,
    bachelor. Administration to sister and only next of kin
    Anne, wife of Edward Skinner. (Jan. 1829).
Fox, William, formerly of Bourton on the Water, Gloucestershire,
    late of New York, bachelor. Administration to mother and
    next of kin Jane Fox, widow. (Aug. 1854). Further grant
    April 1861.
Foxall, Catherine, of George Town, D.C., widow. Administration
    with will to sister Elizabeth Martha, wife of Henry Knight;
    surviving executors Isabella Redin, spinster, Angelletta,
    wife of Francis Lowndes, and William Smallwood Bullock
    renouncing. (Feb. 1848).
Foxcroft, John, of Cambridge, Mass. Administration with will
    to John Lowell, attorney for Abraham Biglow in North America.
    (Mar. 1804).
Foxcroft, Sarah, of Cambridge, Mass. Administration to Samuel
    Savile and William Bourfield, attornies for husband John
    Foxcroft at Cambridge. (Feb. 1802). Revoked on his death

and granted to his administrator with will John Lovell as attorney for executor Abraham Biglow; sister Deborah, wife of Gideon White, cited but not appearing. (May 1804).

Francis, Anne, of Philadelphia, widow. Administration with will to Walter Stirling, attorney for surviving executor William Tilghman at Philadelphia. (June 1818).

Francis, Thomas, of Middletown, Connecticut, bachelor. Administration to brother Abraham Francis. (July 1827).

Fraser, Anna Laughton, of Bordenham, New Jersey, widow. Administration to Charles Frederick Tilstone, attorney for daughter Eliza Smith Fraser at Bordentown (*sic*). (Jan. 1841).

Fraser, James, of Charlestown, North America. Administration to creditor Patrick Macleod; relict Mary Fraser and children Sarah Mary, Richard, Ash, Caroline, George, William, Harriet, John and Alexander Fraser cited but not appearing. (Dec. 1807).

Fraser, John, of St. Simon's Island, Georgia, Lieutenant on half pay of Royal Marines. Administration to Charles Menzies, attorney for relict Anne Sarah Fraser at St. Simon's. (Jan. 1841).

Fraser, Thomas, formerly of St. Bartholomew, Charleston, South Carolina, reduced Major of late South Carolina Regiment of Royalists, late of Philadelphia. Administration with will to Crawford Davison, attorney for daughter Eliza Smith Fraser at Philadelphia; relict Ann Loughton Fraser and daughter Jane Winter Fraser renouncing. (July 1823).

Freed, **nee** Woodgate, Elizabeth, of Palermo, Oswego Co., New York. Limited administration to Edward Millen, attorney for husband Joseph Freed at Palermo. (Oct. 1844).

French, John, of Clarke Co., Alabama. Administration to Henry John Turner, attorney for relict Sarah French at Clarke Co. (July 1846).

Friend, Henry, of New Orleans, bachelor. Administration to brother Charles Friend; mother Ann Friend, widow, renouncing. (May 1857).

Frost, John, formerly of Grove Street, Camden Town, Middlesex, late of New York City, jeweller. Administration to relict Maria Frost. (Dec. 1843).

Fry, George, formerly of Hackney, Middlesex, late of Lake Co., Indiana. Administration to relict Dinah Fry. (May 1846).

Fry, Thomas, formerly of Bristol, late of South Carolina. Limited administration to William Woodgate, attorney for William George Cowdry, Thomas Cowdry and Nathaniel Cowdry. (Feb. 1838).

Fuller, James, formerly of Poplar Cottage, Strouds Vale, Maiden Lane, Islington, Middlesex, carpenter, widower, who died passenger on ship *Charles Bartlett* (bound for New York). Administration to son Frederick Fuller. (Aug. 1849).

Fuller, James Cannings, of Skaneateles, Onandaga Co., New York. Probate to relict Lydia Fuller by her solemn declaration. (Dec. 1851).

Fulton, Mark, of Philadelphia. Administration to relict Sarah Fulton. (Apr. 1822).

Furlong, Joseph, formerly of Woolwich, Kent, late of Cincinnati. Administration to relict Mary Ann Furlong. (Mar. 1854).

Futerell, Catherine, formerly of St. Mary Axe, St. Andrew Undershaft, London, late of Charleston, South Carolina, spinster. Administration to William Williams, attorney for James Ramsay, M.D., at Charleston. (May 1832).

Gale, Thomas, of New York City, bachelor. Administration to
father Richard Gale. (Jan. 1823).
Gapper, Susan Maria, formerly of Bristol, late of Philadelphia,
widow. Probate to Richard Van Heythuysen. (Sept. 1838).
Garden, John, of Philadelphia. Probate to William Blackburn.
(Jan. 1801).
Gardiner, John, of Virginia, bachelor. Administration to Phebe
Gardiner, spinster, attorney for brother Peter Gardiner at
Dundee, Scotland. (Nov. 1816).
Gardner, Richard, formerly of Lyme Regis, Dorset, late of Boston,
North America, bachelor. Administration to brother George
Gardner and sister Mary, wife of Thomas Hodder. (June 1820).
Garnett, Henry, of New Brunswick, New Jersey, bachelor. Admini-
stration to mother Mary Garnett. (June 1835). Revoked on
her death and granted to sister Harriet Garnett. (Aug. 1853).
Garnett, John, formerly of Bristol, late of New Brunswick, New
Jersey. Administration to relict Mary Garnett. (Apr. 1822).
Garratt, Robert, formerly of Clieves in the parish of Mugging-
ton, Derbyshire, late of Ossigon, New York. Administration
with will to Thomas Turton, attorney for sons John and
William Garratt in U.S.A. (Feb. 1832).
Gates, Thomas, of Charleston, South Carolina. Administration
with will to James Alexander Simpson, attorney for Henry
Alexander De Sayssure, George Kinloch and Robert William
Fisher at Charleston. (Mar. 1853).
Gee, William, formerly of Stamford, Lincolnshire, late of
Bennington Centre, Wyoming Co., New York. Administration
to brother Edward Gee; relict Drusilla Gee and mother
Elizabeth Gee renouncing. (June 1853).
Gennins, Anne - see Jennings.
Geoghegan, William, of Concordia, Louisiana, M.D., bachelor.
Limited administration to Thomas Todd, attorney for brother
Richard Geoghegan at Concordia. (Sept. 1845).
Gibbs, Richard, of Bensalem, Pennsylvania. Limited probate to
Richard Lowther with similar powers reserved to Brickwood,
Prattle & Co. (Mar. 1804).
Gibson, Abraham Priest, of Boston, U.S.A., U.S. Consul at St.
Petersburgh, who died at Holles Street, Cavendish Square,
Middlesex. Probate to Thomas Aspinwall. (Dec. 1852).
Gifford, Wearman, formerly of Cliff's End House, Withycombe
Rawleigh, Devon, late of Houston, Texas. Administration to
Charles Gifford, son and executor of father Charles Gifford
deceased; relict Sarah Eliza Gifford renouncing. (May 1855).
Gilchrist, Adam, of Charleston, South Carolina. Administration
to John Hopton, attorney for son James Gilchrist at Charles-
ton; relict Elizabeth L. Gilchrist renouncing. (Feb. 1818).
Gilchrist, Adam the elder, of West Chester, New York, widower.
Administration to John Hopton, administrator to son Adam
Gilchrist the younger and attorney for James Gilchrist, son
of Adam Gilchrist the younger, at Charleston, South Carolina;
son Robert Gilchrist having died. (Apr. 1819).
Gilchrist, James, of Waccaumaw near George Town, U.S.A., doctor
of physic, bachelor. Administration to John Hopton, admini-
strator to father Adam Gilchrist the elder, attorney for
James Gilchrist at Charleston, South Carolina. (Apr. 1819).
Gilchrist, Robert, of New York City. Administration to John
Delafield the younger, attorney for relict Elizabeth Gil-
christ at Albany. (June 1819).
Gildart, Francis, of Washington, Mississippi, Captain on half
pay in Tarlton's Dragoons. Administration with will to
James Tidbury, attorney for relict Sophia Gildart and
Theodore Stark at Mississippi. (July 1816).

Giles, Eleazar, of Beverley, Mass., Master of merchant ship
    Harriot, widower. Administration to creditor William Eppes
    Routh; only child Ebenezer Giles cited but not appearing.
    (Oct. 1809). Revoked on production of will and administra-
    tion granted to Benjamin Giles; relict Sarah Giles cited
    but not appearing. (Dec. 1812).
Giles, Robert, of 22 Dock Street, Philadelphia, seaman of
    merchant ship *Carolina*, who died at sea. Administration to
    Thomas Aspinwall, attorney for relict Martha Giles at Phila-
    delphia. (Mar. 1846).
Gilliat, Thomas, of Richmond, Virginia. Probate to brother
    John Gilliat with similar powers reserved to Joseph Gallego,
    Thomas Dent and M.W. Hancock. (Dec. 1810 & Nov. 1812).
    Revoked on death of John Gilliat and granted to son Alfred
    Gallego Gilliat; executors Joseph Gallego and Thomas Dent
    having also died and Michael W. Hancock cited but not
    appearing. (June 1821).
Glascock, Richard, of Richmond, Virginia. Administration with
    will to William Murdock, attorney for son Milton Syms
    Glascock. (Feb. 1812).
Glass, James William, formerly of Newman Street, Oxford Street,
    Middlesex, late of New York City. Probate to mother Maria
    Hackley Glass, widow. (June 1856).
Glasson, Hugh Dunstan, of California, bachelor. Administration
    to father Josiah Glasson. (Oct. 1854).
Gledhill, Harriet, of Eagle, Wyoming Co., New York, who died in
    1849. Limited administration to Thomas Plowman, attorney
    for husband Joseph William Gledhill at Eagle. (Sept. 1857).
Glessing, Henry, of Newburg, U.S.A. Administration to relict
    Clara Eliza Glessing. (Feb. 1836).
Glynn, John, steward of merchant ship *Columbia* who died at Fort
    Vancouver, Oregon, North America, bachelor. Administration
    to aunt and only next of kin Ellen, wife of James Purcell.
    (Feb. 1852).
Godden, William - see Leggett.
Goe, William, of Philadelphia. Administration with will to
    relict Mary Goe; executor William Brufton having died in
    testator's lifetime. (Aug. 1821).
Goldworth, James Chapman, formerly of Bungay, Suffolk, farmer,
    late of Augusta, Georgia. Administration to George Martin
    James, attorney for relict Frances alias Fanny, now wife of
    William Frederick Smith, at Augusta. (Mar. 1851).
Good, Brent, formerly of Hutton, Somerset, late of Troy, America.
    Administration with will to Fanny Good, daughter of testator
    by his late wife Harriet; brother James Good, Thomas Smith
    and William Sheppard renouncing and residuary legatees Joseph
    Edgar and James Partridge Caple also renouncing. (July 1835).
Goodeve, John, of New York City. Administration to William
    Lemmon, executor to relict Rebecca Goodeve deceased; brothers
    Joseph and William Goodeve, nephews and nieces Ann wife of
    John West, John and James Goodeve, Mary wife of Edward White,
    Edward and Joseph Goodeve, and Winifred Waldron wife of
    Daniel Miall, having all died, nephew Benjamin Goodeve renoun-
    cing and nephew William Daniel Goodeve cited but not appearing.
    (Mar. 1843).
Goodwin, formerly Harwood, widow, Elizabeth, wife of Thomas
    Goodwin, of Van Dam Street, New York. Limited probate to
    Daniel Walker. (Oct 1851).
Goodwin, Thomas Fretwell, of Fat Fields, Hampton, Virginia.
    Administration with will to relict Sarah Ann Goodwin; execu-
    tors Martin Long, Daniel Israel, Abraham Jessie, Parris
    Simkins and Thomas Robins renouncing. (May 1849).

Gordon, Ann, of Goochland Co., Virginia, widow. Administration with will to William Murdock, attorney for children James Harrison Gordon and John Matthews Gordon in North America; brothers and surviving executors Philip, Smith and George Woodson Payne renouncing and Robert Payne having died. (Apr. 1808).

Gordon, James, of Lancaster Co., North America. Administration with will to William Murdock, administrator with will to relict Ann Gordon and attorney for children James Harrison Gordon and John Matthews Gordon in North America. (Apr. 1808),

Gore, Elizabeth Ann, of Newark, U.S.A., widow. Probate to William Gerring and George Crane Ruckel. (Apr. 1851).

Gough, Harry Dorsey and Perry Hall, of Baltimore, North America. Administrations with wills to William Hoffman, attorney for surviving executor James Carroll in North America. (Dec. 1822). Revoked on death of Hoffman and granted to George Carr. (May 1829).

Gough, Harry, of Bel Air, Harford Co., Maryland. Administration to William Henry Clapham, attorney for relict Martha Hilton, formerly Gough, at Baltimore. (Dec. 1829).

Gourlay, John, formerly of Streatham, Surrey, late of Green Township, Harrison Co., Ohio. Administration with will to Richard Cattarns, attorney for brother George Gourlay at Green Township. (Oct. 1857).

Gowan, Alexander, of Weymouth, Dorset, afterwards of Long Acre, St. Martin in Fields, Middlesex, late of New York, bachelor. Administration to aunt and next of kin Jane Burnett, widow. (Oct. 1800).

Gracie, James, Lieutenant in 21st Regiment of Foot who died at Baltimore, North America, bachelor. Administration to mother and next of kin Jean Gracie. (Sept. 1817).

Grafton, Woodbridge, of Philadelphia, Captain in American merchant service. Probate to Francis Barault, M.D. (Oct. 1826).

Graham, Joseph the younger, formerly of Scotby, Wetheral, Cumberland, late of New Orleans, bachelor. Administration to Mary Wilkinson, widow, administratrix to father Joseph Graham deceased. (Aug. 1856).

Graham, Lewis, of Pelham, West Chester, New York. Administration with will to Effingham Lawrence, attorney for Egbert Benson and Thomas Hunt at New York; executor John Parkinson cited but not appearing. (Nov. 1800).

Grave alias Graves, Leonard, of Charles Town, South Carolina. Administration with will of estate unadministered by Leonard Grave deceased to nephew Robert Grave; executors brother William Grave, William Burrowes and father Robert Grave having died. (Mar. 1819).

Graves, Richard, formerly of Sheffield, Yorkshire, late of New York City. Administration to relict Elizabeth Graves. (Apr. 1836).

Green, nee Bennett, Ellen Charlotte, of Baltimore, U.S.A. Administration to James Samuel Bennett, attorney for husband Charles Green at Baltimore. (May 1828).

Green, Matthew, of New York City. Administration with will to relict Jane Green. (June 1852).

Greenslade, Francis, formerly of Martinhoe, Devon, late of Independent Grove, Illinois. Administration to relict Mary Ann Greenslade. (Nov. 1838).

Gregory, George, of Kings Town, U.S.A., bachelor. Administration to sister Eliza, wife of William Latter. (Oct. 1855) Further grant June 1859.

Greive, George, formerly of Swansfield, Northumberland, late
    of Brussels, France, citizen of U.S.A., bachelor. Admini-
    stration to creditor Richard Wilson; all those entitled
    to administration cited but not appearing. (Oct. 1809).
Grice, Peter, formerly of Coalbrook Dale, Shropshire, late of
    Rondout, Ulster Co., New York, barge builder, widower.
    Administration to father Peter Grice. (Dec. 1853).
Grigg, Robert, formerly of Looe, Cornwall, late of Mobile,
    North America. Administration to relict Mary Grigg. (Apr.
    1848).
Grogen, William, formerly of Exeter, Devon, late of Charleston,
    South Carolina. Limited administration with will to Edmund
    Granger and Robert Tothill. (Feb. 1818).
Groom, George, of Boston, U.S.A. Administration to relict
    Lydia Groom. (June 1808).
Groves, Elizabeth, of Charlestown, South Carolina. Probate to
    sister Susannah Hawkins, widow, with similar powers reserved
    to sisters Mary Groves and Ann, wife of John Rous. (June
    1810).
Groves, Peter, of New York, bachelor. Administration to father
    Thomas Groves. (Apr. 1847). Further grant October 1874.
Gruet, Peggy, of Newark, New Jersey, widow. Administration
    with will to Thomas Trevor Tatham and Henry Tatham, attornies
    for son **Frederick** Gruet at Newark. (Jan. 1838).
Gunning, Peter, formerly of London, late of Mead Township,
    Crawford Co., Pennsylvania. Administration with will to John
    Joseph Field, attorney for son William Peter Gunning at
    Pittsburgh, North America; daughter Elizabeth Gunning
    renouncing. (Apr. 1850). Revoked on death of son William
    P. Gunning and granted to daughter Elizabeth Gunning after
    retraction of her renunciation. (Aug. 1851).
Gwinn, James, of Nantucket, Mass. Probate to relict Mary Gwinn.
    (June 1818).

Hadfield, George, of City of Washington, North America, bachelor.
    Administration to sister Charlotte Combe, widow. (Aug. 1827).
Hagen, George, of Ferrisburgh, Addison Co., Vermont, miller and
    gardener. Administration with will to Alfred Brown by his
    solemn affirmation, attorney for Rufus Hazard and Andrew
    Holmes at Vermont. (Feb. 1854).
Haigh, Samuel, formerly of Cloudesley Square, Islington, Middle-
    sex, late of New Orleans, bachelor. Administration to sister
    Jane Haigh; mother Jane Haigh having died. (May 1834).
Hake, Lucy, of Racine, Wisconsin. Administration to husband
    Thomas Gordon Hake. (Mar. 1857).
Hale, Edward, formerly of Highgate, Middlesex, late of Water
    Town near Boston, North America. Probate to Sylvanus Hanley,
    William Robinson and son Edward Hale. (June 1811).
Hale, William, formerly of Alton, Hampshire, late of Philadel-
    phia, bachelor. Administration to sister and next of kin
    Ann Seacocke. (Oct. 1832).
Hall, George, of Norfolk, Virginia, bachelor. Administration
    to brother William Hall, attorney for mother Mary Hall,
    widow, during her lunacy. (Mar. 1828).

Hall, Henry, of Charleston, South Carolina, bachelor. Administration to brother Joseph Hall. (Oct. 1804).

Hall, John, formerly of Poole, Dorset, late of New York, bachelor. Administration to father Charles Hall. (Apr. 1813). Revoked on his death and granted to his daughter and executrix Catherine Parkhouse, widow. (Apr. 1815).

Hallowell, Robert, of Gardiner, Mass., widower. Administration to son and next of kin Robert Hallowell Gardiner (sic). (Dec. 1818).

Ham, Samuel, of Portsmouth, New Hampshire. Administration to creditors Thomas Wilson and William Rowlett; relict Jane Ham and only children Abigail and William Ham cited but not appearing. (June 1815).

Hamilton, John, of Harrisburg, Dauphin Co., Pennsylvania. Administration to Michael Smith Parnther, Richard Grose Burfoot and Charles Robert Turner, attornies for relict Margaret, now wife of Andrew Mitchell, in America. (June 1823).

Hammet, formerly Hutchins, Frances, wife of John Hammet, formerly of Bandon, Cork Co., Ireland, late of Philadelphia. Administration to Reuben Harvey, attorney for only surviving children Emanuel Hammet and Ann, wife of Edward Clayton, at Philadelphia. (Sept. 1819).

Hammond, Abijah, formerly of New York City, late of Westchester, New York, merchant. Administration to George Atkinson, attorney for son Charles Henry Hammond in New York City; relict Margaret Hammond renouncing. (July 1838).

Hammond, James, of Zainsville, Ohio, surgeon of H.M.S. Osprey. Administration to Alexander Haldane, attorney for relict Elizabeth Hammond at Zainsville. (May 1834).

Hammond, John, of Warwick, Rhode Island, master mariner. Administration to George William Oleary, attorney for relict Sarah Hammond at Washington, D.C. (Jan. 1844).

Hammond, Samuel, formerly of Birmingham, Warwickshire, late of Brooklyn, New York. Administration to Isaac Hadley, attorney for relict Maria Hammond at Brooklyn. (Jan. 1852).

Hancock, John, of New Orleans, bachelor. Administration to James Hancock, son and administrator of father Robert Hancock deceased. (May 1836).

Hannam, William, of New York, bachelor. Administration to sister Ann, wife of James May. (May 1806).

Harding, Richard, formerly of Market Harborough, Leicestershire, wool stapler, late of Meade Co., Kentucky, widower. Administration to niece Mary Ann Milner, spinster; sisters and only next of kin Anne wife of Thomas Stevenson and Martha wife of Benjamin Page renouncing. (Dec. 1832).

Hardwick, Mary A. - see Stonier.

Hare, Margaret, of Pennsylvania, widow. Administration with will to Walter Stirling, attorney for Robert Hare and John Hare Powel at Philadelphia; other executor Charles Willing Hare cited but not appearing. (Dec. 1819).

Harford, Samuel, formerly of Bristol, merchant, late of New York. Probate to brother John Harford by his solemn affirmation. (Jan. 1839).

Harriman, William, formerly of Upper Thames Street, London, late of New York City, merchant. Administration to daughter Eliza Harriman; relict Frances Harriman having died. (Apr. 1826).

Harrington, Mary, formerly of Thorncombe, Devon, late of Pike near village of Le Raysville, Bradford Co., Pennsylvania, widow. Administration with will to son William Harrington. (June 1843).

33

Harris, Daniel - see Howard.
Harris, Edward, of Moorestown, Burlington Co., New Jersey.
Limited administration with will to son Edward Harris.
(Aug. 1827).
Harris, John, formerly of Dublin, Ireland, late of Charleston,
South Carolina, bachelor. Administration to sister and
only next of kin Elizabeth Patterson, widow. (Sept. 1804).
Harrison, Charles, Captain in New Jersey Volunteers who died
at Sheffield, New Brunswick. Administration with will to
Evan Davies, attorney for brother James Harrison at Sheffield.
(Dec. 1803).
Harrison, Denise, of New York, widow. Administration to Rev.
William Dupre, attorney for only child Esther, wife of
Edward Shepherd at New York. (Aug. 1819).
Harrison, Elizabeth, of New York City, widow. Administration
to nephew Rev. William Dupre. (Aug. 1821).
Harrison, James, reduced Lieutenant in 2nd Batallion of New
Jersey Volunteers of Sheffield, New Brunswick. Administra-
tion to David Davies, attorney for relict Charity Harrison
at Sheffield. (Dec. 1806).
Harrison, John, formerly planter of Manehack, Louisiana, late
reduced Major in South Carolina Royalists, who died at New
Orleans. Administration with will to John Bannatyne, attor-
ney for surviving executor William Durnford at New Orleans.
(Mar. 1806).
Harrison, Jonas, of Savannah, bachelor. Administration to
father George Harrison. (July 1822).
Harrison, Robert, formerly of Plaistow, Essex, late of Buffalo,
U.S.A. Probate to George Price with similar powers reserved
to John William Cundy. (Oct. 1833).
Harrison, William Cockworthy, formerly of Strensham near Tewkes-
bury, Gloucestershire, late of Crocketts, Texas, bachelor.
Administration to creditor Charles Harrison; father George
Harrison renouncing. (Mar. 1853).
Harrold, Alfred, of Philadelphia, merchant. Probate to brother
Frederick William Harrold and Arthur Ryland. (May 1845).
Hart, Charles, formerly of Stafford, Staffordshire, late of
Philadelphia, bachelor. Administration to Elizabeth, wife
of Charles Boult, administratrix with will to father John
Hart deceased. (Jan. 1853).
Hart, Ephraim, formerly of Mark Lane, London, late of New York
City, having title in New Synagogue, Leadenhall Street,
London. Limited administration to Louis Lucas and Philip
Phillips. (July 1840).
Hart, Samuel, formerly of Russia Row, Moorfields, London, late
of New Orleans, Louisiana, merchant. Limited administration
with will to John Hodgson, attorney for James Ramsay at New
Orleans. (Mar. 1834).
Harvey, Charles, formerly of Bourton House, Flax Bourton, Somer-
set, late of Bath, Mason Co., Illinois. Probate to sister
Mary Robinson, wife of Frederick Palmer. (Apr. 1853).
Harvey, Charles Arbuthnot, of Albany, New York, bachelor.
Administration to mother and next of kin Maria Harvey.
(May 1855).
Harvey, Elizabeth, of Upper Canada, New York, spinster. Probate
to father George Harvey. (Sept. 1807). Revoked on his death
and granted to brother William Harvey; mother Elizabeth
Harvey having died in testatrix's lifetime. (Feb. 1817).
Harvey, John, of Mexico who died in Military Service of U.S.A.,
bachelor. Administration to sister Christiana Harvey. (Aug.
1848).

Harvey, Joseph, of Bellevue, Michigan, bachelor. Administration to John Curry and William Curry, administrators to aunt and only next of kin Hannah Curry deceased. (Feb. 1843).

Hassock, George Fisher, formerly of Wimblington, Isle of Ely, afterwards of Rockford, Illinois, who died passenger on steam ship *Sarah Sands*, bachelor. Administration to father Christopher Hassock. (Oct. 1850).

Haswell, Sarah, of Watervliet, Albany Co., New York, widow. Administration to son John Haswell. (Oct. 1829).

Hawksley, Alfred, formerly of 10 Sidmouth Street, Grays Inn Road, Middlesex, who died passenger on ship *Charles Bartlett* (bound for New York), bachelor. Administration to father Thomas Hawksley. (Aug. 1849).

Haxby alias Axby alias Hicksby, Thomas, of New York, flax dresser and rope maker. Administration to mother Sarah Haxby. (July 1842).

Hay, John, of New York, carpenter of merchant ship *Bolivar*. Administration to only child Christian Hay, spinster; relict Christian Hay alias Brown, widow, having died. (Feb. 1845).

Hayden, Jemima, of Castine, Hancock Co., U.S.A., widow. Administration to Henry Frederick Edward Downes, attorney for only child John Hayden at Castine. (Nov. 1836).

Hayden, Samuel, Captain on half pay of late Lieutenant-Colonel Rogers' Regiment who died at Castine, Hancock Co., U.S.A. Administration to Henry Frederick Edward Downes, attorney for only child John Hayden at Castine. (Nov. 1836).

Hayes, Frederick, of Saratoga Springs, Saratoga Co., New York, bachelor. Administration to brother Edward Hayes; mother and next of kin Frances Hayes renouncing. (Dec. 1855).

Hayes, Thomas, Ensign in General Delancey's Corps of Infantry in North America who died at Georgia, bachelor. Administration to David Thomas, surviving executor of brother Robert Hayes deceased; mother Sarah Hayes, widow, having died. (July 1818).

Hayne, William, formerly of Exeter, grocer, late of New York. Administration to relict Louisa Hayne. (Sept. 1846).

Haynes, John, of Philadelphia, bachelor. Administration to sister Mary, wife of Hugh McBride. (Oct. 1806).

Hayt, James, of Bridgeport, Connecticut, quartermaster on half pay of Prince of Wales' American Regiment. Administration to David Davies, attorney for relict Mercy Hayt at Bridgeport. (Apr. 1807).

Hayt, Monson, of New York City, Lieutenant on half pay in Prince of Wales' American Regiment. Administration to David Davies, attorney for relict Lucretia Hayt in New York City. (Apr. 1807).

Hayward, Margaret - see Agar.

Heacock, Peter, of Middletown, Delaware Co., Pennsylvania, widower. Administration with will to daughter Elizabeth, wife of James Bottomley, by her solemn affirmation; executors Thomas Dutton and Jesse Young renouncing. (June 1837).

Head, William, marine of H.M.S. *Andromache*. Administration to Thomas Head, attorney for relict Barbara Austin, formerly Head, at Pennsylvania. (Jan. 1834).

Heal, Charles, formerly of Bridgwater, Somerset, late of Illinois. Administration to Frederick Charles Foster, attorney for relict Betsey Head in Illinois. (Apr. 1854).

Heal, William, formerly of Church Street, Hackney, Middlesex, late of Baltimore, U.S.A. Administration to relict Elizabeth Heal. (Feb. 1833).

Healy, John, of Albany, New York, bachelor. Administration to
brother Michael Healy. (Nov. 1831).

Heapy, John, of Philadelphia who died in 1809. Limited administration to Charles Rowland Packer of Greenwich, Kent,
attorney for Abraham Nettlefold and James Cronk. (July 1822).

Hearn, Anthony, of Penn Township, Philadelphia Co., Pennsylvania.
Probate to Redmond Byrne, John Carroll and Joseph Smyde.
(Apr. 1818).

Hearsum, Elizabeth, of Albion, Illinois. Administration to
husband David Hearsum. (Apr. 1844).

Hearsum, Mary, of Albion, Illinois. Administration to husband
David Hearsum. (Apr. 1844). *Both sic in Act Book*

Heath, Joseph Thomas, formerly of Millend Farm, Buckinghamshire,
late of Steilcoom, Oregon. Probate to brother Thomas Mason
Heath with similar powers reserved to William Fraser Tolmie.
(Feb. 1851).

Heathcote, John, formerly of Love Lane, Aldermanbury, London,
late of Baltimore, U.S.A. Limited administration with will
to Thomas Edwards, Enosh Durant and George Elwall. (July
1814).

Heighway, John, of New Orleans, bachelor. Administration to
brother and only next of kin Richard Husband Heighway.
(May 1851).

Hemming, George, formerly of Hampstead Marshall near Newbury,
Berkshire, late of Lockport, North America, bachelor.
Administration to brother William Hemming; mother Priscilla
Kimber, formerly Hemming, widow, having died. (Feb. 1853).

Hemsley, William, of Baltimore, North America, millwright,
widower. Administration to son Thomas Hemsley. (Dec. 1834).

Hendrie, James, of Mobile, Florida, widower. Administration
to sisters Jean and Marian Hendrie; mother Jean Hendrie,
widow, having died. (Aug. 1808).

Henley, Peter, Chief Justice of North Carolina, widower.
Administration to Charles Frederick Henley, administrator
to only child John Henley deceased. (Feb. 1825).

Hennessey, Mary Frank, formerly of 33 Baker Street, Portman
Square, Middlesex, afterwards of Philadelphia, who died at
St. Croix, West Indies, widow. Administration to sister
Ann Akers, wife of John Price. (Nov. 1836).

Henry, John, of Richmond, Virginia. Probate to brother James
Henry with similar powers reserved to Conway Whittle. (Dec.
1809).

Henshaw, Sarah Richards, of New York City, spinster. Administration to Percival White, attorney for mother and next of
kin Sarah Richards Henshaw at New York City. (Feb. 1811).

Herault, Elizabeth, of Sherman, Fairfield Co., Connecticut,
widow. Administration to George Goryer, attorney for
natural child Hannah Hubbell at Queensbury, Washington Co.,
New York. (Oct. 1804).

Heron, Andrew, of Augusta, Georgia, bachelor. Administration
to brother Peter Heron. (Feb. 1817).

Herring, James, of New York. Probate to relict Mary Herring
with similar powers reserved to son James Herring. (Aug.
1830).

Hesketh, Henry, of Sacramento, California, bachelor. Administration to brother and only next of kin Robert Hesketh.
(Dec. 1856).

Hewetson, James, of New York State, bachelor. Administration
to brother and next of kin Benjamin Hewetson. (July 1813).

Hewson, Thomas, formerly of College Street, Westminster, Middlesex, late of Charlestown, America, bachelor. Administration
to sister Maria Catharine, wife of James Sanders; mother

and next of kin Fanny Hewson, widow, having died. (July 1836).

Hiatt, James, of Point Township, Northumberland Co., Pennsylvania, purser in Royal Navy. Administration with will to James Park, attorney for James Hepburn in Northumberland Co. (Feb. 1814).

Hibbard, Eliphaz, late of Picton, Nova Scotia, who died at New Orleans. Administration to relict, now Ann Jones. (Aug. 1838).

Hichens, Thomas, Captain of 93rd Regiment of Foot who died at New Orleans. Probate to brother and sole heir Richard Hichens. (Feb. 1816).

Hickman, John, of Columbia, Caldwell Co., Louisiana. Administration to brother Charles Randall Hickman; relict Eliza Hickman cited but not appearing. (June 1847). Revoked on death of Charles R. Hickman and granted to sister Harriet, wife of Francis Arthur. (May 1850).

Hicksby, Thomas - see Haxby.

Hide - see Hyde.

Hill, James, formerly of Tipton, Staffordshire, late of Chicago, Illinois. Administration to John Richardson, attorney for relict Jane Elizabeth Hill at Chicago. (June 1853).

Hill, James Spackman, formerly of Twickenham, Middlesex, afterwards of Old Hall near Ware, Hertfordshire, late of Cincinnati. Probate to Marlow John Francis Sidney. (Dec. 1830).

Hill, Mary - see Lanfear.

Hill, William, Controller of Customs at Sydney, Cape Breton Island. Administration to Alexander Harper, attorney for relict Rebecca Hill at Boston, Mass. (June 1804).

Hilton, Benjamin, of New York City, widower. Administration with will to James Tidbury, attorney for children Edward and John Hilton and Ann Benjamin Halsted, widow, at New York. (Mar. 1834).

Hinckley, William, of Joseph, Calhan Co., Florida, gardener. Administration to brother James Hinckley; relict Ann Hinckley having died. (Nov. 1850).

Hine, Thomas, of New Orleans. Administration with will to brother Michael George Hine. (May 1845).

Hines, Richard Johnston, of New Orleans, bachelor. Administration to mother and next of kin Marrian Hines, widow. (Dec. 1850).

Hipkins, Paris, of Galveston, Texas. Administration to daughter Maryann, wife of John Bush; relict Maryann Hipkins having died. (Aug. 1855).

Hitchcock, nee Wigmore, Elizabeth, formerly of Woolwich, Kent, late of New York City. Administration to Ann, wife of Thomas Bond, attorney for husband William George Hitchcock at New York. (Feb. 1840).

Hocking, John, formerly of Camborne, Cornwall, late of Rockland, Ontario Co., U.S.A. Administration to relict Margaret Hocking. (July 1855).

Hodge, Robert Bickford, formerly of Exeter, Devon, late of Camden, New Jersey, bachelor. Administration to brother Coplestone Edward Hodge and sister Betsy Damerell Bickford Hodge. (Sept. 1845).

Hodges, Frederick Downer, formerly of Victoria Cottage, Farleigh Down near Hastings, Sussex, late of New York City. Probate to relict Elizabeth Hodges. (Nov. 1845).

Hogan, Michael, of New York State. Administration to relict Frances Hogan. (May 1835).

Hogarth, George, formerly of Middle Temple, London, late of
Baltimore, North America. Limited administration to Henry
Farnell. (Apr. 1844).
Hogg, William, formerly of London, jeweller, late of U.S.A.,
bachelor. Administration to nephew and only next of kin
Abraham Hogg. (Apr. 1809).
Holiday, William, of Goose Creek, South Carolina, planter.
Administration with will to William Lee, attorney for
Joan Carlyle alias Bell, wife of Walter Bell, daughter and
administratrix with will to cousin Jean alias Jane Bell
deceased, at Nether Albie, Dumfries, Scotland; executors
Charles Johnson, John Simpson, Jacob Valk, Ziphaniah Kinsley,
William Edwards and relict Sarah Holiday having died;
sister Sarah Paisley Jane, wife of John Carlyle and legatees
Jane Bell and Elizabeth Groves having also died; and sur-
viving legatee William Blacklock having been cited but not
appearing. (May 1810).
Hollis, Thomas Frederick, of Dominica, West Indies, bachelor.
Administration to mother Lucinda Hollis, widow; father
Thomas Pelham Hollis having died. (Feb. 1834).
Hollis, Thomas Pelham, of New York. Administration to relict
Lucinda Hollis. (Feb. 1834).
Holman, Mary - see Sellens.
Holt, Elizabeth, of Washington, North America. Administration
to John Hay, attorney for husband Theophilus Holt at Washing-
ton. (Aug. 1809).
Homfray, Jeston, formerly of Old Swinford, Worcestershire, late
of Spotswood, New Jersey, widower. Administration to only
child Francis Homfray. (May 1803).
Hood, William, formerly of Bristol, late of Charleston, U.S.A.
Administration with will to relict Sarah Hood; executors
John Acraman having died in testator's lifetime and Robert
Jenkins since. (Sept. 1837).
Hooton, George, of Sullivan Street, New York. Administration
to son William Henry Hooton; relict Rachel Hooton having
died. (Sept. 1851).
Hooton, John, of Gloucester Co., New Jersey, Captain of late
Batallion of West Jersey Volunteers. Administration to
Leonard Streate Coxe, attorney for relict Rachel Hooton in
Gloucester Co. (Mar. 1805).
Hopkins, John, of Philadelphia. Probate to Samuel Fatin with
similar powers reserved to Samuel Griffiths. (Aug. 1850).
Hopper, Thomas, of Lyons, Wayne Co., New York. Administration
to relict Mary Hopper. (May 1851).
Hopwood, Jemima - see Rolph.
Horley, John and William, formerly of Croydon, Surrey, late of
Charles Town, South Carolina, bachelors. Probate to mother
Mary White, widow. (May 1804).
Horlock, Joseph, formerly of Southwark, Surrey, late of Charles-
ton, South Carolina. Administration to relict Dorothy Horlock.
(Aug. 1803).
Horrell, Thomas Armstrong, of Texas, North America, widower.
Administration to daughter Mary Ann Horrell. (July 1841).
Hosier, William, formerly of Laverton, Somerset, farmer, late
of Milwankel, Wisconsin, bachelor. Administration to brother
and next of kin Joshua Hosier. (Sept. 1857).
Houghton, Jane, of Fulton Street, Brooklyn, New York, widow.
Administration to Jonathan Stevens, attorney for daughter
Mary Jane Smith, widow, at New York. (Dec. 1854).
Hounslow alias Hunt, Mary Ann, formerly of Exeter Change,
Middlesex, late of Philadelphia Co., Pennsylvania, spinster.

Probate to Henry Hunt with similar powers reserved to Samuel
Hunt. (June 1828).

Houseal, Frances, of Prince William parish, South Carolina,
wife of John Bernard Houseal, formerly of Streatham, Surrey,
late of North America. Limited administration to William
Marsh and Richard Creed. (July 1810).

Howard, Abigail, of Boston, Mass., widow. Administration with
will to Alexander Thomson, attorney for Rev. Samuel Parker
DD, at Boston. (Feb. 1802).

Howard alias Harris, Daniel, formerly of Jamaica, late of
Newport, Rhode Island, bachelor. Administration to father
Thomas Howard. (Apr. 1807).

Howard, Thomas George, of Pulaski, Arkansas, widower. Admini-
stration to mother Mary Calvert Howard. (Oct. 1847).
Revoked on her death and granted to brother Edward John
Howard and sisters Harriet and Margaret Howard. (Aug. 1852).

Howell, Henry, formerly of Bath, late of Savannah, West Indies,
bachelor. Administration to brother Williams Howell and
sisters Catharine wife of William Marks and Elizabeth wife
of John Howell. (Jan. 1818).

Hoyt, Esther, of New York, widow. Administration to James
Tidbury, attorney for son Stephen Hoyt at New York. (Oct.1828).

Hoyt, Stephen, Captain on half pay of Prince of Wales' American
Regiment of Poughkeepsie, New York. Administration to Daniel
Thomas, attorney for relict Esther Hoyt at New York. (July
1810).

Huertis, James - see Hustis.

Hughes, Charles, formerly of Devizes, Wiltshire, afterwards of
Chelsham, Surrey, late of Fairfax Court House, Virginia.
Administration to creditor Richard Miller; relict Nancy
Hughes and children Elizabeth, Sarah Ann, -----, spinster,
------, spinster, and Thomas Hughes cited but not appearing.
(Dec. 1809).

Hughes, John Stokes, of New Orleans, who died at Messina, Sicily,
merchant. Probate to sister and surviving executrix Elizabeth
Mary, wife of Rev. Horatio Moule. (Oct. 1856).

Humble, Edward, of Staten Island, New York, bachelor. Administration to sisters Maria wife of Charles Smith and Jessie Humble;
mother and next of kin Isabella Humble, widow, having died.
(Jan. 1856).

Humphreys, Jane, of Philadelphia, widow. Administration to only
child Thomas Humphreys. (Aug. 1843).

Hunt, Betty, formerly of Derby, late of New York City, spinster.
Administration with will to Edward Leam, attorney for Richard
Brown in New York. (Jan. 1847).

Hunt, Mary A. - see Hounslow.

Hunter, Daniel, of Wilmington, North Carolina. Limited administration with will to Jameson Hunter, attorney for relict
Sarah J., now wife of Nathaniel Potter at Wilmington. (Apr.
1831).

Hunter, Septimus Hewgill alias Robert Edward, formerly of High
Street, Margate, Kent, late of New Orleans, surgeon.
Administration to relict Frances Margaret Hunter. (May 1848).

Huntington, Henry, of New York City, bachelor. Administration
to father Thomas Huntington. (June 1832).

Huntington, formerly Morgan, Sarah, wife of Hezekiah Huntington,
of Hartford, Connecticut. Limited administration to brother
James Francis Morgan, attorney for niece Lucretia Williams
Imlay, wife of William Edward Imlay, in Connecticut. (Mar.
1850).

Huntington, Thomas, formerly of Bristol, late of New Rochelle,
New York. Probate to Peter Shute and Newberry Davenport
with similar powers reserved to Pitcher Huntington. (July
1801). Revoked and granted to son James Pitcher Huntington
(July 1817).

Huntley, Richard, formerly of Newcastle upon Tyne, Northumberland, late of Staten Island, New York, merchant. Administration to Michael Clayton, attorney for relict Susannah
Huntley at Staten Island. (Apr. 1829).

Hurry, Samuel, of Philadelphia. Probate to relict Elizabeth
Ann Hurry with similar powers reserved to son John Hurry.
(May 1824).

Husband, Thomas Craskell, formerly of Manchester, Jamaica,
late of Trenton, New Jersey. Administration with will to
Edward Husband, attorney for relict Adah Ann Husband and
sister Caroline Husband in U.S.A. (Apr. 1838).

Hussey, Ammeill alias Amiel, of Nantucket, North America,
Master of merchant ship *Britannia* employed in Southern
Whale Fishery. Administration to creditor Abraham Lyon
Moses; relict Anis Hussey and only child Lydia Hussey
cited but not appearing. (Oct. 1808).

Hustis alias Huertis, James, of New York City, Lieutenant on
half pay of Loyal American Chasseurs. Limited administration to James Tidbury, attorney for relict Margaret Hustis
in New York. (June 1824).

Hutchins, Frances - see Hammet.

Hutchinson, Anthony John, of Helena, Arkansas, bachelor.
Administration to sister Elizabeth, wife of Joseph Fryer.
(Nov. 1850).

Hyde, Charlotte - see Young.

Hide, Jean - see Bliss.

Ingate, Anne, of 29 Greenwich Avenue, New York City, widow.
Administration with will to George Laurence, attorney for
son James Wright Ingate in New York City. (June 1847).

Innerarity, John, formerly of Montpellier Row, Stockwell, Surrey,
late of Savannah, Georgia. Administration to creditor Andrew
Millar; relict Henrietta Innerarity and daughter Henrietta
Innerarity renouncing, they and sons James and John Innerarity being only persons entitled to administration. (Jan.
1805).

Inwood, John Payne, of Savannah, Georgia, bachelor. Administration to sister Sarah Inwood. (Nov. 1847).

Israel, Israel the younger, of Philadelphia, bachelor. Administration to James Mackenzie, attorney for father Israel
Israel at Philadelphia. (Mar. 1812).

Issit, formerly Forbes, Ann Katherine, of Charleston, South
Carolina. Administration to husband Charles Gorman Issit.
(Apr. 1824).

Ivy, James, of Shoreditch, Middlesex, late of New York City,
widower. Administration to daughter Esther, wife of James
Mills. (June 1800).

Jackson, George Knowil, of Boston, Mass., doctor of music,
widower. Administration to son Charles Jackson. (Mar. 1824).
Jackson, Jane, wife of George Knowil Jackson, of Boston, Mass.
Administration to son Charles Jackson. (Mar. 1824).
Jackson, Theodore, of Boston, Mass., bachelor. Administration
to brother Charles Jackson, administrator to father George
K. Jackson deceased. (Mar. 1824).
Jackson, William, formerly of Wetherden, Suffolk, late of
Kingston, Luzerne Co., Pennsylvania. Administration to
John Seaman, attorney for relict Elizabeth Jackson at King-
ston. (Jan. 1841).
Jacobson, Swansea, of Naval Asylum, Philadelphia, bachelor.
Administration to brother John Jacobson. (Sept. 1844).
Jalland, John, formerly of Lutton, Lincolnshire, late of
Baltimore, North America. Administration to Thomas Gaisford,
attorney for brother and next of kin Joseph Jalland at
Coddington, Nottinghamshire; relict Ruth Jane Jalland cited
but not appearing. (Aug. 1810).
James, Benjamin, of Frankfort, North America. Administration
to daughter Elizabeth Amer, widow; relict Ursula James
having died. (July 1829).
Jardine, Robert S., of Madison Co., Virginia. Limited admini-
stration with will to James Ross with similar powers reser-
ved to John Thom and John Mundell. (Dec. 1815).
Jauncey, Mary, of New York City, spinster. Administration to
brother and next of kin William Jauncey. (Jan. 1822).
Jauncey, William, formerly of Charlotte Street, Portland Place,
Middlesex, late of New York City. Probate to Thomas Barclay
and John Rutherford with similar powers reserved to John
Chambers. (July 1829).
Jenkins, Elizabeth - see Brett.
Jennings alias Gennins, formerly Radcliffe, Anne, of Roxburgh,
U.S.A. Administration to George Cox, attorney for husband
Thomas Jennings in Pennsylvania. (Nov. 1833).
Jerrard, John, formerly of Chideoak, Dorset, late of Boston,
North America. Administration with will to John Perham,
husband and administrator of sister Joan Perham deceased.
(May 1814).
Jimenez, Jose - see Ximenez.
Johnson, Charles, formerly of Calcutta, East Indies, late of
Newcastle, Delaware, bachelor and bastard. Administration
to Samuel Johnson for use of the King. (Mar. 1827).
Johnson, John, of New London, Chester Co., Pennsylvania. Admi-
nistration to William Lumley, attorney for relict Sarah
Johnson at North Milford Hundred, Cecil Co., Maryland.
(June 1827). Revoked on his death and granted to relict
Sarah, now wife of Levin Shockley. (Dec. 1834).
Johnson, Joshua, formerly of Coopers Row, St. Botolph Aldgate,
London, late of Washington City, North America. Administra-
tion to creditor William Taylor; relict Louisa Johnson and
only children Ann Johnson, Louisa wife of John Quincy Adams,
Caroline, Thomas, Harriet, Eliza and Adelaide Johnson cited
but not appearing. (May 1805).
Johnson, Sarah, of Charleston, South Carolina, widow. Admini-
stration with will to Thomas Crowder, attorney for sons
Joseph and James Johnson at Charleston. (July 1838).
Johnson, Simon, of New York City. Administration with will to
Gabriel Shaw, administrator to granddaughter Margaret Johnson
Bibby (formerly McEvers), wife of Thomas Bibby; relict
Margaret Johnson and executors Robert G. Livingston, Gerrard
Beekman the elder and William Neilson having died. (May 1823).

Johnson, Thomas, of Savannah, North America, bachelor. Administration to sister and only next of kin Elizabeth Nicholson.
(Jan. 1808).

Johnson, Uzal, surgeon on half pay of New Jersey Volunteers.
Administration with will to James Tidbury, attorney for
relict Jane Johnson and son Isaac Arthur Johnson in New
Jersey. (Apr. 1828).

Johnsons, George, formerly of Corsham, Wiltshire, late of
Albany, U.S.A., widower. Administration to Thomas Branson,
attorney for daughter Elizabeth Fleet, widow, in America.
(Sept. 1817).

Johnston, Johanna, formerly of Woolwich, Kent, afterwards of
Philadelphia, died passenger on merchant ship *Three Brothers*,
Captain Hargrave, at sea, widow. Administration to nephew
and next of kin George Boston. (Sept. 1839).

Johnstone, John, of Fort Vancouver, City of Columbia, U.S.A.
Probate to surviving executrix Isabella Miller alias Moar,
wife of Jonathan Moar, formerly wife of James Logie. (June
1856).

Jones, Christopher, formerly of St. Asaph, Flint, late of New
York City, plumber, painter and glazier, bachelor. Admini-
stration to mother and next of kin Elizabeth Jones, widow.
(Sept. 1852).

Jones, Eden Henry, formerly of Bristol, chemist, late of New
York. Administration to relict Annatilda Juliet, now wife
of Joseph Haythorne Latcham. (Mar. 1853).

Jones, Henry, formerly of Throgmorton Street, London, late of
Charleston, South Carolina, merchant. Administration with
will to Thomas Crokatt and Charles Alderman, attornies for
John McDowall and James Harper at Charleston; William
Inglesby renouncing. (June 1815).

Jones, John, formerly of Gilfach Wyod, Dolgelly, Monmouth,
farmer, late of New York City, widower. Administration to
mother Catherine Jones, widow. (Aug. 1849).

Jones, John Coffin, of Boston, U.S.A. Limited probate to
Ebenezer Chadwick with similar powers reserved to Isaac
Underhill Coles and Margaret Champlin Coles; relict
Elizabeth Jones having died. (Sept. 1838).

Jones, Losco, formerly of Bethnal Green, Middlesex, late of
California in South Seas. Probate to Dennis Peele with
similar powers reserved to Jane Jones, widow. (Nov. 1829).

Jones, Louisa, formerly of Toronto, Canada, late of Hamilton
Co., Ohio. Administration to husband John Jones. (Jan.
1852).

Jones, William, formerly of Goodge Street, Tottenham Court Road,
Middlesex, late of Nacogdockes, Texas, merchant, widower.
Administration to sister Sarah, wife of Edward Davis. (June
1848).

Jope, Priscilla - see Balsley.

Jope, Sarah - see Williams.

Joseph, Benedictus, of New York. Administration to Henry Joseph,
attorney for relict Jane Joseph at New York. (Mar. 1851).

Joseph, Eliza, of New York, widow. Administration to son John
Joseph. (Oct. 1853).

Joseph, Samuel, formerly of Plymouth, Devon, afterwards of
Philadelphia, late of Cincinnati, Ohio. Administration to
Nathan Joseph, attorney for relict Rebecca Joseph at Phila-
delphia. (July 1827).

Jouett, Daniel Troop, of Philadelphia. Administration to Rev.
William Parker, attorney for relict Margaret Jouett at Philadelphia. (July 1814).

Judd, James, formerly of Wyke Regis, Dorset, late of Cincinnati, bachelor. Administration to sisters Georgiana and Anna Maria Judd; mother and next of kin Mary Judd, widow, having died. (Apr. 1851)

Kane, John the elder, of New York City. Administration with will to Gabriel Shaw, administrator to John Kane the younger deceased, sole executor. (Nov. 1822).
Kane, John the younger, of New York City. Administration to Gabriel Shaw, attorney for relict Maria Kane in New York City. (Nov. 1822).
Kasner, Barnet, of San Francisco, California, bachelor. Administration to father Isaac Kasner. (Nov. 1851).
Kearney, Julia L. - see Morris.
Kearney, Susan alias Susannah, of Newark, New Jersey, widow. Limited administration with will to John James Watts, attorney for daughter Eliza Kearney in New York City. (Aug. 1851).
Keeling, William, of New York, bachelor. Administration to John Keeling, son and executor of Alice Keeling, relict and sole executrix of father Joseph Keeling. (Aug. 1823).
Keen, Mary, formerly of Witney, Oxfordshire, late of New Orleans. Administration to husband Richard Keen. (Apr. 1854).
Keith, Ann - see McAlister.
Keith, Charles, of Georgia, America, Lieutenant of Royal Navy, bachelor. Administration to father William Keith. (Mar. 1818).
Keith, Charlotte - see Barron.
Keith, James, formerly of Charles Town, South Carolina, late of Blairskinnock, Banff, Scotland. Administration with will of estate unadministered by James Irving alias Irvine deceased to Marion Irving, widow, attorney for nephew John Keith at George Town, South Carolina; executors George Gerrard having died and William Irvine and Robert Falder alias Folder cited but not appearing. (Aug. 1810).
Keith, Mary, of George Town, South Carolina, spinster. Limited administration to John Tunno, attorney for brother and only next of kin John Keith. (Aug. 1807).
Kennedy, Rev. John, formerly of East Florida, late of Glasgow, Scotland. Probate to Coll McDonald with similar powers reserved to Alexander McDonald and Charles McPherson. (Dec. 1802).
Kerie, Rev. John Julius, formerly of Island of St. Christopher's, late of Philadelphia. Administration with will to son Julius Samuel Kerie; surviving executor brother Jedediah Kerie renouncing. (Aug. 1847).
Kerr, Alexander, Lieutenant of 62nd Regiment who died at Philadelphia, bachelor. Administration to mother Elizabeth Kerr. (May 1802).
Kidd, Mary Adeline, of Derby, Connecticut. Administration to husband Samuel Kidd. (Mar. 1826).
Killick, Sarah, of Ripley Farm, Rochester, New York. Administration to William Stevens, attorney for husband Thomas Killick at Ripley Farm. (July 1838).

43

King, nee Albin, Catherine, of Charleston, South Carolina.
Limited administration to brother-in-law David Henry King,
attorney for husband William King in New York. (Jan. 1854).
King, John, formerly of High Wycombe, Buckinghamshire, late
of Baltimore, Maryland, bachelor. Administration to father
Edward King. (Mar. 1805). Revoked on his death and granted
to one of his executors Isaac Sheffield. (Feb. 1821).
King, John, formerly of Grays, Essex, afterwards of Hoxton,
Middlesex, but late of Jersey, America. Probate to John
Bourne of Crutched Friars, London, and George Swan with
similar powers reserved to Joan Dyer Dommott Dommott,
spinster. (June 1831).
King, Thomas the younger, of Charles Town, America, widower.
Administration to brother William Robert Wale King, admini-
strator to father Thomas King. (May 1810).
Kingsbury, Jonathan, of Needham, Mass. Probate to son Asa
Kingsbury. (Aug. 1807).
Kirby, James, of Richmond, Virginia. Probate to brother Robert
Kirby with similar powers reserved to Joseph Gallego.
(Apr. 1815).
Kirkman, Thomas, of Dalkey, Dublin Co., Ireland, late of
Nashville, Tennessee. Administration with will to son
Thomas Kirkman, attorney for relict Barbara Carroll Kirkman
at Philadelphia; Ephraim Carroll and Robert Jones renouncing.
(June 1815).
Kirkman, Thomas, of Nashville, Davidson Co., Tennessee. Probate
to relict Eleanor Kirkman with similar powers reserved to
Washington Jackson and Bolton Jackson. (Sept. 1828).
Klingender, Frederick, of New Orleans, bachelor. Administration
to Catharine Martha Klingender, relict and administratrix of
father Frederick Charles Louis Klingender. (July 1836).
Knight, Charles, of Philadelphia. Administration to John
Cryder, attorney for relict Sarah Knight at Berwick, Columbia
Co., U.S.A. (July 1839).
Knott, Elizabeth, of Utica, Oneida Co., New York, widow. Admi-
nistration to Ann Holliday, widow, attorney for son Joseph
Marshall Knott at Utica. (Mar. 1854).
Knowles, John, formerly of Philadelphia, since of Tottenham
Court Road, watch and clock maker late of Trinidad. Admini-
stration to relict Sarah Knowles. (May 1810).
Knowles, John, of Bound Brook, North America, bachelor. Admi-
nistration to mother Sarah Knowles, widow. (Nov. 1835).
Knowles, Richard, formerly of Nailstone, Leicestershire, late
of New York City, bachelor. Administration to brother
Joseph Knowles. (May 1837).
Knox, Frances, formerly of High Park and Levington Park, West-
meath, Ireland, late of Philadelphia, widow. Administration
to Dame Mary Levinge, widow, relict and executrix of father
Sir Richard Levinge. (Sept. 1818).
Kuchenthal, Henry Philip, of Saint Clair, Schuylkill Co., Pennsylvania, widower. Administration to Henry Lindsell, attorney for daughter Julia, wife of George Sebastian Repplier,
at Saint Clair. (Feb. 1853).
Kuper, Heinrich George, of Baltimore, U.S.A., and H.M. Consul
there. Administration to relict Mary Kuper. (Apr. 1857).

Lake, William Walton, of New York, bachelor. Administration
to father William Walton Lake. (Aug. 1838).
Lambert, Walter, of New Orleans who died at sea on board ship
Sampson, widower. Administration to John Cropper, guardian
of children Bridget, Michael, Thomas and Eliza Lambert.
(July 1821).
Lamotte, William Henry, formerly Master of merchant ship *Moray-
shire* of London, late of Wawarsing, Ulster Co., U.S.A.
Probate to surviving executor John Lagier Lamotte. (Mar.1857).
Lanfear, nee Hill, Mary, of New Orleans. Administration to
Henry Dunkin Francis, attorney for husband Ambrose Lanfear
at New Orleans. (Jan. 1842).
Lang, William Giltenan, of Boston, U.S.A. Administration with
will to John Holmes, attorney for relict Elizabeth Frances
Lang at New York City. (June 1856).
Langdon, William, formerly of 19 Penny Fields, Poplar, Middle-
sex, late of New York, depositor in Bloomfield Street Savings
Bank. Administration to brother Anthony Langdon. (May 1842).
Larkins, Thomas, formerly of Old Broad Street, London, and of
Layton, Essex, late of San Francisco, California, merchant,
formerly Master in the Maritime Service of the East India
Co. Limited probate to Thomas Brown Horsley, Thomas
Collingwood and George John Steer. (Sept. 1850).
Latham, William Henry, of New York who died at sea, comedian
and musical composer. Administration to relict Ellen Mary
Latham. (Mar. 1844).
Laugher, Elizabeth - see Worthington.
Laundon, Margaretta, of Elyria Loraine, Ohio. Administration
to William John Woolley, attorney for husband Thomas Winkles
Laundon at Elyria Loraine. (Mar. 1855).
Lawford, Susannah Josephine, formerly of Mill Bridge, Birstal,
Yorkshire, late of Amora, Dearborne Co., Indiana, widow.
Administration to only child Frederick Lawford. (Dec. 1850).
Lawrence, John, formerly of Buckland, Gloucestershire, after-
wards of Liverpool, Lancashire, late of Norfolk, Virginia,
bachelor. Administration to cousins german once removed and
next of kin Diana Kemp, widow, Matthew Wilkinson and Benjamin
Wilkinson. (May 1828). Revoked by decree and granted to
George Maule as nominee of H.M. the King; all others with
an interest cited but not appearing. (Jan. 1833).
Lawrence, John, of Philadelphia. Administration to relict Ann
Lawrence. (Dec. 1857).
Lawton, Joseph, of Charleston, South Carolina, and of Saddle-
worth, Yorkshire. Administration with will to Francis
Frederick Whitehead and John Dickens Whitehead; executors
William Nayler and William Matthews renouncing. (Aug. 1855).
Laxton, Catharine - see White.
Layton, Susannah, of Illinois, widow. Administration to daugh-
ter Mary, wife of Robert Pantall. (Sept. 1842).
Learwood, James, formerly of Esher, Surrey, gardener, late of
New Settlement, Ann Harbour, Michigan. Administration to
relict Mary Ann Learwood. (Jan. 1836).
Lechmere, Anthony, of Charleston, South Carolina, bachelor.
Administration to John Lane, administrator to father Nicholas
Lechmere deceased and attorney for his granddaughter Catherine
Lechmere in America. (June 1823).
Le Cras, Eleanor Treandaphelia Sarah, formerly of Campbell
Terrace, St. Helier, Jersey, late of Buffalo, New York,
spinster. Administration to father Abraham Jones Le Cras.
(Sept. 1841).
Ledger, Matthew, of Sonora, California. Administration to relict
Martha Ledger. (Dec. 1852).

Lee, John, of Granville Court House, South Carolina. Administration to mother and next of kin Elizabeth Belhaven Lee,
widow. (June 1833).

Lee, John, formerly of Birmingham, Warwickshire, late of Boston,
Mass. Probate to son John Francis Lee. (Nov. 1840).

Lee, Joseph, of Cambridge, Mass. Administration with will to
Thomas Dickason the younger, attorney for nephews Thomas and
Joseph Lee in North America. (Apr. 1803).

Lee, Sarah, of Boston, Mass., spinster. Probate to brother
John Francis Lee. (Oct. 1850).

Leeds, Rev. John, of Coteau du Lac, Canada, who died at New
York, bachelor. Administration to brother William Henry
Leeds. (Aug. 1854).

Leggett alias Godden, William, of Rochester, Mass., who died at
Bordeaux, France, master mariner. Administration to John
Hambrook, attorney for relict Sarah, now wife of Nathaniel
Carpenter, at New York; administration as of a bachelor
of July 1817 to father John Leggett revoked. (Dec. 1823).
Further grant May 1871.

Leslie alias Leslee, John, of Richmond, Virginia. Probate to
James Scott with similar powers reserved to James Caskie and
Robert Graham. (Nov. 1820).

Leslie, John, formerly of Wapping, Middlesex, late of Norfolk,
Virginia, who died at sea, mariner and bachelor. Administra-
tion to Charles Lever, attorney for brothers George and Henry
Leslie at Portsmouth, Norfolk Co., Virginia. (Dec. 1831).

Lestourgeon, Susannah - see Shepherd.

Levick, George, formerly of Clayworth, Nottinghamshire, late of
New York, miller, bachelor. Administration to John Levick,
son and administrator with will to father James Levick.
(Jan. 1851).

Levy, Ashur, formerly of Gower Street, Bedford Square, Middlesex,
late of New York City. Probate to Louis Lucas, Philip Lucas
and Jacob Aaron Melhado. (June 1846).

Lewer, nee Cooper, Elizabeth Susannah, of South Amboy, New York.
Administration to husband William Lewer. (Mar. 1836).

Lewis, Ann, formerly of St. James, Bristol, late of New York
City, spinster. Administration to brother and only next of
kin John Lewis. (Feb. 1833).

Lewis, John, of Boston, U.S.A., currier, bachelor. Administration to Mary Lewis, administratrix and daughter of father
Robert Lewis deceased. (Feb. 1836).

Lewis, John William, formerly of Stock Exchange, London, late of
Baltimore, Maryland, bachelor. Administration to brother and
next of kin David Lewis. (Dec. 1805).

Lewis, Warner the younger, of Virginia. Administration with will
to son John Lewis, executors Philip Ludwell Grymes, William
Nelson, Burwell Stark, Mann Page the younger, Matthew Anderson and son Warner Lewis having died and surviving executors
brother Fielding Lewis, brother John Lewis, daughter Mary
Chiswell Nelson (formerly wife of Thomas Lewis the younger),
and daughter Elizabeth, wife of Matthew Whiting Brook,
renouncing. (Mar. 1818).

Lewis, William, of Philadelphia. Administration to relict
Catherine Anne Lewis. (Jan. 1846).

Lewis, William, formerly of Trelleck Grange, Monmouth, late of
Sharon, Hamilton Co., Ohio, bachelor. Administration to
brother John Lewis. (Sept. 1850).

Lightfoot, Frances, of Newport, Rhode Island, spinster. Limited
probate to Rev. William Lloyd Baker with similar powers
reserved to John Bours. (Nov. 1800).

Lindsay, Charles Philip, of Hudson Street, New York City,
Post Office agent. Administration to George Nelson Emmet,
attorney for relict Grace, now wife of Frederick C. Parks
at New York. (Apr. 1855).

Lisle, Margaret Warren, of New Haven, Connecticut, spinster.
Probate to nephew Lisle Lloyd with similar powers reserved
to George Williams. (Jan. 1827).

Livingston, Gilbert Robert, reduced Captain of Cavalry in late
American Legion of Schenectady, New York. Limited admini-
stration with will to James Tidbury, attorney for relict
Patty Livingston at Schenectady. (Jan. 1817).

Livingston, Mortimer, of New York City. Probate to Charles
William Foster and William Sydney Drayton with similar
powers reserved to relict Sylvia Livingston. (Jan. 1858).

Lloyd, Daniel, formerly of Wandsworth, Surrey, late of Saugher-
ties, Ulster Co., New York, widower. Administration to only
child Daniel Lloyd. (Mar. 1840 & Aug. 1842).

Lloyd, Margaret, of New Orleans State, widow. Administration
to daughter Harriet Lloyd. (Sept. 1838).

Logan, William, of Charleston, South Carolina, widower. Limited
administration to William Wynch, attorney for grandson
William Logan in South Carolina. (Sept. 1802).

Long, Elizabeth Burgh, of Culpeper Co., Virginia. Administration to John Dunlop, attorney for husband Armistead Long in
Culpeper Co. (Mar. 1827).

Long, Robert, formerly of Sutton Veny, Wiltshire, late of
Anahuac, Galveston Bay, Texas, bachelor. Administration to
Alfred Long, son and executor of father Stephen Long. (Feb.
1849).

Lord, Thomas, formerly of Bushley, Worcestershire, late of
Gibson's Co., Tennessee, who died at sea passenger on American steam ship *Colonel Thompson*, bachelor. Administration
to John Lord, administrator to father William Lord deceased.
(Apr. 1856). Revoked on presentation of will and probate
granted to Daniel Smith and Thomas Farr. (July 1857).

Loring, William, formerly of Boston, North America, afterwards
of Bordeaux, France, late of Buenos Aires, South America,
bachelor. Administration to James Abel, attorney for
creditor John Ward at Providence Rhode Island; administration of November 1804 to said John Ward revoked. (Mar.1805).

Loveless, Thamar, of New York City, spinster. Probate to John
Marles with similar powers reserved to Thomas Cox. (Jan.
1856).

Lucas, Jonathan, of Charleston, South Carolina, and Whitehaven,
Cumberland. Probate to Richard Sherwin, Peter William Sherwin and Thomas Naylor. (Apr. 1822).

Ludlow, Gabriel Gabriel, President and Commander in Chief of
New Brunswick. Administration with will to Isaac Minet,
attorney for relict Ann Ludlow and sons Gulian and Gabriel
Ludlow at New York City. (Aug. 1809).

Ludlow, Gulian, of New York. Administration with will to John
Stride, attorney for relict Maria Ludlow and Thomas William
Ludlow at New York. (Mar. 1848).

Lungley, Thomas, of Makefield, Buckingham Co., U.S.A., bachelor.
Administration to niece Elizabeth, wife of John Sibley.
(Mar. 1834).

Lynch, Dominick, formerly of New York, late of Paris. Probate
to Nicholas Luquer and daughter Jane, wife of Julius Pringle.
(Dec. 1840).

Lyon, John, of Charles Town, South Carolina. Administration
with will to Robert Naylor, attorney for mother Elizabeth
Hill, widow, at Charles Town; executor Charles Paxton Butler

cited but not appearing. (May 1802).

Lyon alias Lyons, John, formerly of Hammersmith, Middlesex,
late of Philadelphia, botanist and gardener. Administration
with will to James Lee, attorney for Thomas Dobson and David
Landreth in U.S.A. (Oct. 1816).

Lysnar, George, of Brooklyn, New York, goldsmith, widower.
Administration to son George Lee Lysnar. (Nov. 1856).

McAlister, formerly Keith, Ann, of Queenborough, Georgia.
Limited administration to John Tunno, attorney for husband
John McAlister. (Aug. 1807).

McCall, Catharine Flood, formerly of Clydeside, Essex Co., and
of Richmond, Virginia, late of George Town, D.C., spinster.
Limited administration with will to Archibald McCall. (Apr.
1831).

McCartney, Eliza, of Madison Co., Alabama. Administration to
Josiah Roberts, attorney for husband James McCartney in
Alabama. (Dec. 1829).

Macaulay, Daniel, formerly of Charleston, South Carolina, merchant, late of Liverpool, Lancashire. Probate to relict
Mary Leaycroft Macaulay, David Lamb and Duncan Gibb. (Jan.
1856).

McClure, Alexander, of Charles Town, South Carolina. Probate
to uncle Cochrane McClure with similar powers reserved to
uncle William McClure and William Muir. (Dec. 1812).
Revoked on death of Cochrane McClure and granted to Janet,
wife of William McClure, daughter of uncle William McClure.
(July 1813).

McCullok, Eleanor, of Rockland, Baltimore Co., Maryland. Limited administration with will to John Stuart Roupell; husband
Samuel McCullok renouncing. (Nov. 1840).

McCutchon, David, formerly of Dudley, Worcestershire, late of
Davenport, Scott Co., Iowa. Limited administration to creditors Thomas Hunter and James Perram. (Apr. 1852).

McDonald, Alexander, of Aberdeen, Scotland, Captain on half pay
of Florida Rangers, widower. Administration to cousin german
Mary, wife of William Patterson, guardian of only children
Alexia, James and Margaret McDonald; aunts Jane Munro, widow,
and Mary MacLain renouncing guardianship. (Apr. 1805).

McDonald, Ann, of Cumberland Co., North Carolina, widow. Administration to Charles Cooke, attorney for cousin german and next
of kin Daniel Monk at Cumberland Co. (Mar. 1803).

MacDonald, Archibald, formerly surgeon in Regiment of Pioneers
during the American Revolutionary War, late of White Plains,
West Chester Co., New York. Administration to James Tidbury,
attorney for relict Flora MacDonald at New York. (Feb. 1817).

MacDonogh, Thomas, of Charleston, Mass., British Consul in New
Hampshire, Mass., Rhode Island and Connecticut. Administra-
tion to Thomas Dickason the younger, attorney for relict
Harriet MacDonogh at Charleston. (Dec. 1805).

McDuell, Ann, of Frederick Co., Maryland, widow. Administration
to Thomas Aspinwall, attorney for son Robert McDuell at
Frederick Co. (July 1846).

Mackethen, Dugald, of Raleigh, North Carolina, Lieutenant of
Royal North Carolina Regiment. Administration to Robert
Sheddon, attorney for relict Martha Mackethen in America.
(June 1805).

McEvers, James, of New York City. Administration with will to
daughter Dame Elizabeth Myers; relict Elizabeth (afterwards
wife of Robert Baynard) and executors Charles Ward Apthorp
and brother Charles McEvers having died. (July 1811).
Revoked on death of Dame Elizabeth Myers and administration
granted to her sole executrix Margaret Baynard, spinster;
children James, John, Charles, Elizabeth, Catherine wife of
Thomas Palmer, and Mary McEvers (afterwards Myers, who was
born after the testator's death), having all died. (June
1823).

McEvers, Margaret J. - see Bibby.

McFadyen alias McFadzean, John, of Boston, North America.
Administration with will to John Boyd, attorney for Jacob
Rhoades at Boston. (Dec. 1805).

McFarlan, James, formerly of Ivy Place, Hoxton, Middlesex, late
of Cheviot near Cincinnati, Hamilton Co., Ohio. Administration to Thomas Olney, attorney for relict Ann McFarlan at
Cheviot. (Mar. 1850).

McGeorge, Matthew, of Franklinvale near Lyndon, Cattarangus Co.,
New York, hotel keeper. Administration to William Fisher,
attorney for relict Louisa McGeorge at Franklinvale. (Nov.
1857).

McGill, formerly Norry alias Norie, Catharine, of Portsmouth,
New England, widow. Administration to John Anderson and
Alexander Anderson, attornies for Samuel Bowles, guardian of
only children Mary, Margaret and Jane Norie during their
minority. (Feb. 1804).

McGillivray, James, formerly of Savannah, Georgia, late of Inverness, Scotland. Limited probate to brother Lachlan McGillivray with similar powers reserved to Andrew McCudie, William
Mein, Robert Mackay and James Mackintosh. (Nov. 1806).

McGreevy, Peter, of New York City, widower. Administration to
Francis McEvoy, uncle and guardian of only child James Mc
Greevy during his minority. (Jan. 1852).

McIver, Alexander, of Liberty Co., Georgia, planter, widower.
Limited administration to Alexander Carruthers Daubeny,
attorney for daughter Harriette, wife of Samuel Spencer, in
Georgia. (Sept. 1837).

MacIver, Donald, of Augusta, Georgia, who died at St. Bartholomew
Island in West Indies, bachelor. Administration to sister
Helen, wife of Colin Leitch. (Feb. 1817).

McIver, John, formerly of Georgia, late of New York City.
Administration with will to Charles Everett, attorney for
John Taylor at New York City; other executor Amasa Jackson
cited but not appearing. (Nov. 1821).

Mackenzie, Hector, formerly of Bath on Cokerton River, Steubeng
Co., New York, afterwards of Hatton Garden, Middlesex, late
of Trinidad, West Indies. Probate to Daniel Wilson Davison
with similar powers reserved to William MacCaa. (July 1808).
Revoked on production of another will and probate granted to
Robert Davison, doctor of physic, and William McCaa with
similar powers reserved to George Sheviz. (July 1808).

McKinnon, Donald, formerly of North Ouist, Scotland, late of
North Carolina, bachelor. Administration to Charles Cooke,
administrator to sister and only next of kin Ann McDonald,
widow, deceased. (Mar. 1803).

McKinstry, Rev. William, formerly of Goring, Oxfordshire, afterwards of Lingfield, Surrey, late of Concord, Merrimack Co.,

New Hampshire. Administration with will to William Pulsford, attorney for Samuel Sparhawk; Isaac Winslow and John William Stark renouncing. (Mar. 1824).

McLeod, Hector, of Newburgh, Orange Co., New York, Master in Royal Navy, widower. Administration to son William McLeod. (Aug. 1822).

McLeod, Susannah, of Newburgh, Orange Co., New York. Administration to son William McLeod; husband Hector McLeod having died. (July 1822).

Maclure, William, of New Harmony, Posey Co., Indiana. Administration with will to John Christopher Fry, attorney for surviving executor Alexander Maclure at New Harmony. (Sept. 1845).

McMaster, John, of Wiscasset, Lincoln Co., Maine. Administration to brother Daniel McMaster; mother Grizell McMaster, widow, renouncing. (Dec. 1824).

McMaster, William, of Augusta, Kennebee Co., Mass. Limited administration with will to Samuel Williams, attorney for son Daniel McMaster at Augusta. (May 1815).

McMillan, Betty, of Horse Shoe Swamp, Bladen Co., North Carolina, spinster. Administration to David Caldwell, attorney for mother Jane McMillan in North Carolina. (Jan. 1818).

MacNeil, Neil, of Charleston, South Carolina. Administration with will to John Bambridge, attorney for sole executor William Smith in America. (Mar. 1824).

Macpherson, Melville, of New York City. Administration to relict Margaret Macpherson. (Feb. 1839).

Madgwick, Martha - see Street.

Makins, John, of Chicago, U.S.A., widower. Administration to brother Jeremiah Makins. (June 1857).

Maltby, Charles, of Philadelphia. Administration to John Bainbridge, attorney for relict Sarah Maltby at Philadelphia. (June 1808).

Maltby, George, formerly of London, late of Baltimore, North America, widower. Administration to creditor George Cooke; minor sons George Edward Maltby and Thomas William Maltby cited but not appearing. (Jan. 1808).

Mander, William, of Brooklyn, U.S.A. Administration to relict Mary Mander. (Apr. 1849).

Manley, Henry Chorley, of Charles Town, South Carolina, bachelor. Administration to father Rev. Henry Chorley Manley. (June 1800).

Mann, Mary, of Needham near Boston, North America, widow. Administration to only child Mary, wife of Isaac Morrill. (Dec. 1803).

Manning, Francis, formerly of Uley, Gloucestershire, late of Charles Town, North America, widower. Administration to nephew Thomas Smithwick Manning; brother Thomas Fielding Manning having died. (Sept. 1826).

Marchand, Charles Laurent Marie, of New York, proprietor of St. Domingo, bachelor. Administration to sister and only next of kin Clotilde Ursule Marchand. (Oct. 1830).

Marke, John, formerly of Rock House near Taunton, Somerset,
late of Houston, Republic of Texas, cow keeper and farmer,
bachelor. Administration to mother and next of kin Elizabeth
Marke, widow. (Oct. 1839).

Markham, Ann, of Turtle, Wisconsin. Administration to William
Jackson, attorney for husband William Markham at Turtle.
(Dec. 1853).

Marlar, John Thomas, formerly of Baltimore, Maryland, late of
Maguires Bridge, Co. Fermanagh, Ireland. Probate by decree
to Edward Stewart. (Dec. 1804).

Marshall, Charles Henry, formerly of Cambridge, late of New York,
bachelor. Administration to brother Newcombe Marshall. (Feb.
1857).

Marshall, William, of Baton Rouge, River Mississippi. Limited
probate to brother George Marshall with similar powers
reserved to James Profit, Philip Hicky and Charles Norwood.
(Apr. 1804).

Marston, Thomas, of New York City. Probate to Francis Bayard
Winthrop with similar powers reserved to William Bayard.
(Nov. 1814).

Martyn, Henry, of Boston, U.S.A. Administration to Thomas
Aspinwall, attorney for relict Mary Ann Martyn at Boston.
(July 1849).

Martin, Robert, formerly of Tewkesbury, Gloucestershire, late of
New Orleans, private in 41st Regiment of Foot, bachelor.
Administration to father Thomas Martin. (June 1834).

Martin, Robert Anthony, of Louisiana, bachelor. Administration
to Mary Ann Bridget Martin, spinster, attorney for Anthony
Martin at Geelong, Australia, administrator to father Anthony
Crosbie Martin. (Sept. 1857).

Martin, Samuel, of Far Rockaway, Hempstead, Long Island, New
York. Probate to brother William Martin with similar powers
reserved to Thomas Banister. (July 1806).

Martin, William, of Baltimore, North America, bachelor. Administration to sister Mary, wife of Alexander Woodward. (Feb.
1800).

Mason, Caleb, of New York, bachelor. Administration to father
Thomas Mason. (Aug. 1851).

Mather, Samuel, formerly of Boston, late of Milton, America.
Administration with will to John Bainbridge, attorney for
relict Margaret Mather at Cambridge, America. (Mar. 1816).

Mathers, Joseph, of New York City, merchant. Probate to surviving executor Charles Denston. (Jan. 1843).

Matthews, William, of South Carolina, bachelor. Administration
to mother Susannah Tabet. (June 1809).

Mauger, Isaac - see Moger.

Maybery, Charles, of Warren Co., Tennessee, widower. Administration to Henry Maybery, attorney for son Thomas Maybery in
Warren Co. (June 1843).

Mears, John, of Pittsburgh who died on island of St. Domingo,
West Indies. Administration to son John Mears; relict Esther
Mears having died. (June 1818).

Mears, Walter Hunter, of East Baton Rouge, Louisiana. Administration to relict Augustine Verret Mears. (Jan. 1839).

Mears, William, of Pittsburgh, Pennsylvania, who died at Cincinnati, Ohio, bachelor. Administration to John Mears, son
and administrator of father John Mears deceased. (June 1828).

Medland, Jane - see Drexhagen.

Mee, Edward James, formerly of Ludlow, Shropshire, veterinary
surgeon, afterwards of Down House near Bromyard, Herefordshire, veterinary surgeon and farmer, late of Philadelphia
and New York. Administration to relict Sarah Mee. (Apr.1848).

Meier, John Hardenbergh, of Schenectady, New York. Administration with will to Edward Ellice, attorney for surviving executors Sanders Lansing and Gerrit Lansing. (Dec. 1820).

Meier, Rachel, formerly of Clermont, Columbia Co., late of New Palz, Ulster Co., New York, widow. Administration with will to Edward Ellice, attorney for surviving executrix Rebecca Romeyn, widow. (Dec. 1820).

Menzies, Sarah, of New York, widow. Administration to son Gilbert Lester Menzies. (Feb. 1818).

Mesick, Mary, of Hudson, New York. Administration to Robert Samuel Palmer, administrator of husband Peter Henry Mesick deceased and attorney for only child Catharine Mary, wife of Richard Ramsay Jones, in New York State. (Aug. 1836).

Mesick, Peter Henry, of Hudson, New York, merchant, widower. Administration to Robert Samuel Palmer, attorney for only child Catharine Mary Jones in New York State. (Aug. 1836).

Messenger, James, formerly of West Street, North Bermondsey, Surrey, carpenter and builder, late of Goochland Co., Virginia, Deputy Superintendent of the Waller Mines. Probate to relict Maria Messenger with similar powers reserved to Charles Eustace Goldring. (Jan. 1857). Double probate July 1889.

Middleton, Mary Helen, of Philadelphia, widow. Administration to son Henry Middleton. (May 1857).

Middleton, Thomas, of Charleston, South Carolina. Limited administration with will to William Williams, attorney for daughter Mary alias Polly, wife of James Shoolbred, at Charleston; grant of March 1799 revoked. (Aug. 1803). Further grants July 1806 and September 1820.

Middleton, William Thomas, formerly of Frendisbury near Rochester, Kent, late of Cincinnati, North America. Administration to relict Elizabeth Middleton. (Nov. 1839).

Miles, Harriet L. - see Squire.

Mill, Matthew, formerly of Lower Shadwell, Middlesex, late of Philadelphia. Probate to sister Sarah Mill the younger with similar powers reserved to Robert Wright. (May 1830). Revoked on death of Sarah Mill and granted to Ann, wife of James Broadbridge, formerly Ann Hutchings; mother Sarah Mill, widow, having died. (Feb. 1854).

Miller, John, of New Providence who died at New York. Probate to relict Mary Miller with similar powers reserved to Lawrence Brickwood, John Brickwood, Robert Thompson, Abraham Eve and John Stevens. (July 1816).

Miller, Margaret, of Halifax, Nova Scotia, relict of Tobias Miller, Ensign in Regiment of South Carolina Loyalists. Limited administration to Andrew Belcher, attorney for only child Tobias Emanuel Miller in Nova Scotia. (Dec. 1823).

Milligan, William, of Charlestown, South Carolina, merchant. Probate to Alexander Anderson with similar powers reserved to John Black, William Birnie, William Drayton, Charles Edmondstone, William Thompson, Robert Sturgeon, John Sutherland, Benjamin Moodie, William Blacklock and Archibald MacLachlan. (June 1811).

Millington, Mary, of Hempstead Branch, Queen's Co., New York. Administration to Frederick Millington, attorney for husband Matthew Millington at Hempstead. (Apr. 1856).

Mills, John, of Alexandria, North America, bachelor. Administration to cousin german John Mills. (Mar. 1847).

Mitchell, Robert, of Savannah, Georgia. Administration with will to Eliza, wife of Hector Turnbull, daughter of brother John Mitchell; executors Peter Mitchell and James Marshall having died and Norman Wallace renouncing. (Oct. 1846).

Moger alias Mauger, Isaac, formerly of Fairfield, Connecticut, late of Williamstown, Berkshire Co., Mass., widower. Administration to George Gouger, attorney for daughter Elizabeth Herault Moger at Lebanon, New York. (Apr. 1807).

Mogridge, Alexander Augustus Perry, of New Orleans, widower. Administration to son Richard Perry Mogridge. (Aug. 1856).

Molyneux, Anthony Lancaster, H.M. Consul in Georgia. Administration with will to brother William Hargraves Molyneux; surviving executor Anthony Barclay renouncing. (June 1852).

Monk, Samuel, formerly of Ilford, Essex, late of Northern Hotel, New York City, bachelor. Administration to sister Ann Monk. (Mar. 1839).

Montague, George, formerly of Phillack, Cornwall, late of New Orleans. Administration to relict Phillis Montague. (Mar. 1849).

Montgomrey, Malcolm, formerly of Brentford, Middlesex, late of Syracuse, New York. Probate to relict Anna Rosina Montgomrey with similar powers reserved to William Kelly and John Charles Heath. (July 1856).

Moodie, Benjamin, of Charleston, North America, H.M. Consul. Probate to relict Caroline Moodie with similar powers reserved to Adam Tunno, William Birnie and Charles Edmondstone. (Nov. 1825).

Moodie, Caroline, formerly of Liverpool, Lancashire, late of Charlestown, South Carolina, widow. Administration to son James Gairdner Moodie. (Nov. 1844).

Moon, James Lawson, formerly of Brotherton near Ferry Bridge, Yorkshire, late of Princton, Gibson Co., Indiana. Probate to Robert Henry Anderson. (May 1841).

Moon, John Radwell, formerly of Orange Street, Bloomsbury Square, Middlesex, late of Mechanics Farm, Milwaukee Co., Wisconsin, bachelor. Administration to sister Marianne Moon. (Sept. 1846).

Moore, Catharine Charles, of Holmesburg, Philadelphia Co., North America, widow. Administration with will to Alfred Alexander Julius, attorney for daughters Jane and Catharine Mary Moore. (Dec. 1837).

Moore, Jane, of Holmesburg near Philadelphia, spinster. Administration with will to Alfred Alexander Julius, attorney for sister Catharine Mary Moore at Holmesburg. (Dec. 1846).

Moore, John, of Russelville, Kentucky, widower. Administration to Cameron Eneas Quilter, attorney for only child Caroline Balfour, wife of Thomas Wood, at Nelson Co., Kentucky. (Mar. 1852).

Moore, Lambert, of Brooklyn, New York. Administration with will to John Mackenzie, attorney for John H. Moore and Adam Tredwell at New York. (May 1808).

Moore, Maurice alias Morice, formerly of 13 Upper Fitzroy Place, New Road, St. Pancras, Middlesex, papier mache maker, who died passenger on American ship *Charles Bartlett* bound for New York with his wife Julia and six of his children Mary, Margaret, Julia, Maurice, John and Bridget Moore. Limited administration to Owen McCarthy the elder, guardian of only surviving child Catherine, wife of Owen McCarthy the younger, during her minority. (Sept. 1849 & Aug. 1853).

Moorland, Joseph, formerly of Stroud Water, Gloucestershire, late of Boston, North America, bachelor. Administration to sisters and only next of kin Susanna Bamford, widow, and Sarah Ford, widow. (Feb. 1816).

Morehouse, Ann - see Wadup.

Morel, formerly Dunbar, Tryphena, of Savannah, Georgia. Administration to Alexander Mein, attorney for husband Peter Henry Morel at Savannah. (Aug. 1810).

Morgan, Ann, formerly of Galway, Herefordshire, late of Illinois,
spinster. Administration to brother Walter Prosser Morgan;
mother Mary Morgan, widow, having died. (Oct. 1847).

Morgan, Anne, of Stockbridge, Berkshire Co., Mass., widow.
Administration to George Hurrey, attorney for granddaughter
Mary Elizabeth, wife of William Burke Skinner, at Hudson,
North America; son Edmund Cobb Morgan having died and only
other next of kin son Richard Morgan having been cited but
not appearing. (Feb. 1849).

Morgan, Francis, of New London, Connecticut. Administration
with will to James Francis Morgan, attorney for brothers
James Morgan at New York City and John Morgan at New London.
(Nov. 1849).

Morgan, George Cadogan, of Stockbridge, Berkshire Co., Mass.,
widower. Administration to George Hurry, attorney for
daughter Mary Elizabeth, wife of William Burke Skinner, at
Hudson, Columbia Co., New York. (Apr. 1848).

Morgan, Harriet, of New London, Connecticut, spinster. Administration to father William Morgan. (Oct. 1839).

Morgan, Luke Ashburner and John Sextus, of Stockbridge, Mass.,
bachelors. Administration to George Hurry, attorney for
niece Grace Ashburner, spinster, at Stockbridge; mother
Ann Morgan, widow, having died. (July 1848).

Morgan, Patrick, formerly of the Crescent, Minories, London,
afterwards of Bernard Street, Russell Square, Middlesex,
late of New Orleans, Louisiana. Probate to relict Mary Morgan.
(May 1806).

Morgan, Sarah - see Huntington.

Morgan, Thomas, formerly of Red Cross Street, London, late of
New York, widower. Administration to only child William
Morgan. (Mar. 1836).

Morgan, Thomas, of Upwood near Chicago, Illinois. Probate to
son James Morgan with similar powers reserved to relict
Anna Maria Morgan and sons Charles, Thomas Charles, William,
Harry, Francis and John Robert Morgan. (July 1851).

Morison, John, formerly of Jamaica, late of Mount Vernon, Ohio,
Upper Canada, practitioner of physick and surgery. Probate
to William Pirrie with similar powers reserved to Gray
Rutherford, Charles Nockells and James Matthew Whyte. (Aug.
1840).

Morrell, John, of Newark, New Jersey, bachelor. Administration
to Peter Barlow, attorney for father Stephen Haddon Morrell
at St. Nicholas Island in Cape Verde. (July 1823).

Morrell, formerly Crawley, Mary, of Newark, New Jersey. Administration to Peter Barlow, attorney for husband Stephen Haddon
Morrell at St. Nicholas Island, Cape Verde. (July 1823).

Morris, Anna, wife of Cadwallader Morris of Philadelphia, who
died in 1792. Limited administration with will to John Brickwood, attorney for Frances Morris (formerly Stretter or
Strettle) wife of Benjamin Morris, in Pennsylvania. (Jan.
1801).

Morris, Joseph Handford, formerly of Buffalo, Erie Co., New York,
afterwards of Letchurch Lodge, Derbyshire, late of Cleveland,
Ohio. Probate to brother William Morris with similar powers
reserved to brother John Morris. (June 1849).

Morris, nee Kearney, Julia Louisa, of Auburn, Cayuga Co., New
York. Limited administration to William Phillipps, attorney
for husband Joseph Marcus Morris at Auburn. (Apr. 1857).

Morris, Richard, of Richmond, Virginia. Administration to
brother and only next of kin Henry John Morris. (July 1809).

Morse, nee Child, Mary, of Zanesville, Ohio. Limited administration to William Henry King during Chancery suit King v.

Cockill. (Oct. 1829).

Morton, William, formerly of Limehouse, Middlesex, late of New York, bachelor. Administration to Joseph Ashby, administrator with will to half brother Samuel Carter; mother Jane, wife of Elijah Carter and half brothers and half sisters Joshua Carter, Ann Isaacs, widow, Mary wife of John Passey, and Elijah Carter having died. (Feb. 1857).

Moses, Joseph, formerly of Gun Square, Houndsditch, London, late of Charlestown, U.S.A. Administration to relict Sarah Moses. (July 1803).

Mountcastle, John, of Talmadge, Portage Co., Ohio, tinman and brazier. Administration to relict Mary Mountcastle. (Apr. 1833).

Moxon, Martha, of Greece, Monroe Co., New York. Limited administration with will to husband John Moxon. (Aug. 1831).

Mullony, John, of Philadelphia, widower. Administration to Charles Cooke, attorney for only child John Mullony. (Dec. 1800).

Mumford, Brenton, of New Bedford, Rhode Island, bachelor. Administration to sister Frances Augusta, wife of William Henry Yarnold. (Nov. 1817).

Mundy, Ann, formerly of Bradford, Wiltshire, late of Long Island, New York, widow. Administration to Samuel Bowyer, attorney for son William Mundy at Saugerties, New York. (Jan. 1851).

Munn, William, of 62 Grove Street, New York. Administration to Lewis Munn, attorney for relict Louisa Munn in New York. (Oct. 1841). Revoked on her death and granted to son George Duncan Munn. (June 1852).

Munnings, George Garnett Husk, formerly of Thorpe le Soken, Essex, late of New York, master mariner, bachelor. Administration to Caroline Munnings, daughter and administratrix of father George Garnett Husk Munnings. (Feb. 1855).

Murdock, Andrew, of New York, Master of merchant ship *Jane*, who died at sea. Administration to relict Eliza Murdock. (Feb. 1812).

Murray, James, of Newark, New Jersey. Administration with will to William Taylor, attorney for William Murray and Edward Blackford at Newark. (July 1810).

Murray, John, sergeant in 1st Batallion of Royals who died at Buffalo, America. Administration to relict Ann, now wife of Patrick Collins. (July 1817).

Murray, John William Boyles, of New York who died at sea, doctor of physic, bachelor. Administration to Christ Knight Murray, attorney for father George William Murray at New York. (July 1817).

Musgrove, Robert, carpenter on merchant brig *Jarrow* of Liverpool who died at New York, bachelor. Administration to mother Margaret Musgrove, widow. (Aug. 1838).

Nancolas, Anthony, of Iowa Co., Wisconsin. Limited administration to Henry Ford, attorney for relict Anna Nancolas
in Iowa Co. (May 1856).

Nash, Alexander, formerly of Edmonton, Middlesex, late of
Flatbush, New York. Probate to brothers William and Henry
Nash. (Aug. 1845).

Naters, Thomas, formerly of Liverpool, Lancashire, ship master
and ship owner, afterwards of Quebec, Canada, then of New-
town, Long Island, New York, late of Goldenburg near Winter-
thur, Switzerland. Probate to William Mather. (Nov. 1836).

Needham, William, of Montgomery Co., Maryland. Administration
with will to James Oswald, attorney for John Laird at George
Town, North America; son William Abington Needham having
died intestate and nephew and only next of kin Thomas
Marshall Maccubbin renouncing. (July 1826).

Neill, Samuel, of Natchez, Mississippi, merchant. Administration to George Greene, attorney for relict Mary Neill at
New York City. (Feb. 1809).

Nelson, nee Smith, Elizabeth, of Newark, New Jersey, widow.
Administration to John Stables, attorney for only surviving
child Sophia Augusta Preintall at Newark. (Aug. 1848).

Nelson, James, formerly of Little Hampstone, Devon, late of
Philadelphia, bachelor. Administration to father William
Nelson. (Aug. 1813).

Nelson, William, formerly of Little Hampstone, Devon, late
prisoner in France, bachelor. Administration to father
William Nelson. (Aug. 1813).

Ness, William, of New York, bachelor. Administration to
brother Richard Ness. (May 1820).

Neville, Thomas, of Washington Street, New York. Administration to relict Catherine Maxted Neville. (July 1847).

Nevins, John, formerly of Aldermanbury, London, late of East
Port, Maine. Probate to nephew Samuel Gatliff with similar
powers reserved to brother Thomas Nevins. (Oct. 1829).

Newcombe, Richard, formerly of Davenport, Devon, late of
Bermuda, stone mason. Administration with will to Benjamin
Charles Thomas Gray, attorney for relict Sarah Jane Pepper
at Bermuda. (Mar. 1848). Revoked on death of attorney and
granted to Charles William Gray and Benjamin Gerrish Gray,
attornies for relict Sarah Jane, now wife of John Joseph
Coakley at New York. (Aug. 1854).

Newens alias Chaplin, Harriet, of Castleton, Richmond Co., New
York, spinster. Probate to William Chaplin with similar
powers reserved to William Henry Pillow. (Sept. 1846).

Newman, Francis, formerly of Headley Park, Hampshire, and of
Cadbury Castle, Somerset, late of Grange, Charles Co., Maryland. Limited probate to daughter Frances Charlotte, wife of
Robert Albion Cox; surviving executor James Meadowcroft and
relict Frances Newman cited but not appearing. (Sept. 1820).
Revoked by decree and administration with new will granted
to Robert Trower and Francis Smedley, attornies for relict
Elizabeth Hannah Friers alias Newman at Charles Co. (Aug.
1822).

Newton, Elizabeth, formerly of Colchester, Essex, late of New
Orleans. Administration to husband James Newton. (Dec.
1853).

Nicholson, Richard, Ensign in 8th or King's Own Regiment who
died at Chippawa, North America, bachelor. Administration
to John Nicholson, son and executor of father Richard
Nicholson deceased. (June 1820).

Nickolls, James Bruce, of Alexandria, D.C. Probate to Rev.
William Jackson by oath and Phineas Janney by solemn affirmation. (May 1832).

Nickson, Henrietta, of Ithaca, Tompkins Co., U.S.A. Administration to William Walker, administrator to husband William Nickson deceased and attorney for children Jamima, wife of William Turnbull Reid and Richard Nickson at New York City. (Dec. 1852).

Nickson, William, of Ithaca, U.S.A., butcher, widower. Administration to William Walker, attorney for only children Jamima Reid and Richard Nickson at New York City. (Dec. 1852).

Niven, John, of Patterson, Passaic Co., New Jersey. Administration to sister Marion Dunlop, widow; relict Jane Niven renouncing. (June 1843).

Noel alias Bushe, Elizabeth, formerly of New York City late of Edinburgh, Scotland, widow. Probate to mother Elizabeth Harriet Hellyer. (June 1846).

Nowell, Henry Cradock, of Plantersville, Lowndes Co., Alabama, bachelor. Administration to mother Rosamira Nowell, widow. (Apr. 1837).

Norie, Catharine - see McGill.

Norman, John the younger, of Charles Town, North America, who died at sea, bachelor. Administration to sister Ann, wife of Timothy Roper, administratrix to father John Norman deceased. (June 1813).

Norry, Catharine - see McGill.

Norton, Martha, of New York City, widow. Administration to son John Leake Norton. (Feb. 1815).

Norton, Samuel, formerly of North Yarmouth, Norfolk, late of New York. Administration with will of estate unadministered by relict Martha Norton deceased to son John Leake Norton; will registered December 1791. (Feb. 1815).

Nourse, Elizabeth - see Chapline.

Nowell, Henry C. - see Noel.

Nugent, Thomas, formerly of St. Croix, West Indies, afterwards of New York City, late of Dorset Street, Dublin, Ireland. Probate to sister Eliza Skelly, widow, with similar powers reserved to David Rogers and Samuel David Rogers (partners in firm of David Rogers & Son, merchants in New York City) and nephew William Skelly. (Dec. 1833).

Nunez, Aaron, of Cincinnati, Ohio. Administration to relict Julia Nunez. (Nov. 1854).

Oakley, William Smith, formerly of Southwark, Surrey, wool stapler, late of Morganfield, Union Co., Kentucky. Administration to Jacob Mould, attorney for relict Susan Oakley at New York City. (Nov. 1825).

O'Beirne, Rebecca, formerly of Philadelphia, late of Dinan, France, widow. Probate to Joseph Tilstone. (May 1842).

Ogden, Nicholas, formerly of Shelburne, Nova Scotia, late of New York City. Administration with will to Gabriel Shaw, attorney for daughter Alida Ogden in New York City; Thomas Barclay and Edward Brindley and nephews David and Thomas Ogden cited but not appearing, and relict Hannah Ogden having died. (Mar. 1823).

Ogilvie, Alexander, of Virginia, bachelor. Administration to
mother and next of kin Margaret Ogilvie, widow. (Feb. 1843).
Ogilvie, George, of Virginia. Administration to relict Helen
Ogilvie. (Feb. 1843).
O'Gorman, George, formerly of 39 Dorset Street, Portman Square,
Middlesex, late of Galveston, Texas. Administration with
will to Elizabeth Isabel O'Gorman, widow, attorney for son
George Charles Richard O'Gorman at Serajgunge in East Indies;
sole executor nephew Edmond Anthony O'Gorman renouncing.
(Apr. 1855).
Oldmixon, Dame Mary, of Philadelphia, widow. Administration to
son William Henry Oldmixon. (Jan. 1838).
Oliver, John, formerly of St. Martin's, Hereford, who died on
passage from Cuba to New Orleans, bachelor. Administration
to father Thomas Oliver. (Nov. 1854). Revoked on his death
and granted to his relict and administratrix Elizabeth Oliver.
(May 1855).
Onions, John, formerly of Birmingham, Warwickshire, late of New
York, bachelor. Administration to Charles James, administra-
tor to sister Catherina James deceased; mother Mary Onions
and other sisters Sarah wife of William Grove, Mary wife of
Joshua Taylor and Elizabeth Onions having also died. (Feb.
1816).
Onwin, Richard, formerly of Mary Street, Hampstead, Middlesex,
late of Harlem near New York, cabinet maker. Administration
to relict Amalia Sophia Onwin. (July 1840).
Orange, Thomas, of New York City. Probate to surviving executor
Henry Kermit. (Nov. 1824).
Orlton, Griffith, of New York. Administration to brother John
Orlton; relict Jane Orlton having died. (Dec. 1816).
Orne, Susannah, of Marblehead, U.S.A. Administration to Samuel
Williams, attorney for daughter Annis Orne at Salem, North
America; husband Joshua Orne having died. (Feb. 1818).
Osborn, Joseph, of New York City. Probate to son William
Osborn with similar powers reserved to relict Judith Osborn.
(June 1830).
O'Sullivan, Caroline, of New York City. Administration to
Jonathan Outram, attorney for husband Jeremiah O'Sullivan
at New York. (Apr. 1855).
O'Sullivan, John, of New York, who died at sea on board merchant
ship *Dick*. Administration to relict Mary O'Sullivan. (Aug.
1825).
Overington, John, formerly of Belmont Place, Lambeth, Surrey,
late of Oxford Township, Philadelphia Co., Pennsylvania.
Probate to relict Sarah Overington. (Dec. 1810). Revoked
on her death and granted to James Sowton, attorney for son
William Overington at Oxford. (Oct. 1836).
Owen, Edward, of Philadelphia. Administration to brother
Wyriotte Owen; relict Esther Owen having died. (Dec. 1821).
Owen, William, of Adelaide, South Australia, who died at Stockton,
Upper California, bachelor. Administration to mother and
next of kin Grace, wife of Richard Thomas. (Nov. 1850).

Paddock, Adino, of Boston, North America, Army Captain who died
in New Jersey. Probate to James South, James Simpson and
William Forman. (Aug. 1804).

Paine - see Payne.

Palairet, Mary Ann, formerly of Mount Clements near Stanmore,
Middlesex, late of Philadelphia. Limited administration
with will to Rev. Richard Thomas Palairet, brother and
executor to husband Septimus Henry Palairet deceased. (Apr.
1856).

Palmer, John Temple, of Boston, U.S.A., bachelor. Administration to father William Lamb Palmer. (Dec. 1822).

Palmer, Peregrine, formerly of Barnards Inn, afterwards of
Fetter Lane, London, late of New York. Administration with
will to Richard Alexander Price, attorney for daughter Ann,
wife of Hugh McGregor, at Greenock, Scotland. (Mar. 1832).

Panton, Rev. George, formerly of Shelburne, Nova Scotia, and
of New York, afterwards of Kelso, Scotland, late of Edinburgh. Administration to relict Jeane Panton. (Oct. 1810).

Panton, William, of Pensacola, West Florida, who died at sea.
Limited probate to John Forbes and Adam Gordon with similar
powers reserved to John Panton, Thomas Forbes, John Innerarity, James Innerarity and others. (Dec. 1804).

Paradise, Lucy, of Williamsburg, Virginia, widow. Administration to grandson Count Giovanni Alvise Barziza. (Oct. 1815).

Parish, George, of Ogdensburgh, New York. Probate to Joseph
Russell. (Aug. 1839).

Parke, Cuthbert, of Philadelphia. Administration to John
Charles Laycock, attorney for John Bradley, guardian
appointed by Philadelphia Orphans' Court to only children
Ellen and William Parke; relict Martha Ann Parke having
died. (June 1847).

Parker, William, of Staten Island, New York, bachelor. Administration to mother and next of kin Elizabeth, wife of Abraham Filewood. (Aug. 1855).

Parkins, Joseph Wilfred, formerly of London and of Essex Street,
Strand, Middlesex, afterwards of New York City, late of
Newark, New Jersey. Administration with will to Thomas
Colpitts Granger, executor to executor George Best deceased,
after sentence for validity of will. (Dec. 1843). Revoked
on death of Granger and granted to relict of George Best,
Mary now wife of William Simpson. (Feb. 1853).

Parks, Roland, Cornet on half pay in King's American Dragoons,
who died at Westfield, Hampbden Co., Mass. Administration
to James Tidbury, attorney for relict Sarah Parks at Westfield. (June 1830).

Parslow, John, of New Orleans, bachelor. Administration to
brother Edward Parslow; mother Elizabeth Parslow, widow,
having died. (Apr. 1845). Grants in same month in respect
of brothers Daniel Parslow, Lieutenant of 6th Regiment of
Native Infantry at Bombay; Thomas Parslow, naval store-
keeper at Barbados; and James Sharpe Parslow of Kentish
Town, Middlesex, midshipman of H.M.S. *Laurel*.

Parsons, formerly Ewer, Mary, formerly of Charles Street,
Grosvenor Square, Middlesex, late of Boston, North America.
Administration to husband Thomas Parsons. (Feb. 1818).

Parton, Francis, formerly of Queen Anne Street, St. Marylebone,
Middlesex, late of Grand Bank, Newfoundland, and Salem, Mass.
Administration to William Matthews, attorney for relict
Lydia Parton at Salem. (Apr. 1811).

Partridge, John, formerly of Philadelphia, late of New York
City, plasterer. Probate to John Liptrott Graves after
retraction of his renunciation. (Aug. 1827).

Passapae, John Davis, formerly of Baltimore, U.S.A., late of
    Valparaiso, South America, bachelor. Administration to sister
    Mary Ann Hilditch. (June 1853).
Passapae, Joseph, formerly of Baltimore, Maryland, late of Callao
    in Peru, widower. Administration to daughter Mary Ann
    Hilditch. (Apr. 1849).
Passey, Samuel A. - see Plummer.
Patrick, Edward, alias Smith, John Edward, formerly of Peters-
    field, Hampshire, late of Southampton, Suffolk Co., North
    America, rigger. Probate to James Harlow Payne and brother
    James Patrick with similar powers reserved to Henry P. Hedges.
    (Oct. 1855).
Patten, Mary, of Washington Co., New York, widow. Administration
    to David Davies, attorney for son Edward Patten at Washington.
    (Nov. 1811).
Pattinger - see Pettinger.
Pattle, Eliza Henrietta, formerly of Golden Square, Middlesex,
    late of Brooklyn, New York, spinster. Administration with
    will to Edward Beldam, attorney for William Edward Custis
    at New York. (Feb. 1854).
Paine, Elizabeth, of Evansville, Indiana, spinster. Administra-
    tion to William Millard, attorney for father John Paine at
    Evansville. (July 1852).
Payne, Jean, of Goochland Co., Virginia, widow. Administration
    with will to William Murdock, attorney for son George Woodson
    Payne at Goochland Co. (June 1808).
Paine, Samuel, of Worcester, Mass., bachelor. Administration to
    Harrison Gray, attorney for brother William Paine, M.D., at
    Worcester. (Apr. 1808).
Pearne, George, formerly of Dover, Kent, late of Blackwall,
    Poplar, Middlesex, engineer on steam vessel *Great Western*,
    who died at New York, bachelor. Probate to William Crandall.
    (July 1838).
Peel, John, of New York City, widower. Administration to sister
    and only next of kin Ann, wife of Francis Graham. (Sept. 1800).
Pelley, James, of Hobucken, New Jersey, bachelor. Administration
    to brother and next of kin William Pelley. (June 1825).
Penney, William Honeycombe, of New York, seaman on steam vessel
    Oscela, bachelor. Administration to father John Penney.
    (Nov. 1840).
Perman, George, of Charleston, South Carolina, merchant. Admini-
    stration to Rev. Thomas Evans, attorney for relict Isabella
    Perman at Charleston. (Dec. 1847).
Peronneau, Mary Coffin, of Charleston, South Carolina, spinster.
    Probate to William Henry Peronneau. (Nov. 1849).
Perry, Robert, formerly of Birmingham, Warwickshire, late of
    New York, merchant. Probate to Thomas Lamb with similar
    powers reserved to William Shakespear, Henry Pope and William
    J. Bradford. (July 1827).
Perryman, Thomas, formerly of Tottenham Court Road, St. Pancras,
    Middlesex, late of Fernton near Philadelphia. Probate to
    sister Sarah Perryman. (Apr. 1807).
Peter, William, of Philadelphia. Administration with will to
    John Thomas Henry Peter, attorney for relict Sarah Peter at
    Philadelphia. (July 1853). New grant March 1894.
Petrie, Frederick Henry, of Union, Monroe Co., Virginia.
    Administration with will to John Miller, attorney for Eliza-
    beth Clara, wife of Addison Dunlap at Union. (July 1846).
Pettengell, Frederick, of South Carolina, bachelor. Administra-
    tion to sister Ann, wife of Edward William Turner; mother
    Sarah Pettengell having died. (Oct. 1843)

Pettengell, William Henn, of South Carolina. Administration
to relict Ann Pettengell. (Oct. 1843).

Pettinger alias Pottinger alias Pattinger, John, formerly of
New York City, late boatswain of H.M.S. *Caroline*. Admini-
stration to John Fallowfield Scott, attorney for mother Ruth
Pettinger in New York. (July 1820).

Pfeffel, Peter Carl, formerly of Frankfurt on Main, late of
New York, merchant, bachelor, who died at sea passenger on
steam ship *President*. Administration to Adolphus Bach,
attorney for father Carl Friederich Pfeffel at Frankfurt.
(Apr. 1842).

Phelps, Edwin, formerly of Hartpury, Gloucestershire, yeoman,
late of Limaville, Ohio. Administration to Henry Pritchard,
attorney for relict Jane Phelps at Limaville. (Aug. 1854).

Phillips, Ann, formerly of Wapping High Street, Wapping,
Middlesex, late of New York, widow. Administration to
brother John Bluck. (July 1811).

Philips, Frederick, formerly of New York, late of Chester.
Administration of estate unadministered by son Frederick
Philips deceased to daughter Eliza Ann Philips; relict
Elizabeth Philips renouncing. (Feb. 1822).

Philips, Frederick, of Philipstown, Putnam Co., New York.
Administration to Frederick Codd, attorney for only child
Mary, wife of Samuel Gouverneur at New York City; relict
Maria Philips renouncing. (Feb. 1831).

Phillips, Grace Amos, of Cincinnati, U.S.A. Administration to
Joseph Isaac, attorney for husband Isaac Phillips at Pleasant
Hill, Missouri. (Oct. 1857).

Phillips, Henry, of Exeter, New Hampshire. Probate to relict
Elizabeth Phillips. (Aug. 1813).

Phillips, Patrick, formerly of Hungerford Market, Strand, Middlesex, late of Bath Town, Virginia. Administration to brother
Michael Phillips. (Nov. 1827). Revoked on his death and
granted to brother William Phillips. (Mar. 1829). Revoked
because grant was made on false suggestion that deceased was
a childless widower and regranted to only child Patrick
Phillips; relict Susannah Morgan, formerly Phillips, renouncing. (Aug. 1837).

Philpott, Thomas, of Boston, U.S.A., widower. Administration
to son Henry Philpott. (Mar. 1833).

Pinckney, Charles Cotesworth, of Charleston, South Carolina,
General in U.S. Army. Administration with will to Benjamin
Stead, attorney for daughters Maria Henrietta Pinckney,
Harriott Pinckney and Eliza Lucas Izard, widow (formerly
wife of Ralph D. Izard), at Charleston; wife Mary Pinckney
having died in testator's lifetime, and sister Harriott Horry,
widow, and brother Thomas Pinckney renouncing. (Apr. 1827).

Pirsson, Joseph Poole, of New York City, counsellor at law.
Administration with will to William Warren Hastings, attorney
for relict Mary Chapman Pirsson at New York. (Jan. 1848).

Pitcher, James, of New York. Probate to niece Ann, wife of
Thomas Broadbear, executrix of executrix Grace Pitcher;
other executors William Porter and Cornelius Clopper having
died. (Mar. 1800).

Pitt, Samuel Grove, of Ionia Co., Michigan, bachelor. Administration to brother Peter Pitt; father William Pitt renouncing. (Nov. 1854).

Platas, Antonio, of Baton Rouge, Louisiana, widower. Administration to daughter Maria Merced Platas. (June 1831).

Pleasants, James, formerly of Richmond, U.S.A., late of Masanzas,
Cuba, bachelor. Administration to Robert Auld, attorney for
creditor James Ross; all others with an interest cited but
not appearing. (Apr. 1821).

61

Plenderleath, Gabriel George, of New York, bachelor and
    bastard. Administration to George Maule for use of the
    King. (Jan. 1827).
Plumbe, Frances Margaretta, of Du Buque, Iowa, widow.
    Administration to son Richard Plumbe. (Oct. 1857).
Plummer alias Passey, Samuel Aggs, of Philadelphia. Limited
    probate to cousin Francis Gardner. (Aug. 1829).
Plunket, David, of Baltimore, Maryland, merchant. Administra-
    tion with will to Hon. William Conyngham Plunket. (Aug.
    1818).
Pocock, Joseph, of Rochester, New York, widower. Administra-
    tion to Charles Pocock, son and administrator to father
    Thomas Bartholomew Pocock deceased. (Dec. 1856).
Pocock, Sarah, of Rochester, New York. Administration to
    Charles Pocock, administrator to husband Joseph Pocock
    deceased. (Dec. 1856).
Pogson, Rev. George, of Charlestown, North America, bachelor
    and bastard. Administration of estate unadministered by
    Rev. Thomas Preston deceased to Thomas Pogson for use of
    the King. (Nov. 1816).
Poinsett, Fanny alias Frances, formerly of Freshford, Somerset,
    late of Charleston, South Carolina, widow. Limited admini-
    stration with will to Joel Richards Poinsett, attorney for
    daughter Frances Poinsett in Charleston. (Aug. 1806).
Pollard, Edward, of Nashua, Hillsborough Co., New Hampshire.
    Administration to Matthew Forster, attorney for father
    Cumings Pollard at Nashua. (Aug. 1841).
Pollard, Francis, of Grenada and Martinique, who died at Boston,
    New England. Probate to James Inglis with similar powers
    reserved to John Inglis. (July 1800).
Pollard, John, formerly of Carey Street, St. Clement Danes,
    Middlesex, late of Philadelphia. Administration to sister
    and next of kin Sarah, wife of Charles Price; relict Mary
    Pollard cited but not appearing. (Oct. 1809).
Pollock, Thomas, of Paisley, Scotland, merchant, widower.
    Administration to William Swainson, attorney for sons George
    and Thomas Pollock at Boston, U.S.A. (Nov. 1838).
Ponsonby, Richard, formerly of Whitehaven, Cumberland, late of
    Maryland, bachelor. Administration to niece Elizabeth, wife
    of Isaac Nicholson; sisters and only next of kin Elizabeth
    wife of Isaac Brown, Jane Nicholson, widow, Mary wife of
    Richard Clark, Bridget Topping, widow, and Dinah McDougal,
    widow, having died. (Feb. 1837).
Poole, Elizabeth - see Rolfe.
Pope, Charles, formerly of Bishopstone, Wiltshire, farmer,
    late of Newgarden, U.S.A. Administration to sister and only
    next of kin Elizabeth, wife of Isaac Archer; relict Susannah
    Pope renouncing. (Dec. 1830).
Porcher, James, of St. Peter's parish, South Carolina. Admini-
    stration to relict Mary J. Porcher. (Oct. 1824).
Postlethwaite, George, of New York City, bachelor. Administra-
    tion to father Richard Postlethwaite. (July 1803).
Pottinger - see Pettinger.
Powell, Howell, of New York City, widower. Administration to
    daughter Margaret, wife of Griffith Edwards. (Jan. 1842).
Powell, John Parry, formerly of Moor Park, Brecon, late of St.
    Louis, Missouri, widower. Administration to son William
    John Powell. (Dec. 1841).
Powell, Joseph, formerly of Leominster, Herefordshire, late of
    New York, plumber and glazier. Probate to Thomas Brayer the
    younger. (Apr. 1833).

Power, Emily, of Youghall, Cork Co., Ireland, who died at
Utica, New York, spinster. Administration to brother George
Farmer Power; mother and next of kin Emily Bromfield Power
having died. (Nov. 1856). Administration of brother Pierce
Power granted same month.
Powles, Thomas, of Ohio, bachelor. Administration to brother
James Powles; father James Powles renouncing. (Aug. 1856).
Powling, Benjamin, of Illinois. Administration to relict
Elizabeth Powling. (May 1855).
Poyntell, William, of Philadelphia. Administration with will
to son George Poyntell; executors Paul Beck, Robert Alexan-
der Chaldcleugh and son William Poyntell cited but not
appearing. (Mar. 1812). Revoked on death of George Poyntell
and granted to William Taylor, attorney for Robert A. Cald-
cleugh, Paul Beck and son William Poyntell at Philadelphia.
(Oct. 1812).
Pratt, Horace Southworth, of Tuskaloosa, Alabama. Administra-
tion to James Bullock Dunwody, attorney for relict Isabel
Ann Pratt at Tuskaloosa. (May 1843).
Pratt, Jane Farley, of Tuskaloosa, Alabama. Administration to
James Bullock Dunwody, administrator to husband Horace S.
Pratt and attorney for his relict Isabel Ann Pratt at
Tuskaloosa. (June 1843).
Preece, Henry, of California, America, who died at sea, bachelor.
Administration to mother and next of kin Martha, wife of
John James Catton. (Dec. 1850).
Preswick, Mary, of Mount Pleasant, New York, widow. Administra-
tion to William Maryan, attorney for son Christopher Pres-
wick at sea. (Aug. 1815).
Prevost, William, of Cincinnati, Ohio. Probate to Thomas James.
(Jan. 1830). Further grant November 1859.
Price, William, formerly of Beckett, Berkshire, late of New
York, bachelor. Administration to father Barrington Price.
(Apr. 1818).
Prichard, James, of Hyde Park, Dutchess Co., New York. Admini-
stration with will to James Prichard, attorney for Peter
Schryver at Hyde Park. (May 1840).
Priest, Henry, of New York City, widower. Limited administra-
tion to George Dollond, attorney for sons William Henry,
Frederic Dollond and Edward Carleton Priest in New York.
(Dec. 1815).
Prime, Richard Airey, of New Orleans. Probate to sisters Mary
Airey Prime and Cornelia Airey Prime. (Apr. 1818).
Primerose, Catharine, of Charleston, South Carolina, widow.
Probate to Christopher Gadsden Morris with similar powers
reserved to Hugh Perroneau Dawes. (Aug. 1841).
Primerose, Robert, of Charleston, South Carolina. Probate to
Christopher Gadsden and Hugh Perroneau with similar powers
reserved to Adam Tunno and James Lamb. (Aug. 1825).
Prole, George, of Stafford, New York, bachelor. Administration
to niece Marian Elizabeth Harris; brothers and only next of
kin Frederick and Henry Prole renouncing. (Jan. 1844).
Prowell, Joseph, formerly of Demarara and Berbice, late of
Philadelphia. Probate to Robert Pulsford, with similar
powers reserved to John Wilson, John Douglas and David Lenox.
(Feb. 1806).
Puffer, George, of New York, merchant, widower. Administration
to creditor Peter Puffer; son George Shelford Puffer
renouncing for himself and as guardian of other children
Caroline Augusta, Elizabeth, Charles Drevar, Emily and
Joan Parton Puffer. (Aug. 1837).

Puffer, Matilda Brown, of New York, spinster. Administration
to creditor Peter Puffer; brothers and sisters George
Shelford, Elizabeth, Charles Drevar, Emily and John Parton
Puffer renouncing. (Aug. 1837).

Pugh, Eliza, wife of William Pugh, of Philadelphia. Limited
administration with will to Samuel James Blacklow and David
Morrison. (Nov. 1838).

Punfield, Samuel, formerly of Birmingham, Warwickshire, late
of Baltimore, Maryland, bachelor. Administration to sister
and next of kin Elizabeth Punfield. (Dec. 1801).

Purchase, James, formerly of Haselbury Plucknett, Somerset,
late of Arkansas. Probate to Joseph Purchase and Adam
Rendall. (Apr. 1851).

Purdy, David, of New Town, New York, Lieutenant of half pay in
King's American Regiment commanded by General Edmund Fanning.
Administration to James Tidbury, attorney for relict Maria
Purdy at New Town. (Dec. 1827).

Putnam, John Chandler, of Boston, Mass. Limited administration
with will to George Pope, attorney for relict Abigail Smith
Putnam at Boston. (Nov. 1840).

Pye, Edward Henry, of Cornwallis's Neck, Charles Co., Maryland.
Administration with will to William Barksdale, attorney for
brothers James B. Pye and Nicholas Stonestreet in America.
(Jan. 1826).

Quinn, Peter, of Springfield, U.S.A., bachelor. Administration
to brother Philip Quinn; relict Honora Quinn renouncing.
(Oct. 1847).

Rabbeth, nee Bentley, Susannah, formerly of Clay Bridge,
Lincolnshire, late of New York City. Administration to
Frederick Burton, attorney for husband James Rabbeth at New
York City. (May 1845).

Radburn, Thomas, formerly of Chipping Norton, Oxfordshire, late
of Charleston, North (sic) Carolina, widow. Administration
with will to only child Elizabeth, wife of William Faulkener;
wife Mary Radburn having died in testator's lifetime. (June
1826).

Radcliffe, Anne - see Jennings.

Rae, William Glen, of San Francisco, Upper California. Admini-
stration with will to Edward Roberts, attorney for John
McLoughlin at Fort Vancouver, Columbia River; Sir George
Simpson renouncing. (June 1849). Further grant April 1863.

Raitt, Alexander, formerly of Kittery, Maine, who died at sea.
Administration to George Muirson Woolsey, attorney for son
William Raitt at Eliot, Kittery; relict Miriam Raitt having
died. (May 1825).

Ramsay, James, of Charles Town, South Carolina, M.D. Administration to Robert Goulding, attorney for relict Eleanor
Ramsay at Charles Town. (May 1833).

Randolph, Benjamin, formerly of Bristol, late of Virginia.
Administration with will to James Randolph, attorney for
brother Thomas Eston Randolph in Albemarle Co., Virginia.
(Sept. 1818).

Rapp, John, formerly of Holborn, Middlesex, late of Baltimore,
U.S.A., merchant, widower. Administration to only child
John Rapp. (Nov. 1838).

Ratcliffe, John, of Emigrant Refuge, Wards Island, New York,
bachelor. Administration to father Thomas Ratcliffe.
(Jan. 1856).

Reading, Richard, of Aurora, New York. Probate to nephew
Thomas Reading. (July 1851).

Reddicliffe, Ann C. - see Cutmore.

Redmond, Edward, formerly of Bow Church Yard, afterwards of
Milk Street, Cheapside, London, late of Philadelphia.
Probate to Henry Redmond. (June 1804).

Redrup, Abel, formerly of Saunderton, Buckinghamshire, late of
Royalton near Cincinnati, Ohio. Probate to surviving
executor Joseph Allen. (Apr. 1849).

Redwood, Langford, of Flushing, New York. Administration with
will to John Coles Symes, James Trecothick and John Henry
Roper the younger, attornies for John McCahill and David
Maitland in New York City. (Sept. 1844).

Reed, Thomas, of New York, who died at island of Goree.
Administration to David Knor, attorney for relict Euphen
Reed at New York. (May 1802).

Reeve, Ann - see Fenner.

Reeve, Stephen, of New York City, widower. Administration to
Robert Pears, attorney for only child Ann, wife of Richard
Sankey Fenner, at New York City. (May 1838). Revoked on
her death and granted to her administrator Alexander Cowell,
attorney for Richard Sankey Fenner at Baltimore, U.S.A.
(Oct. 1848).

Reeves, Elizabeth, of Chester, Delaware Co., U.S.A., widow.
Administration to George White, attorney for son Hiram
Reeves at Philadelphia. (May 1854).

Reilly, Charles, of Charlestown, North America, merchant.
Limited administration to John Hopton. (June 1807).

Renaud, Charlotte, of Philadelphia, widow. Administration to
only child Charlotte, wife of Francis Gordon. (Jan. 1804).

Renwick, William (*Robert in text of Act*), of New York City.
Administration to John Mountgomery, attorney for relict Jane
Renwick at New York. (Dec. 1816).

Reynell, Emily, of Louisville, Kentucky, spinster. Administration to sister Mary Anne, wife of Elijah Carter; mother
Lydia Reynell, widow, having died. (Dec. 1845).

Reynolds, William, of Philadelphia, widower. Limited administration to Richard Gwynn, attorney for only child Herbert
Reynolds at Philadelphia. (Dec. 1853).

Richards, William Fayting, of Old Providence, North America,
bachelor. Administration to half sister Jane Kirkland,
spinster; mother Ann Kirkland, widow, renouncing. (Dec.
1843).

Richman, Francis Henry, of Philadelphia. Probate to Emanuel
Loury and relict Hannah Richman. (June 1856).

Richmond, George, of Boston, U.S.A., bachelor. Administration
to sister and only next of kin Ord Lind, widow. (Feb. 1819).

Ricketts, Ann, of St. Heliers, Jersey, widow. Administration to James Hampson, attorney for son James Jervis Ricketts at Philadelphia. (May 1843).

Ridd, Francis, formerly of Tawstock, Devon, late of Utica, North America, bachelor. Administration to father Thomas Ridd. (Mar. 1833).

Riddle, Susanna, of Rolls Co., Missouri, widow. Administration to creditor Thomas Aspinwall; only children James Nourse Riddle, William Nourse Riddle, David Hunter Riddle and Catherine Burton wife of William Stone, and nephews and nieces Martha Susan Riddle, William Tabb Riddle, Catherine Burton Riddle, Joseph Nourse Riddle, Mary Matthews Riddle, Elizabeth Frances Riddle, Lavinia Anderson Riddle and David Hoge Riddle renouncing. (July 1850).

Ridley, Matthew, formerly of Essex Street, Strand, Middlesex, late of Baltimore, Maryland. Administration to Samuel Montague Sears, son and administrator to creditor Samuel Sears deceased; relict ---- Ridley cited but not appearing and ----- Ridley having died a bachelor before administering. (May 1806).

Riggs, William, of Fairfax, Vermont. Administration to John Stuart, attorney for relict Nancy Riggs at Vermont. (Nov. 1855).

Ring, James, of New York, bachelor. Administration to Mary Ring, relict and administratrix of brother and only next of kin Thomas Ring deceased. (Jan. 1818).

Ring, John, formerly of Bath, late of New York, bachelor. Administration to nephew and only next of kin Thomas Ring. (Mar. 1840).

Rioch, Kenneth, of Boston, New England, bachelor. Administration to sister Ann Rioch. (Oct. 1802).

Roberts, Jane, of Rochester, U.S.A., widow. Administration to Mary Davies, widow, attorney for daughter Mary Roberts at Oberlin, U.S.A. (July 1852).

Robertson, John, of Charles Co., Maryland. Administration with will to John Blair, attorney for son John Robertson at Claiborne Co., Mississippi; executors Alexander Green and Henry Henley Chapman cited but not appearing. (Dec. 1824).

Robins, Clementine, of New York, widow. Administration to Edward Colston Hague, administrator to only child Emily Robins deceased. (Sept. 1857).

Robinson, George, formerly of Scarborough, Yorkshire, late of New York City. Probate to mother Margaret Robinson. (Mar. 1802).

Robinson, Joseph, formerly Lieutenant in South Carolina Royalists, late of Charlotte, Prince Edward Island. Administration with will to Goodinch Murray Thompson, attorney for relict Lilly alias Lilia Robinson, Robert Hodgson and Ralph Brecken at Prince Edward Island. (Jan. 1808).

Robinson, Margaret - see Taylerson.

Robinson, Sarah, formerly of Gloucester Place, New Road, Middlesex, late of Vermillion Co., North America. Probate to Henry Callaway. (Dec. 1851).

Rodaway, Aaron Miller, formerly of Pontypool, Monmouth, late of Philadelphia, widower. Administration to brother and next of kin Alfred Biggs Rodaway. (Oct. 1852).

Rodman, Thomas Rotch, formerly of New Bedford, Mass., late of Havana, Cuba, bachelor. Administration to Thomas Dickason the younger, attorney for father Samuel Rodman at New Bedford. (June 1810).

Roe, John the elder, of Hazlewood in Madison Township, Licking Co., Ohio. Probate to son Thomas Henry Roe, M.D. (Dec. 1849).

Roe, Sarah, of Hazlewood near Newark, Licking Co., Ohio.
Administration to husband John Roe. (July 1847).

Rogers, Ann, of Charleston, South Carolina, widow. Administration to daughter Elizabeth, wife of Robert Barlow. (Sept.
1805).

Rogers, Fanny, of New York, widow. Administration to Richard
Rogers, attorney for son William Rogers at New York.
(Apr. 1841).

Rogers, John Morris, of New York City. Administration to
Edward Henry Rickards, attorney for relict Ann Rogers at
New York. (Jan. 1846).

Rogers, Mary - see Stevenson.

Rogers. Samuel, of St. Marylebone, Middlesex, late of Boston,
Mass. Administration to son John Rogers. (Aug. 1805).

Rogers, Samuel, of Boston, U.S.A., merchant. Administration
to Timothy Wiggin, attorney for relict Nancy Rogers at Boston.
(Nov. 1833).

Rogers, William, formerly of Bristol, late of New York City.
Probate to John Wesley Hall with similar powers reserved to
James Maize and Benjamin W. Rogers. (Oct. 1829).

Rolfe, nee Poole, Elizabeth, of Brooklyn, New York. Administration to John Poole, attorney for husband John Rolfe at
Brooklyn. (Mar. 1839).

Rolph, nee Hopwood, Jemima, of Williamsburgh, New York. Administration to William Hopwood, attorney for husband John Adey
Rolph at New York City. (Nov. 1844).

Rooke, John Bolton, of Charles Town, South Carolina. Probate
to relict Sarah Rooke with similar powers reserved to William
Palmer. (Mar. 1802).

Rose, John Wallington, of New Orleans, bachelor. Administration
to uncle Thomas Rose. (Nov. 1851).

Rose, William, formerly of Bromsgrove, Worcestershire, late of
New Brunswick, New Jersey, who died in 1792. Limited
administration to John Irvine Glennie. (Sept. 1825).

Rose, William James, of New York City. Administration to relict
Mary Ann Margaret Rose. (Dec. 1849).

Ross, David, of Richmond, Virginia. Administration with will to
John Fallowfield Scott, attorney for Thomas T. Bouldin in
U.S.A.; son Frederick Augustus Ross and Jacob Myers cited
but not appearing. (Apr. 1822).

Rossiter, Eliza, of Cleveland, Cuyahogo Co., Ohio. Administration to husband William Rossiter. (Jan. 1836).

Rossiter, John, of Scranton, Luzerne Co., Pennsylvania, labourer,
bachelor. Administration to father John Rossiter. (Oct.
1852).

Round, George, of Mobile, Alabama. Administration to James
Flavell, attorney for relict Mary Round at Mobile. (Mar. 1850).

Rowe, James, formerly of New Brunswick, late of Whampoa, China,
bachelor. Administration to Edmund Clarke, attorney for
mother and next of kin Catherine Rowe, widow, at Boston,
U.S.A. (Dec. 1853).

Rowland, Thomas, formerly of Salford, Lancashire, late of Sacramento, California. Administration to William Webb, attorney
for relict Caroline Rowland at Sacramento. (Feb. 1853).

Rowley, George, formerly of Staple Inn, London, late of Philadelphia, bachelor. Limited administration to Mylam Garling,
attorney for Elizabeth, wife of William Garrett. (Mar. 1802).

Royle, William, of Williamsburg, Virginia, widower. Administra-
tion to Benjamin Blake, minor; brother of whole blood
Hunter Royle and brothers and sister of half blood Henry St.
John Dixon, John Dixon, Mary Dixon and George Washington
Dixon having died. (July 1852).

Ruddy, John, formerly of Killala, Mayo Co., Ireland, late of
    Springfield, Mass. Administration to relict Bridget Ruddy.
    (Mar. 1856).
Rudge, Jonathan, of Ross, Herefordshire, afterwards of Bristol,
    late of New Orleans, bachelor. Administration to brother
    Thomas Rudge. (Mar. 1805).
Rusk, Hugh, of Baltimore, Maryland, bachelor. Administration
    to William Brown, attorney for brother and only next of kin
    Robert Rusk at Baltimore. (Nov. 1829).
Russell, Elizabeth, of Marblehead, Mass. Administration with
    will of estate unadministered by son Russell Trevett decea-
    sed to Samuel Russell Trevett and Samuel Hooper; executors
    William Gray having died and Daniel Waldo renouncing.
    (Sept. 1803).
Russell, James, of Charleston, North America, widower. Admini-
    stration to son James Russell. (Feb. 1810).
Russell, Thomas, of Boston, North America, bachelor. Admini-
    stration to James Russell, son and administrator of father
    James Russell deceased. (Feb. 1810).
Rutherford, John, of Edgerston, New Jersey. Probate to daughter
    Mary Rutherford with similar powers reserved to Peter
    Augustus Jay, his wife Mary Rutherford Jay, Peter Gerard
    Stuyvesant, his wife Helen Stuyvesant, daughter Louisa Morris
    Rutherford, daughter Anna Watts, widow, granddaughter Helen
    Russell, her husband Archibald Russell, son Robert Walter
    Rutherford and grandson John Rutherford the younger. (Oct.
    1841).
Rutledge, Sarah Motte, formerly of Brighton, Sussex, late of
    Charleston, South Carolina, widow. Limited administration
    to Charles Francis Cobb, attorney for son John Rutledge at
    Charleston. (July 1852).

Sabatier, Richard, formerly of Shepton Mallet, Somerset, late
    of Mass., U.S.A., brewer, widower. Administration to Elisha
    Hayden Collier, attorney for only children Sarah Staines,
    wife of William Gardiner, Anna Maria Housley, divorced wife
    of William Housley, and Jane Sabatier in Mass. (Aug. 1819).
Salkeld, George, formerly of Liverpool, Lancashire, late of New
    Orleans, widower. Administration to William Collins, attor-
    ney for son Frederick Salkeld now on passage to Peru, South
    America. (Dec. 1834).
Salmonson, Frederick, of New York. Administration to relict
    Eugenia Salmonson. (May 1854).
Salter, James, of Knox Co., Ohio, widower. Administration to
    son Samuel Salter. (Aug. 1846).
Sampson, John, of Marysville, Upper California, bachelor.
    Administration to sister Augusta Sampson; mother Anna
    Sampson, widow, renouncing. (Feb. 1851).
Sanders, Edward William, formerly of Columbus, Colorado, Texas,
    late of Havana, Cuba, bachelor. Administration to brother
    George Lee Sanders. (Sept. 1849).
Sandford, Thomas James Harris, formerly of Rotherham, Yorkshire,
    late of Marietta, Ohio. Probate to relict Mary Sandford,

brother Charles Samuel Roberts Sandford and sister Anna
Maria Yonge, widow. (Nov. 1825).

Sansom, Joseph, of Philadelphia. Limited administration with
will to Richard Van Heythuysen, attorney for relict Beulah
Sansom in Philadelphia. (May 1828).

Sargeaunt, John, formerly of Newnham, Gloucestershire, late of
Philadelphia. Probate to mother Margaret Sargeant, widow.
(Dec. 1822).

Sarti, Antonio, formerly of Spur Street, Leicester Square,
Middlesex, late of Boston, U.S.A., modeller. Probate to
surviving executrix, Selina Isabella, wife of Daniel Barker.
(Feb. 1851).

Saubere, Samuel, of Philadelphia. Administration with will to
Henry Lloyd Magan, attorney for Mary, wife of David Simpson
at Philadelphia; sole executor Peter Keller renouncing.
(Apr. 1849).

Savage, Patrick, British Vice-Consul at Norfolk, Virginia.
Administration to James Savage, uncle of only children John,
Emma Ann and Amelia Stewart Savage during their minority;
mother Ann Savage, widow, renouncing. (Dec. 1818).

Saviche, Matias, of Pueblo de los Angeles, California, who died
at sea on steam ship *Orinoco*, widower. Administration to
Joseph Rodney Croskey, attorney for Ignacio Franco Coronel
at Los Angeles, grandfather and guardian of only children
Matias and Francisco Saviche during their minority. (Feb.
1853).

Scaife, Elizabeth and Sarah Fell, spinsters, of Maryport,
Cumberland, who died at New York. Administration to mother
Sally Scaife, widow. (Mar. 1844).

Scantlebury, Joanna - see Barritt.

Schmitz, Franz Jacob, formerly of Keppel, late of Olpe, both in
Prussia, who died at San Francisco, California. Administra-
tion with will to daughter Mathilda Schmitz; relict Amalia
Schmitz having died. (Dec. 1853).

Scholes, James, of Brooklyn, New York. Administration with
will to William Pike, attorney for relict Maria Scholes at
Brooklyn. (July 1850).

Schouborg, Ann, of Yonkers, New York. Administration with will
to Joseph Delevaute, attorney for husband Anders Jenson
Schouborg at New York City. (Jan. 1857).

Scott, Alexander, of Lancaster City, Pennsylvania. Administration with will to Charles Robert Turner, attorney for relict
Mary Snyder, widow, in America. (Mar. 1824).

Scott, John, of Barboursville, Virginia, Ensign of 85th Regiment
of Foot. Administration to relict Janet Scott. (Jan. 1821).

Scott, formerly Farr, Sarah, formerly of Hampton Court, Middlesex, then of North Shields, Northumberland, late of New York,
widow. Administration to brother and only next of kin
Edward Farr. (Apr. 1820).

Seager, Stephen, formerly of Birmingham, Warwickshire, late of
Canonsburgh, Washington Co., Pennsylvania. Probate to
Andrew Munro. (Jan. 1808).

Seager, Rev. William, of Williamsburgh, New York. Administration to relict Catherine Seager. (Dec. 1856).

Seckamp, Albert, of Baltimore, North America. Administration
to Alexander Glennie, attorney for relict Sophia Seckamp at
Baltimore. (July 1811).

Seguin, Arthur Edward Sheldon, formerly of King William Street,
Strand, Middlesex, late of New York. Administration to
relict Anne Seguin. (Sept. 1853).

Selby, Skeffington, late of New York who died at Hitcham,
Suffolk. Probate to Rev. George Edis Webster, Edward Compton
and nephew Robert Johnson. (June 1821).

Selfe, Abraham, formerly of Little St. Thomas the Apostle,
London, late of Sharon Richfield, Washtenow Co., Michigan,
widower. Administration to nephew Thomas Selfe. (Mar.
1857).

Selkirk, Andrew, seaman of H.M.S. *Drake*, bachelor. Administration to James Ferguson, attorney for mother Jean Selkirk,
widow, at Barnet, Caledonia Co., North America. (Jan. 1822).

Sellens, nee Holman, Mary, of Cicero Corners, Onandaga, U.S.A.
Administration to husband John Sellens. (July 1851).

Semple, Robert, of Rupertsland, North America, bachelor. Administration to father Robert Semple. (Aug. 1818).

Sewell, Adam, formerly of Milton near Gravesend, Kent, late of
New York City. Administration to Mason Neale, attorney for
relict Ann Sewell at New York City. (Apr. 1807).

Shakespear, Elizabeth S. - see Docker.

Shapton, Thomas, formerly of Union Row, Pill, Somerset, late of
Staten Island, New York, steward of merchant ship *J.W. Paine*.
Administration to relict Rebecca Shapton. (June 1856).

Sharples, James, of New York City. Probate to relict Ellen
Sharples. (July 1811).

Shaw, James Southby, of Columbus, Missouri, bachelor. Administration to brother Charles Southby Shaw and sister Mary
Southby Shaw; mother Frances Naomi Shaw having died. (Dec.
1847).

Shedden, William Ralston, of Roughwood, Ayr, Scotland, who died
at New York. Administration with will to son Patrick Ralston
Shedden now aged 21; executors James Farquhar, David Hosack
and nephew John Patrick having died. (July 1852).

Shell, Richard, formerly of Leend, Wiltshire, late of Sullivan,
Madison Co., New York. Administration to son Steven Shell;
relict Ann Shell renouncing. (July 1857).

Shepperd, James Nutley, of Key West, Florida, bachelor. Administration to Sarah Shepperd, widow, administratrix to father
James Shepperd deceased. (Apr. 1846).

Sheppard, nee Lestourgeon, Susannah Mary, of Kendall Co., Illinois. Administration to husband David Chever Sheppard.
(Sept. 1857).

Sheppard, William, formerly of Old Street Road, Middlesex, tea
dealer, late of New York. Limited administration to Henry
Hutchins, attorney for relict Mary Ann Sheppard at New York.
(Feb. 1839).

Sherwood, Joseph Thomas, of Portland, Cumberland Co., Maine.
Probate to sons Charles Deering Sherwood, William Richard
Sherwood and Edward Preble Sherwood with similar powers
reserved to relict Dorcas Sherwood. (Dec. 1849).

Sheward, William, of Ohio Province, U.S.A., bacehlor. Administration to sister Mary Ann Sheward. (May 1836).

Shield, Benjamin, formerly of Stamford Hill, Middlesex, late of
Baltimore, North America, seaman of American merchant ship
Two Friends, bachelor. Administration to brother John Shield,
and sisters Rebecca Robinson, widow, and Mary Watkins, widow.
(Apr. 1820).

Shipley, George, of New York City. Administration with will to
William Remington, attorney for relict Hannah Shipley at New
York. (May 1804).

Shirley, Thomas Frederic, formerly of Carlisle Lane, Westminster
Road, Surrey, who died with his wife Hannah and only children
Emma and Hannah Shirley as passengers on American ship *Charles
Bartlett* when she was run down on passage to New York by steam
ship *Europa*. Limited administration to Joseph Eugene Shirley.
(Sept. 1849).

Shoolbred, Mary alias Polly, of Charleston, South Carolina.
Administration to husband James Shoolbred. (Sept. 1820).

Short, John, formerly of Barnstaple, Devon, ropemaker, late of
Pleasant Grove near Tremont, Fazewell Co., Illinois. Probate
to William Gribble with similar powers reserved to Richard
Tepper. (Aug. 1842).

Short, Mary, of Stafford, Gennesee Co., U.S.A. Administration
to William Gribble, executor to husband John Short deceased.
(Jan. 1856).

Shoveler, Sarah, of Southwark, Philadelphia, widow. Administration with will by his solemn affirmation to Joseph Hancock,
attorney for sister Mary McNeran in Philadelphia. (Mar. 1800).

Shubrick, Richard, of St. Philip's, Charles Town, U.S.A., who
died in 1777. Limited administration on death of relict
Susannah Shubrick to Edward Western Wright, attorney for
daughter Susannah, wife of Roger Pinckney. (Oct. 1841).

Shubrick, Sarah - see Smith.

Shurlock, Robert, of Easton, Northampton Co., Pennsylvania,
physician, bachelor. Administration to James Stuart, attorney for brother Samuel Shurlock at Bigg Beaver, Pennsylvania.
(June 1831). Further grant December 1878.

Silvester, Joseph Hooper, formerly Captain of main top of H.M.S.
Lily, late seaman of American merchant ship *Massasoit*, who
died at sea, bachelor. Administration to sister Frances
Hannah, wife of William David Charles Read. (Apr. 1846).

Simpson, Frances, formerly of Whitby, Yorkshire, afterwards of
New York, then of Sligo, Ireland, but died on board ship
Agenoria at sea, spinster. Administration to nephew and
only next of kin Robert Simpson. (Feb. 1838).

Simpson, Frederick Godwin, of 212 Bowery, New York. Administration to William Frederick Simpson, attorney for relict
Catherine Simpson at 160 Spring Street, New York. (Mar. 1857).

Simpson, Samuel, formerly of Lowestoft, Suffolk, late master of
brig *Ellen*, who died at New York, bachelor. Administration
with will to sister Delia, wife of William Woods; executor
William Woods renouncing. (Jan. 1827).

Simpson, Thomas, of Lagan Co., Ohio. Administration to Robert
Abbott, attorney for relict Keziah, now wife of Thomas
Sullivan, at Washington, America. (Mar. 1854).

Skey, George, of the Wilderness near Stockton, California.
Administration with will to John William Partridge, attorney
for relict Myra Skey near Stockton. (Dec. 1853).

Skinner, Alexander, of St. Augustine, East Florida, Superinten-
dent for Indian Affairs in Southern District of North America.
Administration with will to James Simpson, attorney for
daughter Margaret, wife of Nathaniel Munro, at New Providence,
Bahamas; executors Hon. John Moultrie, Rev. John Forbes,
William Alexander and Robert Pain alias Payne having died.
(Feb. 1800).

Skinner, Richard, formerly of London, late of New Orleans.
Probate to Thomas Wilson. (Nov. 1817).

Skinner, Stephen, of Shelburne, Nova Scotia, claimant as American
Loyalist. Limited administration with will to Gabriel Shaw,
attorney for relict Catherine Skinner and Thomas Crowell at
Shelburne. (Nov. 1822).

Skinner, William Stephens, of Boston, Mass. Administration to
Edward Clarke, attorney for relict Sarah Skinner at Roxbury,
Mass. (Oct. 1845).

Skull, Sarah, formerly of Lower Homerton, afterwards of Hammer-
smith, Middlesex, afterwards of Tours, France, then of New
York, who died on merchant ship *William and Elizabeth*, widow.
Administration to only child Joseph Skull. (Apr. 1839).

Slaughter, Richard Hampton, of Pensacola, Florida, bachelor. Administration to brother William Shewen Slaughter; mother Sophia Mary Slaughter having died. (Sept. 1842).

Slaughter, Sophia Mary, of Port Hudson, Louisiana, widow. Administration to son William Shewen Slaughter. (Sept. 1842).

Smith, Abraham Lynsen, of New York, Cornet on half pay with British Legion under Brigadier-General Benedict Arnold. Administration to James Tidbury, attorney for relict Diana Smith at New York. (Dec. 1827).

Smith, Ann, of Cook Co., Illinois. Administration to John Christian Wilson, attorney for husband John Charles Smith in Illinois. (Sept. 1852).

Smith, Boyd, of New Orleans, Louisiana. Administration to Boyd Miller, attorney for relict Margaret Ann Smith at New Orleans. (Nov. 1844).

Smith, Caroline, of Cambridge, Lanawa Co., Michigan, spinster. Administration to John Lacey, attorney for father Joseph Smith at Chicago. (Jan. 1847).

Smith, David, of Norfolk, Virginia, bachelor. Administration to brother Elijah Smith; father Allison Smith renouncing. (Jan. 1811).

Smith, Elizabeth - see Nelson.

Smith, Frederick, formerly of Cotton Court, Manchester, Lancashire, late of Charles Town, South Carolina, merchant. Probate to brother Thomas Smith with similar powers reserved to Henry Gourdin and brothers John Benjamin Smith and Joseph Smith. (Oct. 1839).

Smith, George Clement Fearn, formerly of 287 Regent Street, Middlesex, engraver, late of Philadelphia. Administration with will to relict Harriot Elizabeth, now wife of William Lake. (Dec. 1844).

Smith, James, formerly of Hammersmith, Middlesex, late of South Carolina, bachelor. Administration with will to sister and only next of kin Mary Lapworth, widow; sole executor Henry Flint having died. (Feb. 1820).

Smith, John, formerly of Sapcote, Leicestershire, framework knitter, late of 608 North Third Street below Franklin Avenue, Philadelphia. Administration to daughter Eliza, wife of Ephraim Morley; relict Elizabeth Smith renouncing. (Dec. 1856).

Smith, John Laxon, formerly of Whittlesey, Cambridgeshire, late of Lever Street, Lafayette City, Louisiana. Probate to brother Simon Smith, sister Alice wife of John Grounds, and William Searle with similar powers reserved to brother William Edward Steven Smith and sister Janette, wife of Joseph Gibbs. (July 1840).

Smith, Joseph, of New York City. Administration with will to John Stables, attorney for daughter Elizabeth, wife of George Nelson, at New York; grant of September 1795 to Keene Stables revoked on his death. (Feb. 1822). Revoked on death of Elizabeth Nelson and granted to John Stables as attorney for her only surviving child Sophia Augusta Breintnall, widow, at Newark, New Jersey. (Aug. 1848).

Smith, Martha, of Chicago, Illinois, spinster. Administration to John Lacey, attorney for father Joseph Smith in Chicago. (Jan. 1847).

Smith, Mary M. - see Stone.

Smith, Richard, of Williamsburg, Virginia, bachelor. Administration to aunt Susan, wife of Matthew Lester. (Oct. 1804).

Smith, Rt. Rev. Robert, Bishop of South Carolina. Limited administration with will to Edward Western, attorney for daughter Sarah Motte Rutledge and son Robert Smith at Charleston. (Feb. 1842).

Smythe, Samuel, formerly of Baltimore, Maryland, afterwards of
Queen Street, Brompton, Middlesex, late of Belfast, Ireland.
Probate to relict Elizabeth Smythe and daughters Mary and
Ellen Smythe. (May 1827).
Smith, formerly Shubrick, Sarah, wife of Rt. Rev. Robert Smith,
Bishop of South Carolina. Limited administration to Edward
Western, attorney for Sarah Motte Rutledge, widow, and
Robert Smith at Charleston. (Feb. 1842).
Smith, Sarah, of Newport, Rhode Island. Administration to
husband William Smith. (June 1856).
Smith, Thomas, of Hebron, Washington Co., U.S.A. Administration
to George Wildes, attorney for relict Jane Smith at Hebron.
(Mar. 1831).
Smith, Thomas, formerly of Woolwich, Kent, late of Ceres Town,
McKean Co., Pennsylvania, farmer. Administration
to son Christopher Hill Smith. (Apr. 1836).
Smith, Thomas, of Pittsburgh, Pennsylvania. Administration to
Anne Todhunter, widow, attorney for relict Maria Smith at
Pittsburgh. (Nov. 1851).
Smith, Whitefoord, formerly of Charlestown, South Carolina,
late of Cowper Street, North Leith, Scotland. Probate to
Robert Brunton, Charles Spence and Rev. Charles Clowston.
(Sept. 1826).
Smith, William, formerly of Bedford, England, late of Henderson,
Kentucky, widower. Administration to son Richard Smith.
(Dec. 1831).
Smith, William Barlow, of British Hollow near Potosi, Wisconsin,
brewer. Administration with will to Edwin Chadwick, attorney
for relict Sarah Chadwick, now wife of George Walker Sutten-
field, in California. (Dec. 1856).
Southgate, Lydia, of Richmond, Virginia, widow. Administration
to William Taylor, attorney for son James Southgate at
Richmond. (Mar. 1823).
Sparhawk, Susannah, of New York City, widow. Administration to
William Limbey Grosvenor, attorney for only child Elizabeth
Sparhawk at Halifax, Nova Scotia. (Dec. 1800).
Sparkes, William, formerly of Hereford, late of Brooklyn, North
America, bachelor. Administration to father Thomas Sparkes.
(July 1821).
Sparling, John, of Liverpool, Lancashire. Limited administration
with will of estate other than in America to Edward Chaffers
and John Bolton. (May 1800).
Sparrow, Edwin, of Burlington, U.S.A., blacksmith. Administra-
tion to relict Elizabeth Sparrow. (Feb. 1857).
Sparrow, Samuel, formerly of Peckham, Surrey, afterwards of
merchant ship *Industry*, late of Charleston, South Carolina.
Administration with will to relict Sarah, now wife of John
Edward Acres; grant of February 1801 to sister Elizabeth
Stansbury revoked. (Jan. 1804). Revoked on death of Sarah
Acres and granted to her husband John Edward Acres. (Mar.
1804).
Speyer, John, formerly of New York, late of Paris, merchant,
widower. Administration to George Law, attorney for mother
and next of kin Amalia Speyer, widow. (Dec. 1816).
Spurzheim, Gaspar, formerly of Gower Street and Highgate,
Middlesex, afterwards of Paris, late of Boston, U.S.A., M.D.,
widower. Administration with will to Mathias Hermesdorf,
attorney for brother Earl Theodor Spurzheim at Vienna.
(Feb. 1835).
Squire, nee Miles, Harriet Louisa, of Philadelphia. Administration to George Squire, attorney for husband Henry John Squire
at Philadelphia. (July 1844).

Stanford, Joseph, of Detroit, U.S.A. Administration with will
to brother John Stanford; relict Susan Stanford and only
child George Stanford cited but not appearing. (Feb. 1851).
Stanford, Samuel, formerly of Lingfield, Surrey, late of Fort
Leavenworth, who died at Buffalo, North America, bachelor.
Administration to father John Stanford. (Jan. 1852).
Stanley, Margaret, of Vauxhall Cottage near Camptown, Essex
Co., New Jersey, widow. Administration to brother John
Reynolds. (Aug. 1851).
Stansbury, Samuel, of East Haven, New Haven Co., Connecticut.
Administration to Samuel Williams, attorney for relict
Elizabeth Stansbury at East Haven. (Feb. 1825).
Staples, William, formerly of Sevenoaks, Kent, late of Utica,
New York. Administration with will to son Thomas Staples;
executors John Barringer and Samuel D. Lamatter having died.
(Jan. 1826).
Stares, Alfred Guildford, formerly of Titchfield, Hampshire,
late of New York, bachelor. Administration to brother
Thomas Cartwright Stares; mother Mary Stares, widow,
renouncing. (Apr. 1856).
Starr, Anna, of New London, Connecticut. Limited administra-
tion to James Morgan, attorney for husband Jonathan Starr
in New London. (July 1838).
Steele, Edward, of Albion, Illinois. Administration to son
Arthur Steele; relict Sophia Steele renouncing. (July 1855).
Stephenson - see Stevenson.
Stevens, Charles, formerly of Two Waters Mill, Hemel Hempstead,
Hertfordshire, late of Cumberland Street, Brooklyn, New York.
Probate to sisters Eliza Ann and Angelina Margaret Stevens.
(Nov. 1857).
Stevens, Clement William, of Jefferson, Florida. Administration
to John Horsley Palmer, attorney for relict Sarah Johnson
Stevens at Pendeton District, Anderson State, South Carolina.
(Jan. 1839).
Stevens, Ontario Brook Bridges, formerly of Hamilton, Canada,
late of Keyport, New Jersey, bachelor. Administration to
mother and next of kin Elizabeth Stevens, widow. (Apr. 1852).
Steevens, Thomas, of New Orleans, mariner. Probate to Christopher
Young by his solemn declaration and to Benjamin Meredith.
(July 1823).
Stevenson, Cornelius, of New York City. Administration with
will to Effingham Lawrence, attorney for nephews and niece
and only next of kin Robert Bartow, Anthony Bartow, Thomas
Bartow and Charity Wright, spinster, now in New York; no
executor having been named and relict Susannah Stevenson
having died. (Mar. 1806). Revoked on death of Effingham
Lawrence and granted to William Effingham Lawrence as attor-
ney. (Sept. 1806).
Stevenson, John, of Albany City, North America. Probate to
James Stevenson and Dudley Walsh with similar powers reserved
to relict Magdalen Stevenson and daughters Sarah, wife of
said Dudley Walsh, and Anne Stevenson. (Dec. 1810).
Stephenson, John, formerly of Hamborough, Yorkshire, late of
Whitesborough, Oneida Co., New York. Administration to
relict Elizabeth Stephenson. (July 1856).
Stevenson, nee Rogers, Mary, formerly of Wadhurst, Sussex, late
of Henrietta, Munro Co., New York. Administration to John
Rogers, attorney for husband Henry Stevenson at Henrietta.
(Apr. 1844).
Stewart, Alexander, formerly Major of New Jersey Volunteers,
late of Stirling, Scotland. Probate to William Stewart with
similar powers reserved to John Stewart. (Nov. 1820).

Stuart, Charles, formerly of Gateshead, Durham, late of Phila-
delphia, bachelor. Administration to brother and next of
kin Edward Stuart; mother Ann Stuart, widow, having died.
(June 1809).
Stewart, David, of Doden, late of Ann Arundel Co., Maryland.
Administration to William Murdoch, attorney for brothers
and next of kin William and James Stewart in Maryland.
(Dec. 1816).
Stewart, Elizabeth A. - see Clendinen.
Stuart, Hugh, of Mount Pleasant, West Chester Co., North
America, Lieutenant on half pay of Donkins Royal Garrison
Batallion. Administration to William Tustin, attorney for
relict Mary Stuart in New York City. (Sept. 1812).
Stuart, Isaac, Captain on half pay of Dunlap's Corps of
British Provincials in U.S.A., widower. Limited administra-
tion to James Tidbury, attorney for children Martha, wife
of William Kendricks, and Hannah Bown, widow. (Mar. 1821).
Stewart, James, of New Jersey, Captain on half pay of New
Jersey Volunteers. Administration with will to James Tidbury,
attorney for Eleanor Stevens, widow, at New Jersey. (Apr.
1820).
Stewart, John, Lieutenant in Regiment of Carolina Highlanders,
who died at Woodville near New Orleans, bachelor. Admini-
stration to brother Alexander Stewart. (Oct. 1827).
Stewart, Kenneth, of Edinburgh, Captain in late North Carolina
Highland Regiment. Probate to John Cameron with similar
powers reserved to Hector MacLean, Alexander Stewart, Robert
Burt, Kenneth McCashill and Donald McCashill. (July 1815).
Stewart, Peter, of Stewart Lodge, Canton, Greene Co., New York.
Administration with will to Robert Samuel Palmer, attorney
for relict Catherine Desmont Stewart at island of St. Martin,
West Indies. (Aug. 1836).
Stickney, Caleb, of Newbury Port, Mass. Administration to
relict Sarah Stickney. (Oct. 1801).
Stickney, Sarah - see Coleman.
Stickney, William, of Salem, Mass., bachelor. Administration
to father Samuel Stickney. (June 1835).
Stiebel, Bernhard, of Baltimore, Maryland, bachelor and bastard.
Administration to George Maule for use of the Queen. (Feb.
1848).
Stockwell, James, formerly of Boston, U.S.A., late of Madras,
East Indies, officer in service of Wallajah, late Nabob of
Arcot. Administration to nephew Rev. William Batchelder,
administrator to relict Jane Stockwell deceased; all others
with title cited but not appearing. (Feb. 1818).
Stodhart, Samuel Lake, of Brunswick, Maine, bachelor. Admini-
stration to sister Charlotte Stodhart. (Sept. 1851).
Stone, nee Smith, Mary Maria, of Brooklyn, New York. Admini-
stration to Amos Fielding, attorney for husband Robert Stone
at Nauvoo, Hancock Co., U.S.A. (May 1847).
Stonier, nee Hardwick, Mary Ann, of Benton, Yates Co., New York.
Administration to husband Joseph Stonier. (Jan. 1850).
Stooke, Richard, formerly of Exeter, Devon, late of America,
bachelor. Administration to brother Pinder Luke Stooke;
mother Patience Stooke renouncing. (Jan. 1808).
Stowe, Rev. Solomon John, formerly of Bermuda, late of Staunton,
Virginia. Probate to niece Sophia Malvina Cox, spinster;
other executor William John Cox renouncing. (Apr. 1856).
Stowers, James, formerly of Bridgenorth, Shropshire, late of
Poughkeepsie, U.S.A., bachelor. Administration to mother
and next of kin Anna Maria Stowers, widow. (Mar. 1837).

Strachan, James, formerly of Montrose, Scotland, afterwards of
London, late of U.S.A., widower. Administration to son
George Blair Strachan. (June 1844).
Stratton, Gordon, formerly of Villiers Street, Strand, Middlesex,
late of Charleston, South Carolina. Probate to relict
Albertina Mary Anna Theresa Maria, now wife of Robert Harrison,
with similar powers reserved to William Gordon. (Feb. 1802).
Strawbridge, William, formerly of Warren Street, Tottenham
Court Road, Middlesex, late of Lower Providence, Montgomery
Co., Pennsylvania. Limited administration with will to
Horatio G. Jones at Roxborough, U.S.A. (Dec. 1830).
Streatfield, Louisa Jane, of Varick Street, New York. Admini-
stration to Edward Hockley, attorney for husband William
Everest Streatfield at New York. (July 1851).
Street, formerly Madgwick, Martha, of Mount Pleasant, Westchester
Co., New York. Administration to Elizabeth Sarah, wife of
Joshua Gilbert, daughter and administratrix to husband
William Street the elder deceased. (Aug. 1839).
Street, William the elder, of New York, widower. Administration
to daughter Sarah Street. (Mar. 1824).
Street, William the younger, of Philadelphia, bachelor. Admini-
stration to sister Elizabeth Sarah Street. (Mar. 1824).
Streeter, Edward, formerly of Buxted, Sussex, yeoman, late of
Philadelphia, labourer, widower. Administration to Robert
Hoffman Faulconer, attorney for only surviving child Abel
Streeter at Philadelphia. (Nov. 1839).
Stretton, Henry, formerly of Midland Cottage, Hampshire, after-
wards of Mont Cassell in French Flanders, late of New Orleans.
Probate to surviving executor Thomas Bourdillon. (July 1853).
Strong, Thomas J., of Baldwin Co., Alabama. Administration with
will to creditor James Jones; executors Henry Toulmin and
Henry B. Slade having died and executor James Alexander
Torbert, daughter Hannah S. Strong and her mother Ann Strong
cited but not appearing. (Jan. 1826).
Strong, William, of New York who died at Savannah, bachelor.
Administration to nephew James Strong. (Aug. 1828).
Strudwick, Martha, of Orange Co., North Carolina, widow.
Administration with will to Peter Browne, administrator to
sole executor William Francis Strudwick deceased and attorney
for son Samuel Strudwick in Orange Co. (Sept. 1820).
Strudwick, William Francis, of Orange Co., North Carolina.
Administration to Peter Browne, attorney for son Samuel
Strudwick in Orange Co.; relict Martha Strudwick having
died. (Sept. 1820).
Stuart - see Stewart.
Sturge, Thomas, formerly of Weston super Mare, Somerset, cabinet
maker, late of Mill Farm, Warren Co., New York, farmer.
Administration to creditor Thomas Marshall Sturge by his
solemn declaration; relict Emma Sophia Sturge for herself
and as mother of Ellen, Hannah, Thomas Marshall and Rebecca
Sturge, renouncing. (July 1853).
Sutherland, Alexander Smith, formerly of New Orleans, late of
New York, widower. Administration to Jane Webb, aunt and
guardian of only children Jane, Ann, William and Mary Suther-
land during their minority; grandfather and only next of kin
of said children being in a state of mental imbecility.
(Oct. 1828).
Swanwick, Mary, of Alexandria, D.C., widow. Administration to
George Wharton Marriott, attorney for only child Mary, wife
of James Bruce Nicholls, at Alexandria. (Dec. 1821).
Swanwick, Thomas, formerly of Chester, tobacconist, late of
Kaskasia, Illinois. Limited administration to Edward Fricker
and James Stansfeld. (Jan. 1843).

Swift, Benjamin, of Nantucket, North America, mariner. Administration to Paul Pease, attorney for relict Elizabeth Swift at Nantucket. (July 1805).

Swift, Joseph, retired Captain of Pennsylvania Loyalists in North America. Administration to David Davies, attorney for relict Ann Swift in Pennsylvania. (Nov. 1810).

Swinnerton, Sarah, of 2 Congress Street, Newark, New Jersey, widow. Administration to only children George and James Swinnerton. (Feb. 1845).

Syme, Andrew, of New Orleans, bachelor. Administration to brother Hugh Syme; mother Anthony (sic) Syme, widow, renouncing. (Jan. 1821).

Symes, Rev. Robert, formerly of Rye, Sussex, late of America. Administration to relict Mary Symes. (May 1813).

Tait, George, formerly of Wapping High Street, Wapping, Middlesex, late of New York City, merchant, formerly a master mariner, bachelor. Administration to brother Charles Tait. (July 1819).

Talcott, Noah, of New York. Administration to Frederick Westell, attorney for relict Elizabeth Talcott in New York City. (Apr. 1843).

Tamlyn, George, formerly of Testwood, Eling, Hampshire, late of Oysterbay, New York, widower. Administration to son Charles Tamlyn. (Jan. 1853).

Tapin, James Alfred, of Pensacola, East Indies (sic), bachelor. Administration to mother Theodosia Tapin, widow. (Feb. 1801).

Tapscott, George Loveless, formerly of Minehead, Somerset, afterwards of New York, late of Republic of Texas, bachelor. Administration to Amos Greenslade and Thomas Porsford, assignees of father John Tapscott who was cited but did not appear. (Dec. 1840).

Tate, John, formerly of Orkneys, late of Fort Vancouver, Oregon. Probate to Archibald McKinlay and Forbes Barclay. (Jan. 1855).

Tattnall, Edward Fenwick, of Chatham Co., Georgia. Administration with will to brother Josiah Tattnall; executor William Coffee Daniell renouncing. (Aug. 1846).

Tatnall, Samuel, formerly of London, late of Boston, Mass. Administration to John Sturges, attorney for relict Ann Tatnall at Boston. (Oct. 1830).

Tayler - see Taylor.

Taylerson, Ann, formerly of Sedgefield, Durham, afterwards of London, who died at sea, spinster. Administration to George Jackson, executor to brother Daniel Taylerson deceased; mother Margaret Taylerson and sister Margaret Taylerson alias Robinson having also died. (Dec. 1835).

Taylerson alias Robinson, Margaret, formerly of Sedgefield, Durham, afterwards of U.S.A., spinster. Administration to George Jackson, executor to brother Daniel Taylerson deceased; mother Margaret Taylerson, widow, having died. (Dec. 1835).

Taylor, Charlotte Anne, of Detroit, Michigan, spinster. Probate to Thomas Bagnall and Thomas Metcalfe. (July 1840).

Taylor, George, formerly of New York City, late of Soder Hill, New Jersey, gold beater. Administration to relict Sarah Taylor. (June 1836).

Taylor, Jane, of Red River Settlement, North America, widow.
Probate to Sir George Simpson. (Nov. 1845).

Taylor, John Chisim, formerly of Crediton, Devon, late of
Shepherdsville, Bullitt Co., Kentucky, civil engineer,
bachelor. Administration to father John Taylor. (May 1854).

Tayler, Thomas, formerly of Clements Inn, Middlesex, late of
Cortlandt Street, New York. Administration to relict Sarah
Tayler. (Oct. 1852).

Taylor, Thomas Matthew, of Jacksonborough, South Carolina,
bachelor. Administration to father Christopher Taylor.
(Aug. 1807).

Taylor, William, of Perth Amboy, New Jersey. Administration
with will to Daniel Coxe, attorney for relict Elizabeth
Taylor at Perth Amboy. (July 1808).

Taylor, William, of New York City. Administration to relict
Hepzibah Elizabeth Taylor. (Nov. 1845).

Taylor, William Blackwell, formerly of Upper Seymour Street,
Connaught Square, Middlesex, late of Dean Street, Brooklyn,
New York. Administration to relict Emma Taylor. (June 1857).

Taylor, William Swain, formerly of Great Canterbury Buildings,
Lambeth, Surrey, afterwards of New York City, late of Berwick
upon Tweed, Scotland, who died at sea passenger on merchant
ship *Ceres*, widower. Administration to only child Mary
Taylor. (May 1840).

Temple, Dame Elizabeth, of Boston, U.S.A., widow. Probate to
Thomas Sendal Winthrop with similar powers reserved to
James Bowdoin and James Temple Bowdoin. (May 1816).

Temple, Sir John, Consul-General to U.S.A. Administration with
will to Thomas Sendall Winthrop, executor to relict Dame
Elizabeth Temple; administration of February 1799 withdrawn.
(May 1816).

Thatcher, Bartholomew, of Hunterdon Co., New Jersey. Administration with will to James Tidbury, attorney for Henry Clifton
in New Jersey; Hezekiah Waterhouse renouncing. (May 1818).

Thayer, Arodi, of Dorchester, Norfolk Co., U.S.A., widower.
Administration to Thimothy Wiggin, attorney for daughter
Charlotte Thayer at Dorchester. (Mar. 1832).

Thayer, John, of Greenwich, U.S.A. Administration to Thomas
Holme Bower, attorney for relict Achsah Thayer at Greenwich.
(July 1819).

Thomas, John, formerly of Cornwall Road, Lambeth, Surrey, who
died passenger on ship *Charles Bartlett* (bound for New York),
carpenter, bachelor. Administration to father Thomas Thomas.
(Aug. 1849).

Thomson, Ann, of New Jersey, widow. Administration to daughter
Anna Maria, wife of Michael Honseal. (Apr. 1801).

Thompson, Anna, of Charleston, South Carolina, widow. Probate
to daughters Susan Eliza Gaillard, widow, and Sarah Maria
Kiddell, widow, and son Robert Thompson. (Aug. 1849).

Thompson, George, of New York City, hatter, bachelor. Administration to father Thomas Thompson the elder. (July 1841).

Thompson, William, formerly of Newbridge, Radnor, late of
Bathurst, New York, bachelor. Administration to sister
Elizabeth Thompson; mother and next of kin Ann Thompson
having died. (Feb. 1854).

Thorn, Elizabeth, formerly of Brenchley, Kent, late of Albany,
America, widow. Probate to John Martin with similar powers
reserved to John Fuggle. (Oct. 1820).

Thornton, George, formerly of Oxford Street, Middlesex, iron-
monger, late of Buffalo, New York. Administration to relict
Mary Ann Thornton. (July 1843).

Thornton, Robert, formerly of Clapham Common, Surrey, late of
New York. Limited administration to John Thornton; relict
Maria Thornton renouncing. (Apr. 1839).

Thorpe, William, of Bangor, Maine, bachelor. Administration to
sister Catherine Simmons, widow; mother Isabella Thorpe
having died. (July 1848).

Throckmorton, Richard Samuel, of New York City. Administration
to sister Catherine, wife of John Wesley Bartleson; relict
Sarah Jane, now wife of John Wells Littlefield, renouncing.
(Apr. 1851).

Tice, Susannah, of Sinoinattic (sic), Ohio. Administration to
husband William Tice. (Apr. 1826).

Tindall, Ann, of Mansfield, Pennsylvania, widow. Administration
to daughter Mary Ann, wife of George Snoad. (Apr. 1839).

Tisdale, James, of Boston, North America, who died in 1796.
Limited administration to Ebenezer Maitland. (Jan. 1809).

Tobias, Henry, of New York. Administration to relict Augusta
Tobias. (June 1847).

Todhunter, Sarah Anne, of Germanstown, Pennsylvania, widow.
Administration to William Hewetson, attorney for Esther,
wife of Dundass Taylor, in Philadelphia, aunt and guardian
of children Mary Elizabeth, Helen and John Todhunter during
their minority. (Jan. 1853).

Tolfrey, Martha, formerly of Portsea, Hampshire, late of New
York City, minor. Administration to father Joseph Tolfrey.
(Aug. 1842).

Tolfrey, Sarah Anne, of New York, who died at sea, infant.
Administration to father Joseph Tolfrey. (Aug. 1842).

Tolfrey, William, of Toronto, Canada, minor. Administration to
father Joseph Tolfrey. (Aug. 1842).

Tomlins, James, formerly of Shrewsbury, Shropshire, afterwards
of Bath, Somerset, late of Baltimore, U.S.A. Administration
to William Tomlins, attorney for relict Ann Tomlins at
Baltimore. (June 1827).

Tomlins, Sarah, of Philadelphia. Probate to Jesse Brush. (July
1856).

Tooley, nee Fry, Susannah, of New York City. Limited administration with will to James Eldridge, attorney for husband John
Tooley in New York City. (Aug. 1854).

Toulmin, Harry, of Washington Court House, Washington Co.,
Alabama. Probate to relict Martha Toulmin and brother John
Butler Toulmin. (Feb. 1825).

Tovey, William, formerly of Rotherhithe, Surrey, late of New
York, bachelor. Administration to brother and sister and
only next of kin George John Tovey and Martha, wife of John
Stevens. (Sept. 1800).

Trevett, Russell, of Marblehead, Mass. Probate to son Russell
Trevett and Samuel Hooper. (Sept. 1803).

Trickett, Sarah, formerly of Snow Hill, London, late of New
York City, widow. Administration to sister Mary Collins,
widow. (June 1810).

Troke, Martha, formerly of Handsworth, Staffordshire, late of
Brooklyn, U.S.A., widow. Administration to Rowland Neate,
attorney for children Martha Maria, wife of Horatio Shepheard
Moat, at Brooklyn and Mary Eliza Troke at New York. (Feb.
1840).

Truefitt, formerly Cass, Jane, of Philadelphia. Administration
to Peter Truefitt, attorney for husband Henry Paul Truefitt
at Philadelphia. (June 1832).

Tucker, Edward, formerly of Gosport, Hampshire, late of New York
City. Administration to sister Hannah Elizabeth, wife of
Richard Lacy. (Sept. 1820).

Tuite, Robert, of St. Croix, West Indies, who died at Baltimore, Maryland. Limited administration with will to nephew Charles MacCarthy with similar powers reserved to Joseph Blake Chabert, George B. Kelly and Justin MacCarthy. (Dec. 1813). Further grant to creditor Richard Stephens to promote claim against estate in Chancery. (Feb. 1832).

Tunstall, William, formerly of Leeds, Yorkshire, late of Mount Sinai near Petersburg, Virginia. Administration to Francis Witham, attorney for relict Margaret Tunstall at Ghent. (Feb. 1823).

Turnbull, George, of New York City. Administration with will to David Davies, attorney for Frederick Depeyster at New York; other executor Charles Wilkes renouncing. (Jan.1812).

Turnbull, George, formerly of New York City, late of New Haven, Connecticut, Commander in Royal Navy. Probate to relict Margaret Turnbull, John Day and Henry Wilkes. (July 1826).

Turner, Ann - see Wadup.

Turner, Hannah, formerly of Croydon, Surrey, late of Charlestown in America. Probate to Stephen Tapster. (Sept. 1811).

Turner, William, formerly of Hounslow, Middlesex, late of Philadelphia Co. Administration to Thomas Bennett, attorney for relict Sophia Turner at Philadelphia Co. (July 1852).

Turner, Zachariah, of Harlem, New York, farmer. Administration to relict Susanna Turner. (Mar. 1835). Revoked on her death and granted to daughter Mary Alicia, wife of James Thorne. (Nov. 1850).

Tyler, John, of Philadelphia, bachelor. Administration to creditors Joseph Roper and Joseph Townsend; those entitled to administration cited but not appearing. (Nov. 1804).

Vanderburgh, Richard, Captain on half pay of Emerick Chasseurs at New Town, Long Island, New York. Administration to James Tidbury, attorney for relict Sally Venderburgh at New York. (Nov. 1829).

Van Dyke, John, of Somerset Co., New Jersey. Limited administration with will to David Davies, attorney for son Riclif Van Dyke, Abner Houghton and Abraham Van Arsdal. (Jan. 1812).

Van Wyck, Elizabeth, of Baltimore, North America, widow. Administration with will to Rebecca Hutchinson Thomas, widow, attorney for Richard Cooke Tilghman, John Charles Van Wyck and Louis Barney in North America. (Aug. 1821).

Van Wyck, Elizabeth Linnington, of Baltimore, North America, who died in 1819. Limited administration to Harry Barker pending Chancery suit Akers v. Manning. (Mar. 1841).

Vaughan, Charles, of Hallowell, Maine, widower. Administration to son Rev. John Apthorp Vaughan. (Aug. 1842). Further grants August 1874 and February 1879.

Vaughan, Frances Western, of Hallowell, Maine. Administration to Rev. John Apthorp Vaughan D.D., administrator to husband Charles Vaughan deceased. (Aug. 1842). Further grant March 1879.

Vaughan, Petrus V. - see Vink.

Venner, Samuel, former Secretary to Board of Customs in America, late of Rotherham and Sheffield, Yorkshire. Probate to son Morris Venner. (July 1802).

Vincent, nee Evelyn, Martha Boscawen, of Charlestown, South
    Carolina, widow. Administration to creditor Hugh Evelyn;
    children Hugh and Nicholas Vincent cited but not appearing.
    (June 1815). Revoked as having been obtained under false
    suggestions and granted to sons and only next of kin Hugh
    Edward and Nicholas William Vincent; husband Nicholas
    Vincent having died. (Nov. 1818).
Vincent, Nicholas, of Charlestown, South Carolina, widower.
    Administration to sons Hugh Edward and Nicholas William
    Vincent. (Nov. 1818).
Vink alias Vaughan, Petrus Wynard, of New York, furrier.
    Administration to relict Sarah Vink. (Oct. 1845).
Volans, William, of Oswegatchie, St. Lawrence Co., U.S.A.,
    bachelor. Administration to Francis William Calvert,
    attorney for mother and next of kin Sarah Volans at Oswega-
    tchie. (June 1855).

Waddington, John, formerly of Leeds, Yorkshire, late of Phila-
    delphia, merchant. Administration with will to creditor
    John Hain; relict Sarah Waddington renouncing for herself
    and children Sophia, William Henry, Edward Crosley and
    Charles John Waddington; other children Lydia Elizabeth
    and Robert Waller Waddington also renouncing. (Dec. 1815).
Wadup alias Morehouse, nee Turner, Ann, formerly of Newcastle
    Court, Strand, Middlesex, late of Spatenburgh, South Caro-
    lina, widow. Administration to brother and only next of kin
    William Turner. (Mar. 1817). Revoked on his death and
    granted to his executor William Hewitt. (Dec. 1837).
    Revoked on his death and granted to his surviving executor
    Mary Ann Hewitt, widow. (Aug. 1843).
Wagstaff, Charles Eden, formerly of Argyle Street, New Road,
    Middlesex, late of Boston, Mass., engraver. Probate to
    relict Ann Randall Wagstaff. (Feb. 1853).
Wagstaff, Daniel, formerly of Kidderminster, Worcestershire,
    late of Delaware, North America. Administration to relict
    Hannah Housman Wagstaff. (Dec. 1830).
Wake, George Daniel, of Sing Sing near New York City, bachelor.
    Administration to James Wake, son and executor of father
    Daniel Wake deceased. (Oct. 1857).
Walbridge, Henry, formerly of Puddletown, Dorset, late of
    Baltimore, U.S.A., widower. Administration to children
    Henry William and Mary Eliza Walbridge. (Sept. 1825).
Waldo, Samuel, of Portland, Mass. Limited administration to
    George William Erving, attorney for relict Sarah Tyng Waldo
    at Portland. (June 1803).
Walford, John, formerly of Halford, Warwickshire, late of
    Quarantine Ground, Staten Island, New York, bachelor.
    Administration to sister and next of kin Elizabeth, wife of
    William Fletcher. (Dec. 1844).
Walker, George Henry, of Longford near Holmsburg, Philadelphia.
    Administration to daughter Louisa Letitia Walker; relict
    Marianne Douglass Walker renouncing. (July 1850).
Walker, Henry, of Birmingham, Warwickshire, and Philadelphia,
    merchant, bachelor. Administration to John Walker, son and
    executor of father William Walker deceased. (Aug. 1829).

Wallace, James, H.M. Consul at Savannah, bachelor. Administration to Charles Robert Simpson, attorney for brother and next
of kin Michael Wallace at Halifax, Nova Scotia. (Nov. 1829).

Wallace, William, formerly of St. Croix, West Indies, late of
New Haven, North America, merchant. Probate to relict
Catherine Wallace. (Mar. 1831).

Wallace, William Alexander, of New York City, merchant. Probate
to relict Susan Wallace. (July 1840).

Waller, Henry, of Mount Pleasant, West Chester Co., New York.
Probate to son Joseph Fernando Waller with similar powers
reserved to son Henry Waller and Edward Kemlys. (Mar. 1835).

Walter, Eleanor Elizabeth, of Jersey City, New Jersey. Administration to husband James Walter. (Sept. 1856).

Walter, Rev. William, D.D., of Boston, Mass., chaplain of 2nd
Batallion of New York Volunteers. Administration with will
to John Lane, attorney for sons Lynde Walter and William
Walter and for Nathaniel Smith in Mass. (June 1801).

Walters, Emily - see Charlton.

Walton, Matilda Carolina, of New York. Administration to
husband Henry Walton. (Mar. 1825).

Walton, William the elder, of New York City, merchant, widower.
Limited administration to Sir Francis Molyneux Omanney,
attorney for James De Lancey Walton in New York. (Aug. 1822).

Warburton, Rev. Charles, formerly of London, late of Boston,
U.S.A. Probate to Thomas Paul. (Aug. 1815).

Ward, Benjamin, of Peekshill, West Chester Co., New York,
Lieutenant on half pay of Royal American Regiment. Admini-
stration to James Tidbury, attorney for relict Phebe Ward at
New York. (June 1818).

Ward, Moses, of New York, Lieutenant on half pay of a Provincial
Regiment. Administration to relict Abigal Ward. (Oct.1816).

Warder, Jeremiah, of Philadelphia, merchant. Administration to
Thomas Samuel Girdler, attorney for relict Hannah Warder at
Philadelphia. (Jan. 1842).

Wareham, John, of New York. Administration to nephew and next
of kin Thomas Farmer. (Nov. 1823).

Waring, Ellen, formerly of Royal Row, Lambeth, Surrey, late of
Boston, North America, widow. Administration with will to
sister and next of kin Margaret, wife of Thomas Cruse.
(June 1827).

Warre, Francis Whitehead, formerly of Rugby, Warwickshire, late
of New York, bachelor. Administration to sister Caroline
Lucy, wife of Rev. William Harriott. (Feb. 1846).

Warren, formerly Wignell, Anna, of Philadelphia. Administration to John Cole Brooke, attorney for husband William Warren
at Philadelphia. (Sept. 1813).

Warren, nee Clare, Charlotte Susannah, of Galveston, Texas.
Administration to Edwin Albery, administrator to husband
John Warren deceased and attorney for daughter Mary Earnest,
wife of William Prewitt Boidstone. (Dec. 1855).

Warren, John, of Mayoville, De Kalb Co., Missouri, farmer and
merchant, widower. Administration to Edwin Albery, attorney
for daughter Mary Earnest, wife of William Prewitt Boidstone,
at Mayoville. (Dec. 1855).

Warren, Samuel, of Detroit, Michigan. Probate to Charles
Christopher Trowbridge. (Sept. 1850).

Warren, Thomas, formerly of Portsea, Hampshire, late of Boston,
America. Probate to son Thomas Benjamin Warren with similar
powers reserved to relict Clarissa Warren. (Oct. 1850).

Waters, Humphrey, formerly of St. Ann, Westminster, Middlesex,
late of New York, bachelor. Administration with will to
nephew Humphrey Waters; mother Mary Waters and brother James
Waters having died in testator's lifetime and sister Ann,

wife of Richard Mawby, renouncing. (Mar. 1809).

Waterson, Catherine, of Newark, New Jersey, widow. Administra-
tion to William Parkin, attorney for only children Benjamin
Joseph Waterson and Elizabeth Catherine Robins, widow, in
U.S.A.

Waterton, Anne, formerly of Woodlands, Yorkshire, afterwards
of Demarara, West Indies, late of New York City, widow.
Limited administration with will to son Edward Birmingham
(commonly called Lord Athenry); executors John Wright
renouncing and brother John Waddell, Sir Richard Bedingfield
and James Forrest cited but not appearing. (Mar. 1834).
Limited further administration to James and Thomas Croft.
(Aug. 1840). Administration of estate unadministered by sons
Francis and Edward Birmingham granted to son Henry Waterton.
(Aug. 1845).

Watkins, Elijah, formerly of Penbiddle, Llanfihangel Crucorney,
Monmouth, late of Cleveland, North America, who died at sea
passenger on steam ship *City of Glasgow*, bachelor. Administration to father James Watkins. (Oct. 1857).

Watkinson, Samuel, formerly of Lavenham, Suffolk, late of
Middletown, Connecticut. Probate to son David Watkinson with
similar powers reserved to sons John Revel and Edward
Watkinson. (Nov. 1819).

Watson, John James, of New York, bachelor. Administration to
brother and next of kin Robert Mackie Watson. (Jan. 1853).

Watt, John, formerly of Mincinhampton, Gloucestershire, late of
Pittsburgh, Pennsylvania, hawker and peddler. Administration
with will to George Cox, attorney for Samuel Trew and John
Turbitt. (June 1837).

Watts, Mary, of New York, widow. Administration to daughter
Sarah Maria, wife of Bertram Peter Cruger. (Feb. 1852).

Watts, Robert, of Westchester, New York. Administration with
will to Sarah Maria, wife of Bertram Cruger, administratrix
of relict Mary Watts deceased. (Feb. 1852).

Weatherley, Robert, formerly of Newcastle upon Tyne, late of
Detroit, North America. Limited administration to Edward
Gatly. (July 1848).

Weaver, Edward, formerly of Nottingham, late of Philadelphia,
merchant. Administration to daughter Anne Christian, wife
of William Berridge. (Mar. 1824).

Webb, Edward, formerly of Stoke Bishop, Westbury on Trim,
Gloucestershire, afterwards of Adwell, Essex, late of New
York. Administration with will to daughter Elizabeth Frances
Webb; executors Sir Berkeley William Guise and John Webb
having died in testator's lifetime. (Dec. 1839).

Webb, Elizabeth - see Bell.

Webb, Gilbert, of Cornwall, Orange Co., New York. Probate to
Peter Roe with similar powers reserved to John Eastmond.
(Nov. 1824).

Webb, William, of New Orleans. Administration to relict Margaret Proctor Webb. (Oct. 1848).

Webber, Stephen, of Penobscot, Hancock Co., Mass., seaman of
H.M.S. *Leviathan*, bachelor. Administration to Joseph Westcot,
attorney for father Joseph Webber at Penobscot. (Sept. 1805).

Welch, Mary Ann, of Chestertown, Kent Co., Maryland. Administration to husband John Day Welch. (Feb. 1856).

Welchman, Edward, formerly of Kington, Warwickshire, surgeon,
late of New Albion, U.S.A., widower. Administration to
daughter Emma Jemima, wife of Barnabas Henry Bartol. (Dec.
1845).

Welsh, Charlotte, of Philadelphia. Administration to husband
James Welsh. (Mar. 1842).

Wentworth, John, formerly of Portsmouth, New Hampshire, late
of Paris. Administration to relict Martha Wentworth. (May
1833).

West, Hannah, of Chester, Delaware Co., Pennsylvania, widow.
Administration to Benjamin West the younger, attorney for
son Samuel West at Delaware. (Nov. 1819).

West, Silas, formerly of Nantucket, U.S.A., late Master of
merchant ship *Indian* who died at sea, widower. Administration to John Thompson, attorney for brother and next of kin
Paul West. (Oct. 1822).

Weston, Francis Marion, of All Saints, George Town, South
Carolina. Administration with will to William John Slade
Foster, attorney for son Plowden Charles Jennett Weston and
Rev. Alexander Glennie at George Town. (Nov. 1855).

Weston, formerly Weston, Mildred, formerly of Portman Square,
Middlesex, late of South Carolina. Administration to
husband Francis Marion Weston. (July 1825).

Whalley, John, of Charleston, U.S.A. Administration to brother
Joseph Wilkinson Whalley; relict Mary Whalley cited but not
appearing. (Feb. 1820).

Wheatcroft, William, formerly of Ditchford, Worcestershire,
late of Plymouth, Connecticut. Administration with will
to mother Anne Wheatcroft, widow; no executor named. (Feb.
1825).

Wheaton, Henry, formerly Minister of U.S.A. at Berlin, late of
Providence, Rhode Island. Administration to son Robert
Wheaton; relict Catherine Wheaton renouncing. (Mar. 1849).

White, Betty, formerly of Huish Champflower, Somerset, late of
Cleveland, Cuyahoga Co., Ohio, widow. Administration with
will to William Rossiter, husband and administrator of
daughter Eliza Rossiter deceased. (Jan. 1836).

White, formerly Laxton, Catherine, of Cincinnati, Ohio, widow.
Administration to Sarah Gilford, widow, attorney for daughter Elizabeth Attlesey, widow, at Cincinnati. (Dec. 1845).

White, Charles, formerly of Baldock, Hertfordshire, surgeon,
late of Millageville, North America. Administration to only
surviving child Matilda Freshfield, wife of John Winkley;
relict Margaretta White having died. (Apr. 1840).

White, Daniel, formerly of Blakeney, Gloucestershire, late of
Albany, New York. Administration to son James White;
relict Sarah White renouncing. (May 1841).

White, John, formerly of Northampton, draper, who died on steam
ship *Pacific* at sea on passage to New York with wife Hepzibah and only child Elizabeth when all on board perished.
Limited administration to sister Emma White. (Mar. 1857).

White, Marmaduke John Horton, of Franklin Street, New York City,
artist. Administration to John Shadwell White, attorney for
relict Mary White at New York City. (Apr. 1846). Further
grant September 1860.

White, Thomas, of New York City. Administration with will to
Matthew White, attorney for relict Ann White at New York.
(Aug. 1822).

Whittingham, Heber, of Princess Ann Town, Maryland, widower.
Administration to Thomas Thorns, attorney for son John
Whittingham at Montpellier Wharf, St. James parish, Jamaica.
(Oct. 1801).

Whittle, Conway, of Norfolk, Virginia, widower. Administration
to daughter Mary Neale, widow. (Nov. 1819).

Widdop, George, of Dear Island, U.S.A. Administration to relict
Caroline, now wife of Joseph Read the younger. (Aug. 1857).

Wiggins, Emily, of Bond Street, New York City. Administration
to Francis Rivington, attorney for husband William Wiggins
at New York. (Aug. 1843).

Wightman, Shardlow, formerly of Aldersgate Street, London,
late of Kentucky, North America, bachelor. Administration
to nephew Joseph Brownell. (July 1817).
Wigmore, Elizabeth - see Hitchcock.
Wignell, Anne - see Warren.
Wigston, William, of 176 Mercer Street, Bleecher Street, Broad-
way, New York. Administration to relict Mary Wigston.
(Dec. 1855).
Wilkes, Israel, of New York, widower. Administration to John
De Ponthieu, attorney for only children John De Ponthieu
Wilkes, Charles Wilkes and Frances, wife of Lewis Simond
in New York. (Sept. 1809).
Wilkes, John De Ponthieu, formerly of London, late of New York
City, notary public. Administration with will to Edmund
John Scott, attorney for children Eliza Henry, widow, Henry
and Edmund Wilkes at New York; brother and executor Charles
Wilkes having died. (Mar. 1846).
Willcox, Elizabeth - see Windeyer.
Willett, Margaret, of West Chester, New York, widow. Admini-
stration with will to Effingham Lawrence, administrator with
will to nephew and surviving executor Lewis Graham deceased
and attorney for Egbert Benson and Thomas Hart at New York.
(Dec. 1800).
Williams, Joseph, formerly of New Street, Chelsea, Middlesex,
late of New York, carpenter. Administration to relict Mary
Ann Williams. (Mar. 1842).
Williams, Margaretta Marian, formerly of Trinity Terrace, South-
wark, Surrey, late of Greenville, Bond Co., Illinois, spin-
ster. Probate to Rev. Clement Dawsonne Strong with similar
powers reserved to Rev. Paul Hyman Sternchuss. (Oct. 1857).
Williams, Samuel, of Finsbury Square, Middlesex, who died at
Boston, U.S.A., bachelor. Administration to brother and
next of kin Francis Williams. (Dec. 1841).
Williams, nee Jope, Sarah, of Pittsburgh, Pennsylvania.
Administration to George Cox, attorney for husband Rev.
John R. Williams at Pittsburgh. (June 1852).
Williamson, Richard, formerly of Covington, Kentucky, late of
Mormon Diggings, California. Administration to relict
Bridget, now wife of Martin Molloy. (Jan. 1856).
Willing, James, of Haverford Township, Cleveland, Delaware Co.,
Pennsylvania, bachelor. Administration with will to Walter
Stirling, attorney for brother Thomas Willing at Philadelphia;
executors Richard Willing and Thomas Willing Francis having
died. (Sept. 1819).
Willing, Richard, of Delaware Co., Pennsylvania. Administration with will to Walter Stirling, attorney for surviving
executor Thomas Mayere. (June 1820).
Willis, Ann Packer, formerly of Grovesend, Alverton, Gloucestershire, late of Charleston, North America, spinster. Administration with will to sister Temperance Jane Willis; executrix Diana, wife of Richard Lubbock, renouncing. (Dec. 1808).
Willis, Benjamin Winthorne, formerly of Poole, Dorset, afterwards of Liverpool, Lancashire, late of North America,
merchant seaman, bachelor. Administration to James Revans,
administrator to sister Martha Revans deceased; mother Martha
Willis and sisters Eliza wife of William Dicker Stroud and
Susanna Durell wife of George Chappel Snock having also died.
(May 1849).
Willis, Eliza, of St. Domingo. Administration to Anna, wife of
James Furber, administratrix of husband Robert Willis
deceased. (Nov. 1849 & Mar. 1850).

Willis, Robert, formerly of St. Domingo, late of Newark, New
Jersey, widower. Administration to aunt Anna, wife of James
Furber, guardian of only child Robert James Furber Willis
during his minority. (Nov. 1849). Revoked on his death
and granted to said Anna Furber. (Mar. 1850).
Willis, Robert James Furber, of Philadelphia, bachelor. Admini-
stration to aunt Anna, wife of James Furber. (Mar. 1850).
Wilmer, Jonathan, of Baltimore, North America, widower.
Administration to Richard Bell, administrator to brother
Simon Wilmer deceased and attorney for Elizabeth Graves
Worrell at Chestertown, Maryland; mother Mary Wilmer, widow,
having also died. (June 1833).
Wilmer, Lambert, of Kent Co., North America, bachelor. Admini-
stration to Richard Bell, administrator to brother Simon
Wilmer deceased and attorney for Elizabeth Graves Worrell,
widow, at Chestertown, Maryland; mother Mary Wilmer, widow,
and brother Jonathan Wilmer having also died. (June 1833).
Wilmer, Simon, of Kent Co., North America. Administration to
Richard Bell, attorney for only child Elizabeth Graves
Worrell, widow, at Chesterborough, Maryland; relict Mary
Wilmer having died. (June 1833).
Wilson, Benjamin, of Baltimore, U.S.A., bachelor without parent.
Administration to brother and next of kin Charles Wilson.
(May 1828).
Wilson, Daniel, of New York City, mason. Probate to brother
Charles Thomas Wilson. (June 1849).
Wilson, James the younger, of Alexandria, Virginia. Administra-
tion to creditor James Wilson the elder; relict Elizabeth
Wilson and children James, Eliza, William, Maria, Ann,
Malvina and Robert Wilson cited but not appearing. (Jan.
1807).
Wilson, Mary, of Laminburgh, New York, spinster. Administration
to father John Christian Wilson. (Sept. 1852).
Wilson, Samuel, of Nashville, Tennessee, bachelor. Administra-
tion to brother Richard Wilson; mother Jane Wilson, widow,
having died. (Dec. 1835).
Windeyer, nee Willcox, Elizabeth, of Muscatine, Iowa. Administration to husband Richard Cunningham Windeyer. (June 1856).
Winniett, Charles, formerly of Lowestoft, Suffolk, late of New
York, who died at sea, bachelor. Administration to son
Benjamin Winniett, executor to mother Elizabeth Winniett
deceased. (Nov. 1804).
Wise, Edward, of Somerset, Pennsylvania, bachelor. Administra-
tion to sister Lucy Wise. (June 1853).
Wood, Edward, of Steubenville, Jefferson Co., Ohio. Administra-
tion with will to Mary Ann Wood, spinster, attorney for
relict Susan Wood at Steubenville. (Sept. 1855).
Wood, Juliana, of Philadelphia. Administration to Charlotte
Howis, widow, attorney for husband William Burke Wood in
Philadelphia. (July 1837).
Wood, William, H.M. Consul at Baltimore, North America. Admini-
stration to Gabriel Wood the younger, attorney for father
Gabriel Wood the elder at Greenock, Scotland. (Aug. 1816).
Woodney, James, formerly of Bath, late of New York City, mason,
widower. Administration to daughter Sarah, wife of Joseph
Phillips. (July 1820).
Woodward, Elizabeth, of Hector, Tompkins Co., New York, widow.
Administration to son William Woodward. (Apr. 1849).
Woodward, John, of New York City. Probate to son John Woodward
with similar powers reserved to son Charles Woodward. (July
1850). Double probate to son Rev. Charles Woodward. (Sept.
1850).

Wormeley, Ralph Randolph, of Newport, Rhode Island, Rear
Admiral in Royal Navy. Administration to relict Caroline
Wormeley. (Dec. 1852).

Worth, Obed, of Nantucket, Mass., Master of merchant ship
Brook Watson. Administration to Andrew Worth, attorney for
relict Janet Worth at Nantucket. (Mar. 1816).

Worth, Shubael, of Nantucket, Mass. Administration to Paul
Pease, attorney for relict Anna Worth at Nantucket. (June
1806).

Worthington, formerly Laugher, Elizabeth, widow, formerly of
Stourbridge, Worcestershire, afterwards of Hartford,
Connecticut, late of Altrincham, Cheshire. Administration
with will to James Smith Hancox, son of brother James Hancox
deceased; executor Joseph Hancox and husband John Worthington renouncing. (Nov. 1813).

Wragg, William, of Charles Town, South Carolina, who died at
sea passenger on ship *Caesar*. Limited administration with
will to George Curling, attorney for sisters Henrietta wife
of Rev. Milward Pogson, and Charlotte wife of William
Loughton Smith at Charles Town; grant of April 1779 revoked.
(Sept. 1807). Revoked on death of George Curling and granted
to Alexander Simpson as attorney for sisters Henrietta Pogson,
Elizabeth Wragg and Charlotte Wragg Smith, widow. (July 1826).

Wright, John, of St. James Wasamtam, South Carolina. Probate
to surviving executrix Keating Simons; administration as
of intestate of July 1791 revoked on production of will.
(July 1828).

Wright, John Joseph Thomas, formerly of Robleston Farm, Pembrokeshire, late of New York City, who died at sea. Probate to
father Joseph Wright. (Oct. 1855).

Wright, Peter, of New Orleans, Lieutenant in Royal Engineers
Corps, bachelor. Administration with will to mother Ann
Wright, widow. (Feb. 1816). Revoked on her death and granted
to sister Martha Wright; James Bogue Lobb, sole executor to
said Ann Wright, renouncing. (Feb. 1816).

Wylly, Margaret, of St. Simon's Island, Georgia, widow. Limited
administration with will to Charles Robert Simpson, attorney
for son Alexander William Wylly and James Hamilton Couper in
Georgia. (Oct. 1852).

Ximenez alias Jimenez, Jose, of Baton Rouge, Louisiana.
Administration with will to Jose Ventura de Aguirre Solarte
and Cristobal de Murrieta, attornies for Diego Dias at Monte
Morelos, Mexico. (June 1832).

Yarnold, Benjamin, of Augusta, Georgia, widower. Administration to Ann Faver, widow, administratrix of only child
Harriot, wife of James Faver deceased. (July 1847).
Young, Alexander, of Mobile, Alabama, widower. Limited administration to George Young of Pimlico, Middlesex, attorney
pending Chancery suit Young v. Young. (Dec. 1828).
Young, Benjamin, of Baltimore, Maryland, widower. Administration to niece by sister Henrietta Montgomerie, spinster;
sisters Ann wife of James Calder, Laetitia wife of Stead
Lowe, and Mary Young, and half brother Notley Young all
having died. (May 1805).
Young, nee Hyde, Charlotte, of Baltimore, Maryland. Administra-
tion to Henrietta Montgomerie, niece and administratrix of
husband Benjamin Young; mother Hon. Jane Hyde having died.
(May 1805).
Young, George, formerly of Copthall Court, London, late of
New York, merchant. Probate to brother John Young, nephew
James Young and Margaret Lyell, widow, with similar powers
reserved to nephew John Young the younger. (Sept. 1827).
Young, Henry Blackburn, of Richmond, Virginia, bachelor.
Administration to brother James Young. (Mar. 1811).
Younie, James, formerly of Theobalds Road, St. George the
Martyr, Middlesex, late of Freedom, Dutchess Co., New York.
Limited probate to Joshua Needham. (Mar. 1829).

Index of Executors, Administrators, Attorneys, etc.

Abbott, Charles J 17
    Joseph 14
    Robert 71
Abel, James 47
Achelis, Thomas 25
Acraman, John 38
Acres, John E 73
    Sarah 73
Adam, Benjamin 20
Adams, John Q 9,41
    Louisa 41
    Peter 15
    Richard 21
Albery, Edwin 82*
Alcock, William 22
Alderman, Charles 42
Alexander, William 71
Allen, Joseph 65
Ambrose, Isabella 26
    Robert M 26
Amer, Elizabeth 41
Anderson, Alexander 49,52
    John 49
    Rev Joseph 17
    Matthew 46
    Robert H 53
Apthorp, Charles W 49
Archer, Christian 11
    Elizabeth 62
    Isaac 62
Argote, Pedro M 21
Arnold, Benedict 72
Arrieta, Maria J 21
Arthur, Francis 37
    Harriet 37
Ashburner, Grace 54
Ashby, Joseph 55
Aspinwall, Thomas 15,19,
    29,30,48,51,66
Athenry, Edward Lord 83
Atkinson, George 33
Attlesey, Elizabeth 84
Auld, Robert 61
Austin, Barbara 35

Bach, Adolphus 61
Bacon, John F 5
Bagnall, Thomas 77
Bainbridge, George 23
    John 7,26,50,51
    Thomas 27
Baker, Rev William L 46
Balfour, James 14
Bambridge, John 50
Bamford, Susanna 53
Banister, Thomas 51
Bannatyne, John 34
Banner, Thomas 20
Barault, Francis 31
Barclay, Anthony 53
    Forbes 77
Barkly, Henry 2
Barclay, Robert 12
    Thomas 41,57
Baring, John 15
Barker, Daniel 69
    Harry 80
    Selina I 69
Barkly - see Barclay

Barksdale, William 64
Barlow, Elizabeth 67
    Peter 17,54*
    Robert 67
Barney, Louis 80
Barringer, John 74
Bartleson, Catherine 79
    John W 79
Bartol, Barnabas H 83
    Emma J 83
Bartow, Anthony 74
    Robert 74
    Thomas 74
Barziza, Count Giovanni 59
Batchelder, Rev William 75
Baxter, William 18
Bayard, William 51
Bayliss, William H 9
Baynard, Elizabeth 49
    Margaret 49
    Robert 49
Beauchamp, William M 7
Beck, Paul 63*
Beckman, James 23
    Lydia 23
Bedingfield, Sir Richd 83
Beekman, Gerrard 41
Belcher, Andrew 52
Beldam, Edward 60
Belk, Mary 8
    William 8
Bell, Jane 38
    Jean 38
    Joan 38
    Richard 86*
    Walter 38
Bennett, James S 31
    Thomas 80
Benson, Egbert 31,85
    Rev Jonathan 24
Bergne, John B 4
Berridge, Anne C 83
    William 83
Best, George 59
    Mary 59
Bibby, Margaret J 41
    Thomas 7,41
Biglow, Abraham 27,28
Birkett, John 15
Birmingham, Edward 83
    Francis 83
Birnie, William 52,53
Black, Rev. James 22
    John 52
Blackburn, William 29
Blackford, Edward 55
Blacklock, William 38,52
Blacklow, Samuel J 64
Blackmore, Rev Thos W 13
Blair, John 66
Blake, Benjamin 67
Bluck, John 61
Bogue, John 21
Boidstone, Mary E 82*
    William P 82*
Bolton, John 73
Bond, Ann 37
    Thomas 37
Boosey, Thomas 4
Bordenave, Anthony 7
Borrers, Diego J 16
Boston, George 42

Botson, Elizabeth 20
Bottomley, Elizabeth
    1,2,35
    James
    1,2,35
Boudinet, Elisha 17
Boulderson, Joseph 10
Bouldin, Thomas T 67
Boult, Charles 34
    Elizabeth 34
Bourdillon, Thomas 76
Bourfield, William 27
Bourne, John 44
Bours, John 46
Bowdoin, James 78
    James T 78
Bower, Thomas H 78
Bowles, John 18*
    Samuel 49
Bown, Hannah 75
Bowyer, Samuel 55
Boyce, Sarah B 8
Boyd, John 49
Bradford, William J 60
Bradley, James 10
    John 59
    Louisa 10
Branson, Thomas 42
Brayer, Thomas 62
Brearley, Robert 26
Brecken, Ralph 66
Breed, Richard F 24
Breintnall, Sophia A 72
Brend, John 12
Brickwood, John 52,54
    Lawrence 52
    Prattle & Co 29
Brimar, Henry 6
Brindley, Edward 57
Britton, William 24
Broadbear, Ann 61
    Thomas 61
Broadbridge, Ann 52
    James 52
Brook, Elizabeth 46
Brooke, John C 82
Brook, Matthew W 46
Brown, Alfred 32
    Christian 35
    Elizabeth 62
    Hannah 3
    Isaac 62
Browne, Peter 76*
    Peter A 13
Brown, Richard 39
    William 68
Brownell, Joseph 85
Brufton, William 30
Brunton, Robert 73
Brush, Jesse 79
Bryan, John 20
Bullock, William S 27
Bulow, John 15
Burfoot, Richard G 33
Burke, Patrick 19
Burnett, Jane 31
Burr, George 1
Burrowes, William 31
Burt, Robert 75
Burton, Frederick 64
Bush, John 37
    Maryann 37

Busher, John 21
Buswell, Mary 11
    Nathaniel 11
Butler, Charles P 47
Byrne, Redmond 36

Caldecleugh, Robert 63*
Calder, Ann 88
    James 88
Caldwell, David 50
Callaway, Henry 66
Callis, Henry A 1
Calver, James C 16
Calvert, Francis W 81
Cameron, John 75
Campbell, Archibald 19
    Quinton 7
Cann, James C 26
    William 26
Caple, James P 30
Carlyle, Joan 38
    John 38
    Sarah P J 38
Carpenter, Nathaniel 46
    Sarah 46
Carr, George 31
Carroll, Ephraim 44
    James 31
    John 36
Carter, Charles 18
    Elijah 55,65
    Jane 55
    Joshua 55
    Mary A 65
    Samuel 55
Caskie, James 46
Cattarns, Richard 31
Catton, John J 63
    Martha 63
Cauderon, Jean B L A 22
    Marie A E S 22
Cavell, Alexander 26
Chabert, Joseph B 80
Chadwick, Ebenezer 42
    Edwin 73
    Sarah 73
Chaffers, Edward 73
Chalk, John 7
Chambers, John 41
Champion, Thomas 17
Champney, Joseph 9
Chaplin, William 56
Chapman, Henry H 66
    William R 6
Church, Ann 6
Clapham, William H 31
Clarke, Edmund 67
    Edward 71
Clark, Mary 62
    Richard 62
Clayton, Ann 33
    Edward 33
    Michael 40
Clifton, Henry 78
Clopper, Cornelius 61
Close, Mary A 3
    Valentine M 3
Clowston, Rev Charles 73
Coakley, John 27
    John J 56
    Sarah J 56

Cobb, Charles F 68
Coburn - see Cockburn
Cockburn, James 2,26
Coburn, John 6
Codd, Frederick 61
Coglan, Rev. Lucius 23
Colden, Cadwallader D 26
Coles, Isaac U 42
    Margaret C 42
Collard, William F 11
Collier, Elisha H 68
Collingwood, Thomas 45
Collins, Ann 55
    John 14
    Mary 79
    Patrick 55
    William 68
Combe, Charlotte 32
Compton, Edward 69
    William 13
Cooke, Charles 48,49,55
    George 50
Cook, Joseph 13
    Patience 13
Cooper, Robert 25
Cope, Francis 5
Corbett, Rosanna 12
    William 12
Coronel, Ignacio F 69
Corrie, Edgar 6
    Thomas 6
Couper, James H 87
Courtney, Thomas 14
Cowdry, Nathaniel 28
    Thomas 28
    William G 28
Cowell, Alexander 65
Coxe, Daniel 4,12,78
Cox, Edward 6
    Frances C 56
    George 3,4,6*,8,27†
    41,83,85
Coxe, Leonard S 12,38
Cox, Robert A 56
    Sophia M 75
    Thomas 47
    William J 75
Crandall, William 60
Crawford, Frances S 23
    Jacob 23
    James 7
Creagh, John 15
Crease, Ann C 17
    Orlando 17
Creed, Richard 39
Croft, James 83
    Thomas 83
Crokate, Thomas 21
Crokatt, Thomas 42
Crockett, Edward 17
Cronk, James 36
Cropper, John 45
Croskey, Joseph R 69
Crowder, Thomas 41
Crowell, Thomas 71
Cruger, Ann 21
    Bertram P 83*
    John 21
    Sarah M 83*
Cruse, Margaret 82
    Thomas 82
Cryder, John 44
Cundy, John W 34
Curling, George 87

Curran, John 14
    Patrick 14
Curry, Hannah 35
    John 35
Currie, William 17
Curry, William 35
Cushing, Caleb 8
Custis, Nathaniel 9
    William E 60

Da Costa, Benjamin M 5
    Charles M 5
    Jacob M 5
Dalton, John S 4
Danby, Sophia D 19
Daniell, William C 77
Daubeny, Alexander C 49
Davenhill, John S 18
    Mary N C 18
Davenport, Newberry 40
Davies, Daniel 22
    David 2,8,23,34,
    35*,60,77,80*
Davis, Edward 42
    Elizabeth 8
Davies, Evan 34
    Jane 16
Davis, John S 8
Davies, Mary 10,66
Davis, Sarah 42
Davies, Thomas 16
Davison, Crawford 28
    Daniel W 49
    Robert 49
Dawes, Hugh P 63
Dawson, William 10
Day, John 80
Dean, Charles 3
De Arrogave, Anselmo 21
De Beales, Dolores S 25
    John C 25
De Bellanger, Alexander 22
    Jean E A 22
de Bryas, Countess F 16
    Count F 16
De Freyster, Robert 5
Delafield, John 29
De La Leata, Andres 21
De La Quintana, Pedro 21
Delevaute, Joseph 69
de Lizardi, Joseph J 5
de Murrieta, Cristobal 87
Denston, Charles 51
Dent, Thomas 30
Depeyster, Frederick 80
De Ponthieu, John 85
De Sayssure, Alexander 29
de Vos, Auguste 6
Dias, Diego 87
Dibley, George 3
Dickason, Thomas 5,46,48,
    66
Dickins, Asbury 8
Dixon, George W 67
    Henry St J 67
    John 67
    Mary 67
Dobson, Thomas 48
Dollond, George 63
Dommott, Jean D D 44
Douglas, Howard 2

Douglas, John 63
  Louisa 2
Downes, Charles 21
  Henry F E 35*
Downie, Robert 6
Drayton, Rebecca 8
  William 52
  William S 47
Dry, Edward 3
Drysdale, Sarah 25
Dulany, John P 20
Duncan, Ebenezer 20
Dundas, Lady Charlotte 21
  Sir David 21
Dunlap, Addison 60
  Elizabeth C 60
Dunlop, James 8
  John 16,47
  Marion 57
Dunwody, James B 63*
Dupre, Rev William 21,34*
Durnford, William 34
Durant, Enosh 36
Durrant, John 12
Dutton, Thomas 35

Eastmond, John 83
Edgar, Joseph 30
Edmondstone, Charles 52,
  53
Edwards, Griffith 62
  Margaret 62
  Thomas 36
  William 38
Eldridge, James 79
Ellice, Edward 52*
Elwall, George 36
Emmet, George N 47
Erving, George W 81
Evans, Joseph J 1
  Mary 9
  Rev Thomas 60
Eve, Abraham 52
Evelyn, Hugh 81
Everett, Charles 49
Ewing, George 8
Exall, Rev George G 5

Falder, Robert 43
Fanning, Edmund 64
Farmer, Thomas 82
Farnell, Henry 38
Farquhar, James 70
  William 12
Farr, Edward 69
  Thomas 47
Fatin, Samuel 38
Faulconer, Robert H 76
Faulkener, Elizabeth 64
  William 64
Faver, Ann 88
  Harriot 88
  James 88
Fenner, Ann 65
  Richard S 65
Ferguson, James 70
Field, John J 32
Fielding, Amos 75

Filewood, Abraham 59
  Elizabeth 59
Fisher, Horatio N 21
  Robert W 29
  William 49
Fitch, William S 19
Flavell, James 67
Fleet, Elizabeth 42
Fletcher, Elizabeth 81
  William 81
Flint, Henry 72
Flower, John W 25
Folder, Robert 43
Foran, Mary 12
Forbes, John 59
  Rev John 71
  Thomas 59
Ford, Henry 56
  Sarah 53
Forman, William 59
Forrest, Henry 1
  James 83
Forster, Matthew 62
Foster, Charles W 47
  Frederick C 35
  William J S 84
Foulke, Mary 18
Francis, Arthur E 11*
  Henry D 45
  Thomas W 85
Fraschini, Clotilde 20
  Gaetano 20
Frazar, George 25
Fricker, Edward 76
Friers, Elizabeth H 56
Fry, John 10
  John C 50
Fryer, Elizabeth 40
  Joseph 40
Fuggle, John 78
Furber, Anna 85,86*
  James 85,86*

Gadsden, Christopher 63
Gaillard, Susan E 78
Gaisford, Thomas 41
Gallego, Joseph 30,44
Gardiner, Robert H 33
  Sarah S 68
  William 68
Gardner, Francis 62
  Samuel P 24
Garling, Mylam 67
Garrett, Elizabeth 67
  William 67
Gatliff, Samuel 56
Gatly, Edward 83
Geib, George H 3
  Sarah 3
Gerrard, George 43
Gerring, William 31
Gibb, Duncan 48
Gibbons, Barton 21
  Caroline 21
  Emily 21
  Frederick 21
  Robert 21
  Sir William 21
Gibbs, Janette 72
  John 18
  Joseph 72

Giffing, William 15
Gilbert, Joshua 76
  Sarah 76
Gilford, Sarah 84
Girdler, Thomas S 82
Glen, Jacob 19
Glennie, Alexander 69
  Rev Alexander 84
  James S 26
  John I 67
Goldring, Charles E
Goodman, John 15
Gordon, Adam 59
  Alexander 22
  Charlotte 65
  Francis 65
  James 22
  Richard 11
  William 76
Goryer, George 36
Gouger, George 53
Goulding, Robert 65
Gourdin, Henry 72
Gouverneur, Mary 61
  Nicholas 7
  Samuel 61
Graham, Ann 60
  Francis 60
  John 22
  Lewis 85
  Robert 46
Granger, Edmund 32
  Thomas C 6,59
Grant, Robert 21
Graves, John L 59
Gray, Benjamin C T 56
  Benjamin G 56
  Charles W 56
  Harrison 60
  William 68
Green, Alexander 66
Greene, Copley 3
  George 56
Greenslade, Amos 77
Gribble, John 10*
  William 71*
Grierson, John 13
Griffith, Thomas 17
Griffiths, Samuel 38
Grosvenor, William L 73
Grounds, Alice 72
  John 72
Grove, Sarah 58
  William 58
Groves, Elizabeth 38
Grymes, Philip L 46
Guise, Sir Berkeley 83
Gumbrell, Ann 4
  Robert 4
Gurney, Samuel 23
Gwynn, Richard 65

Hadley, Isaac 33
Hague, Edward C 66
Hain, John 81
Haldane, Alexander 33
Hall, Jenny 4
  John W 67
Halsted, Ann B 37
Hambrook, John 46
Hampson, James 66

Hancock, Joseph 71
    Michael W 30
Hancox, James 87
    James S 87
    Joseph 87
Hanley, Sylvanus 32
Harper, Alexander 37
    James 42
Harriott, Caroline L 82
    Rev William 82
Harris, Marian E 63
Harrison, Albertina 76
    Charles 34
    Elizabeth 21
    Robert 76
Hart, Thomas 85
Harvey, Reuben 33
Haslewood, George 18
Hastings, William W 61
Hawkins, Susannah 32
Hay, James 17
    John 38
Hazard, Rufus 32
Heacock, Peter 1
    Sarah 1
Heath, John C 53
Hedges, Henry P 60
Heinert, Fredericke 6
Hellyer, Elizabeth H 57
Henderson, Robert 3
Henrichsen, Henry 23
Henry, Eliza 85
Hepburn, James 37
Hermesdorf, Mathias 73
Hester, Emm 24
    John 24
Hewetson, William 79
Hewitt, Mary A 81
    William 81
Hewlett, Richard 5
Hewson, Fanny 37
Hicky, Philip 51
Hilditch, Mary A 60*
Hill, Elizabeth 1,47
Hilton, Martha 31
Hobson, Campbell 5
Hockley, Edward 76
Hodder, Mary 29
    Thomas 29
Hodgson, John 34
    Peter 24
    Robert 66
Hoffman, William 31
Holland, John 19
Holliday, Ann 44
    Maria 20
Hollingsworth, Nathaniel 3
Holmes, Andrew 32
    John 45
Holy, Thomas 7
Honseal, Anna M 78
    Michael 78
Hooper, Samuel 68,79
Hooton, Sarah B 4
Hoppe, James 22
Hopton, John 29*,65
Hopwood, William 67
Horry, Harriott 61
Horsley, Thomas B 45
Hosack, David 70
Houghton, Abner 80
Housley, Anna M 68
    William 68

Howis, Charlotte 86
Hubbard, William J 3
Hubbell, Hannah 36
Hughes, Henry 14*
    Mary 14
    Richard 14
Hume, Joseph 21
    Robert 14
Hunt, Henry 39
    Samuel 39
    Thomas 31
Hunter, Elizabeth 22
    John 22
    Thomas 48
Hurry, George 54*
Hutchings, Ann 52
Hutchins, Henry 70
Hutton, Timothy 15
Hyde, Hon Jane 88

Imlay, Lucretia W 39
    William E 39
Inglesby, William 42
Inglis, James 62
    John 62
Innerarity, James 59
    John 59
Ironside, Isaac 12
Irvine, Elizabeth 25
    William 43
Irving, James 43
    Marion 43
Isaac, Joseph 61
Isaacs, Ann 55
Isaacson, John F 24
Israel, Daniel 30
Izard, Eliza L 61
    Ralph D 61

Jackson, Amasa 49
    Bolton 44
    George 77*
    Washington 44
    William 51
    Rev William 56
James, Catherina 58
    Charles 58
    George M 30
    Thomas 63
    Thomas s 11
Janney, Phineas 56
Jay, Mary R 68
    Peter A 68
Jenkins, Robert 38
Jennings, Joseph 3
Jessie, Abraham 30
Johnson, Benjamin B 6
    Charles 38
    Robert 69
Johnston, Rachel 25
Jones, Ann 37
    Arthur T 26
    Catharine M 52*
    Edward W 12
    Horatio G 76
    James 76
    Margaret 12
    Rebekah 17

Jones, Richard R 52
    Robert 44
Judah, Benjamin S 23
Julius, Alfred A 53*

Keith, John 4
Keller, Peter 69
Kelly, George B 80
    William 53
Kemlys, Edward 82
Kemp, Diana 45
Kendricks, Martha 75
    William 75
Kermit, Henry 58
Key, Edward 5
Kiddell, Sarah M 78
Kilgour, James 5
Kimber, Priscilla 36
King, William H 54
Kinloch, George 29
Kinsley, Ziphaniah 38
Kirby, Elizabeth 23
Kirkland, Ann 65
    Jane 65
Kissam, Benjamin R 24
    Richard V 24
Knight, Elizabeth M 27
    Henry 27
Knor, David 65
Krause, William H 18

Lace, Ambrose 19
Lacy, Hannah E 79
Lacey, John 72*
Lacy, Richard 79
Laird, John 56
Lake, Harriot E 72
    William 72
Lamatter, Samuel D 74
Lamb, David 48
    James 63
    Thomas 60
Landreth, David 48
Lane, John 9,45,82
Lanford, Isabella 25
Langham, James G 1
Langslow, Lydia 15
    Richard 15
Lansing, Gerrit 52
    Sanders 52
Lapworth, Mary 72
Latcham, Annatilda J 42
    Joseph H 42
Latham, Thomas 8
Latter, Eliza 31
    William 31
Lausing, Sanders 9
Law, George 73
Laurence, George 40
Lawrence, Effingham 25,
    31,74,85
    William E 74
Laycock, John C 59
Leam, Edward 39
Leaycraft, Elizabeth 12
    William 12
Leburn, Thomas 7
Lee, George 8

Lee, James 48
William 38
Leitch, Colin 49
Helen 49
Lemmon, William 30
Lenox, David 17,63
Lester, Matthew 72
Susan 72
Lever, Charles 46
Levinge, Dame Mary 44
Sir Richard 44
Lias, Henry J 2
Lind, Ord 65
Lindsell, Henry 44
Lister, Joseph J 24
Littlefield, John W 79
Sarah J 79
Livingston, Robert G 41
Lloyd, Lisle 47
Lobb, James B 87
Lockey, George 18
Locoak, Jane 24
Lodington, Sarah 20
William 20
Logie, Isabella 42
James 42
Long, Martin 30
Lord, Daniel 17
Isabella 11
Loury, Emanuel 65
Lovell, John 27,28
Lowe, Laetitia 88
Stead 88
Lowndes, Angelletta 27
Francis 27
Lowther, Richard 29
Lubbock, Diana 85
Richard 85
Lucas, Louis 34,46
Philip 46
Luguer, Nicholas 47
Lumley, William 41
Lyell, Margaret 88

McAllister, John 7
McBride, Hugh 35
McCall, John 24
Philly M 24
McCaa, William 49
McCahill, John 65
McCarthy, Catherine 53
MacCarthy, Charles 80
Justin 80
McCarthy, Owen 53
McCartley, Justin 23
McCashill, Donald 75
Kenneth 75
McClintock, James 1
McClymont, Hugh 22
Samuel 22
Maccubbin, Thomas M 56
McCudie, Andrew 49
McCullock, William 22
McDonald, Alexander 43
Ann 49
Coll 43
McDougal, Dinah 62
McDowall, John 42
McEvers, Margaret J 41
McEvoy, Francis 49
McGregor, Ann 59
Hugh 59
Mackay, Robert 49

McKenna, Philip 20
Mackenzie, James 17,40
John 53
MacKillop, James 10
McKinlay, Archibald 77
Mackintosh, James 49
MacLachlan, Archibald 52
MacLain, Mary 48
MacLean, Hector 75
MacLeod, Patrick 28
McLoughlin, John 64
McNeran, Mary 71
McPherson, Charles 43
McQueen, John 17
Margaret 17

Magan, Henry L 69
Maitland, David 65
Ebenezer 79
Maize, James 67
Malleson, John 22
Mandeville, William 15
Marks, Catharine 39
William 39
Marles, John 47
Marriott, George W 76
Marsh, William 39
Marshall, James 52
Martin, Edward 25
Francis 25
John 78
Maryan, William 63
Mason, Nathaniel 1
Massey, Alexander 15
Mather, William 56
Matthews, William 45,59
Maule, George 45,62,75
Mawby, Richard 83
May, Ann 33
James 33
Mayere, Thomas 85
Meadowcroft, James 56
Mein, Alexander 53
William 49
Melhado, Jacob A 46
Menzies, Charles 28
Meredith, Benjamin 74
Catherine 5
Merton, Alexander 7
Messenger, Maria 52
Metcalfe, Thomas 77
Miall, Daniel 30
Winifred W 30
Micoll, Sarah 17
Millar, Andrew 40
Millard, William 60
Millen, Edward 28
Miller, Boyd 72
Francis 11
Isabella 42
John 60
Richard 39
Robert 20
William 17
Mills, Esther 40
James 40
Milner, Mary A 33
Minet, Isaac 47
Mitchell, Andrew 33
Margaret 33
Mitchelson, Bartholomew 25
Elizabeth 25

Moar, Isabella 42
Jonathan 42
Moat, Horatio S 79
Martha M 79
Molloy, Bridget 85
Martin 85
Money, Mary A 13
Richard 13
Monk, Daniel 48
Montgomerie, Henrietta 88*
Moodie, Benjamin 52
Moodey, John A 16
Nancey C 16
Moon, Samuel 12
Moore, William C 12
Morgan, James 74
James F 39
Susannah 61
Morley, Eliza 72
Ephraim 72
Morrill, Isaac 50
Mary 50
Morris, Christopher 63
George 7
Morrison, David 64
Morton, Alexander 5
Moses, Abraham L 40
Mould, Jacob 57
Moule, Elizabeth M 39
Rev Horatio 39
Moultrie, Hon John 71
Mountgomery, John 65
Muggleworth, Jane 24
William 24
Muir, William 48
Mundell, John 41
Munro, Andrew 69
Jane 48
Margaret 71
Nathaniel 71
Peter J 10
Murdoch, William 13*,75
Murdock, William 30,31*, 60
Myers, Dame Elizabeth 49
Jacob 67
Mary 49

Napier, William F P 27
Naylor, Robert 47
Thomas 47
Nayler, William 45
Neale, Mary 84
Mason 70
Neate, Rowland 79
Needham, Joshua 88
Neilson, William 41
Nelson, Elizabeth 72
George 72
John W 20
Mary C 46
William 46
Nethersole, Henry 25
Nettlefold, Abraham 36
Nicholls, James B 76
Mary 76
Nicholson, Elizabeth 42, 62
Isaac 62
Jane 62
Nockells, Charles 54
Nolan, James 20

Norry, Jane 49
        Margaret 49
        Mary 49
Norwood, Charles 51

Oleary, George W 33
Oliver, John 17
        Robert 17
Olney, Thomas 49
Omanney, Sir Francis 82
Ord, John 14
Osterwald, Daniel F 22
Oswald, James 56
Outram, Jonathan 58
Overing, Charlotte M 22
        Henry 22
Owen, Eben 4
        Mary 4

Packer, Charles R 36
Page, Benjamin 33
        Mann 46
        Martha 33
        William B 11
Paine - see Payne
Paleske, Charles G 13
Palmer, Catherine 49
        Frederick 34
        John H 74
        Joseph E 24
        Mary R 34
        Robert S 52*,75
        Thomas 49
        William 67
Pantall, Mary 45
        Robert 45
Park, James 37
        Thomas 12
Parker, Rev Samuel 39
        Rev William 42
        William P 14
Parkhouse, Catherine 33
Parkin, William 83
Parkinson, John 3,31
Parks, Frederick C 47
        Grace 47
Parlby, Elizabeth 16
        John 16
Parnther, Michael S 33
Partington, Charles J 16*
Partridge, John W 71
Passey, John 55
        Mary 55
Patrick, John 70
Patterson, Eliza J 17
        Elizabeth 34
        Mary 48
        William 17,48
Paul, Thomas 82
Payne, George W 31
        James H 60
        Philip 31
        Robert 31,71
Paine, Samuel 13
Payne, Smith 31
Pears, Robert 65
Pearson, Enoch 9
Pease, Paul 13,77

Peele, Dennis 42
Pepper, Sarah J 56
Percival, James 13
Perham, Joan 41
        John 41
Perram, James 48
Perroneau, Hugh 63
Phillips, Joseph 86
        Philip 34
        Sarah 86
        William 9,54
Philpot, John 2
Phipps, Pownal 2
Pike, William 69
Pillow, William H 56
Pinckney, Roger 71
        Susannah 71
Pirrie, William 54
Platt, Isaac 26
Plowman, Thomas 30
Plummer, Joseph 15
        Mary W 15
Pogson, Henrietta 87
        Rev Milaward 87
Poinsett, Joel R 10
Poole, John 67
        Joseph R 24
Poot, Jonathan 7
Pope, George 64
        Henry 60
Porsford, Thomas 77
Porter, William 61
Potter, Nathaniel 39
        Sarah J 39
Powel, John H 33
Power, Rev John 10
Preintall, Sophia A 56
Preston, Rev Thomas 62
Pretto, Isaac 5
Price, Ann A 36
        Charles 62
        George 34
        John 36
        Richard 10
        Richard A 59
        Sarah 62
Pringle, Jane 47
        Julius 47
Pritchard, Henry 61
Profit, James 51
Pulsford, Robert 63
        William 50
Purcell, Ellen 30
        James 30

Quilter, Cameron E 53

Ramsay, James 28,34
Rance, Henry 19
Read, Caroline 84
        Frances H 71
Reid, Jamima 57*
Read, Joseph 84
        William D C 71
Reid, William T 57
Redin, Isabella 27
Rees, Margaret 11
        Rees 11

Reid - see Read
Remington, William 70
Remsen, Henry 12
Rendall, Adam 64
Repplier, Julia 44
        George S 44
Revans, James 85
        Martha 85
Reynolds, John 74
Rhoades, Jacob 49
Richardson, Christopher 6
        John 37
Rickards, Edward H 67
Riley, William 4
Risque, Elizabeth 4
Rivington, Francis 84
Roberti, Ursula E 7
Roberts, Edward 64
        Josiah 48
Robins, Elizabeth C 83
        Thomas 30
Robinson, Margaret 18
        Rebecca 70
        William 32
Roe, Peter 83
Roebuck, John 12
Rogers, Ann 18
        David 17,57
        John 74
        Samuel D 57
        William 18
Romeyn, Rebecca 52
Ronalds, Hugh 27
Rooke, Henry W 20
Roper, Ann 57
        John H 65
        Joseph 80
        Timothy 57
Roscoe, Henry 19
Rose, Hickman 20
Ross, James 41,61
        Malcolm 1
Rossiter, Eliza 84
        William 84
Rothery, John 15
Roupell, John S 48
Rous, Ann 32
        John 32
Routh, William E 30
Rowlett, William 33
Ruckel, George C 31
Rudd, John 23
        Mary 23
Rudge, Jonathan 24
Russell, Archibald 68
        Helen 68
        James G 21
        Joseph 59
Rutherford, Gray 54
        John 41
Rutledge, Sarah M 72,73
Ryland, Arthur 34

Salt, Thomas 5
Sanders, James 36
        Maria C 36
Saunders, Robert 5
Sands, Christian H 25
        Henry 11
Saunders - see Sanders
Saunderson, Ann 1

Saunderson, John 1
Savadge, John 18
    Mary N C 18
Savery, John T 19
Savile, Samuel 27
Schryver, Peter 63
Scott, Edmund J 85
    James 46
    John 10
    John F 61,67
Scudamore, Rowles 7
Seacocke, Ann 32
Seaman, John 41
Searle, William 72
Sears, Samuel 66
    Samuel M 66
Shakespear, William 60
Shaw, Charles 19
Shaw, Gabriel 5*,6,41,
    43*,57,71
Sheddon, Robert 49
Sheffield, Isaac 44
Shepherd, Edward 34
    Esther 34
Sheppard, William 30
Sherwin, Peter W 47
    Richard 47
Sheviz, George 49
Shine, Jeremiah 10
Shockley, Levin 41
    Sarah 41
Shoolbred, James 52
    John 10
    Mary 52
    Polly 52
Shrigley, Mary 11
Shrive, Caleb 20
Shute, Peter 40
Sibbald, Rev John 22
Sibborn, James 25
Sibley, Elizabeth 47
    John 47
Sidney, Marlow J F 37
Simkins, Parris 30
Simmons, Catherine 79
Simond, Frances 85
    Lewis 85
Simons, Keating 87
Simpson, Alexander 87
    Charles R 8,82,
           87
    David 69
    Sir George 64,
           78
    James 59,71
    James A 29
    John 38
    Mary 59,69
    William 59
Singleton, John 3
Sisson, Jesse 13
Skelly, Eliza 57
    William 57
Skinner, Anne 27
    Edward 27
    Mary E 54*
    William B 54*
Slade, Henry B 76
Slaney, Mary 26
    Zachariah 26
Slaughter, John H 1
Smedley, Francis 56
Smith, Ann 24
    Charles 39

Smith, Charlotte 87
    Daniel 47
    Frances'30
    Hannah 10
    Henry 24
    Kathrine 22
    Maria 39
    Mary J 38
    Nathaniel 82
    Richard 18
    Robert W 8
    Susanna E 8
    Thomas 30
    William 50
    William F 30
    William L 87
Smyde, Joseph 36
Snoad, George 79
    Mary A 79
Snock, George C 85
    Susanna D 85
Snowdon, Joseph 8
Snyder, Mary 69
Solarte, Jose V de A 87
Somerville, John 27
South, James 59
Southgate, John 22
    Thomas 22
Sowton, James 58
Sparhawk, Samuel 50
Sparrow, Charles R 23
Spaulding, Charlotte 27*
    Nicholas 27*
Spaw, Richard 16
Spegle, John V 9
Spence, Charles 73
Spencer, Harriette 49
    Samuel 49
Stables, John 56,72
    Keene 72
Stansbury, Elizabeth 73
Stansfeld, James 76
Staple, John 16
Stark, Burwell 46
    John W 50
    Theodore 29
Stead, Benjamin 61
Steer, George J 45
Stephens - see Stevens
Stephenson - see Stevenson
Sternchuss, Rev Paul 85
Stevens, Elianor 75
    John 8,52,79
    Jonathan 38
    Martha 79
Stephens, Richard 80
Stevens, William 43
Stevenson, Anne 33
    Cornelius 18
Stephenson, Samuel 17
Stevenson, Thomas 33
Steward, Samuel 12
Stewart, Edward 51
Stuart, James 71
    John 66
Stickney, John 15
Stirling, Walter 11,28,
    33,85*
Stogdon, John 26
Stone, Aaron 24
    Catherine B 66
    William 66
Stonestreet, Nicholas 64

Stotlar, Ann 18
    Mathias D 18
Stoughton, Anna M 21
    John 21
Stretter, Frances 54
Strettle, Frances 54
Stride, John 47
Strong, Rev Clement 85
Stroud, Eliza 85
    William D 85
Stuart - see Stewart
Sturgeon, Robert 52
Sturges, John 77
Stuyvesant, Helen 68
    Peter G 68
Sullivan, Keziah 71
    Thomas 71
Sutherland, John 52
Suttenfield, George 73
    Sarah C 73
Swainson, William 62
Swan, George 44
Swigert, Jacob 1
Symes, John C 65

Tabet, Susan 51
Tally, John 14
Tapster, Stephen 80
Tatham, Henry 32
    Thomas T 32
Tavel, Elizabeth 7
    John 7
Taylor, Ann 4
    Dundass 79
    Esther 79
    John 4,12,49
    Joshua 58
    Mary 58
    William 41,55,
           63,73
Teesdale, John 21
Tepper, Richard 71
Thatcher, George 14
Thom, John 41
Thomas, Ann 11
    Daniel 39
    David 4,11,35
    Grace 58
    Rebecca H 80
    Richard 58
Thomson, Alexander 39
Thompson, Andrew 12
    Goodinch M 66
    John 19,84
    Robert 52
    William 52
Thorne, James 80
    Mary A 80
Thorns, Thomas 84
Tidbury, James 6,12,16,
    29,37,40,42,47,
    48,59,64,72,
    75*,78,80,82
Tilghman, Richard C 80
    Walter 28
Tilstone, Charles F 28
    Joseph 57
Todd, Thomas 29
Todhunter, Anne 73
Tolmie, William F 36
Topping, Bridget 62

Torbert, James A 76
Tothill, Robert 32
Toulmin, Henry 76
Townsend, Joseph 80
Traill, John 15
Trappes, Henry 22
Travers, Ann 21
Trecothick, James 65
Tredwell, Adam 53
Trevett, Russell 68
     Samuel R 68
Trew, Samuel 83
Troke, Mary E 79
Trowbridge, Charles C 82
Trower, Robert 56
Tunno, Adam 53,63
     John 4,43,48
Turbitt, John 83
Turnbull, Eliza 52
     Hector 52
Turner, Ann 60
     Charles R 33,69
     Edward W 60
     Henry J 28
     William 81
Turton, Thomas 29
Tustin, William 75

Urquhart, Thomas 21

Valk, Jacob 38
Van Arsdal, Abraham 80
Van Cortlandt, Pierre 5
Van Heythuysen, Richard
     29,69
Vaughan, Petty 8,9,18
     William 9
Veazey, Edward 27
     Elizabeth 27
Vidal, John G 2

Waddell, John 83
Waddington, Henry 22
Waldo, Daniel 68
Walker, Daniel 30
     George F 26
     William 57*
Wallace, Norman 52

Wallas, John 11
Walsh, Dudley 74
     Sarah 74
Walther, Philip 6
Ward, John 47
Warren, John 25
Waterhouse, Hezekiah 78
Watkins, Charles 23
     Mary 70
     Samuel 23
Watmough, Jonathan 6,7
     Mary 6,7
Watson, James 6
Watts, Ann 15
     Anna 68
     John 18
     John J 43
     Josiah H 15
     Robert 18
Webb, Jane 76
     William 67
Webster, Rev George 69
Weisiger, Joseph 1
Welby, Richard E 20
West, Anne 30
     John 30
Westcot, Joseph 83
Westell, Frederick 77
Western, Edward 72,73
White, Deborah 28
     Edward 30
     George 65
     Gideon 28
Whyte, James M 54
White, John C 10
     Mary 30,38
     Percival 36
Whitehead, Francis F 45
     John D 45
Whittle, Conway 36
Wiggin, Timothy 67,78
Wildes, Edward 1
     George 73
     Henry A 1
Wilkes, Charles 26,80
     Henry 80
Wilkinson, Benjamin 45
     Mary 31
     Matthew 45
Williams, Elizabeth 16
     George 16,47
     Hyde 4
     John 10
     Robert W 20
     Samuel 21,50,
      58,74
     William 28,52

Willing, Richard 10
Wilmot, William 22
Wilson, Benjamin 12
     John 63
     John C 72
     Melvil 1
     Richard 32
     Thomas 15,33,71
Winkley, John 84
     Matilda F 84
Winslow, Isaac 4,50
Winstanley, Thomas 8
Winthrop, Francis B 51
     Thomas S 78*
Winwood, Edward 9
Witham, Francis 80
Withers, Elizabeth 15
     William 15
Woddrop, John 7
Wood, Caroline B 53
     James 24
     Thomas 53
Woodgate, William 28
Woods, Delia 71
     William 71
Woodward, Alexander 51
     Mary 51
Woolley, William J 45
Woolsey, George M 64
Worrell, Elizabeth G 86*
Wright, Charity 74
     Edward W 71
     Jesse 17
     John 83
     Robert 52
Wynch, William 47

Yarnold, Frances A 55
     William H 55
Yates, John B 12
Yonge, Anna M 69
Young, Christopher 74
     Jesse 35
     William 2,5
Younger, John 16

Zobriskie, John A 11

Index of Places

UNITED STATES OF AMERICA

Alabama

Baldwin Co. 76
Clarke Co. 28
Jefferson Co. 18
Madison Co. 48
Mobile 5,8,21,32,36,67,
    88
Plantersville 57
Tuskaloosa 63*
Washington Court House 79

Arkansas 64

Helena 40
Pottsville 7
Pulaski 39

California 30,42,63,73

Canyon 3
Hopkins Creek 1
Los Angeles 69
Marysville 68
Mormon Diggings 85
Pueblo de los Angeles 69
Sacramento 27,36,67
San Francisco 3,43,45,64
    69
Sonora 45
Stockton 58,71

Connecticut 48

Bridgeport 35
Derby 43
East Haven 74
Fairfield 53
Greenwich 78
Hartford 39,87
Hebron 73
Middletown 28,83
New Haven 14,47,80,82
New London 13,15,54,74
Norwalk 5
Plymouth 84
Sherman 36

District of Columbia

Alexandria 52,56,76
Alexandria Co. 20
George Town 27,48
Washington 8,15,27,32,33,
    38,41,71

Florida 1,12,43,48

Jefferson 74
Joseph 37
Key West 70
Pensacola 52,72,77
St.Augustine 22,71

Georgia 35,43,49,53

Augusta 22,30,36,49,88
Chatham Co. 77
Liberty Co. 49
Milledgeville 84
Pleasant Retreat 16
Queenborough 48
Savannah 8*,9,13,14,17,
    22*,25,26,34,39,40*,
    42,49,52,53,76,82
St.Simon's Island 28,87

Illinois 35,45,54,63

Adams Co. 3
Albion 7,14,27,36*,74
Bath 34
Beardstown 12
Bristol 7
Burnt Prairie 15
Cass Co. 26
Chicago 8,10*,37,50,72*
Cook Co. 72
Edwards Co. 27
Frankfort 41
Greenville 85
Independent Grove 31
Kaskasia 76
Kendall Co. 70
Lasalle 19,24
Nauvoo 75
New Albion 83
Peoria Co. 14
Rockford 35
Tazewell Co. 3
Tremont 71
Upwood 54
Vermillion Co. 66

Indiana

Amora 45
Evansville 60
Lake Co. 28
Lost Creek 9
Medicine 14
Napoleon 26
Newburgh 30
New Harmony 50
Oxford 4
Princton 53
Union Township 3

Iowa

Davenport 48
Dubuque 19,62
Muscatine 86
Wappelow 24

Kansas

Fort Leavenworth 74

Kentucky 1,85

Covington 85
Henderson 73
Louisville 7,10,12,65
Meade Co. 33
Morganfield 23,57
Nelson Co. 53
Russelville 53
Shepherdsville 78
Springfield 4

Louisiana 51

Baton Rouge 51*,61,87
Columbia 37
Concordia 29
Lafayette City 72
Manehack 34
New Orleans 1*,4,6*,9,10,
    13,14,20*,21*,22*,25,28,
    31,32,33,34*,36,37*,39*,
    43,44,45*,47,51,53*,54,
    56,58,59,63,67,68*,71,
    72,74,76*,77,83,87
Pass Christian 24
Port Hudson 72
Woodville 75

Maine

Bangor 79
Brunswick 75
Castine 35*
Deer Island 84
East Port 56
Hallowell 80*
Kittery 64
Portland 70
Wiscasset 50

Maryland 20,62

Ann Arundel Co. 75
Baltimore 1,2*,4*,5*,6,
    12,15,16,18,19,20*,23,
    26,31*,36*,38,41,44*,
    46,50,51*,60*,62,64,
    65*,66,68,69,70,73,75,
    79,80*,81,86*,88*
Baltimore Co. 23
Bel Air 31
Charles Co. 66
Chestertown 83,86*
Cornwallis's Neck 64
Frederick Co. 15,48
Grange 56
Kent Co. 86*
Montgomery Co. 56
North Milford Hundred 41
Prince George's Co. 1,20*
Princess Ann Town 84
Rockland 48
Somerset 9

Massachusetts 68

Augusta 50
Beverley 30
Boston 2,8,9,10,12,13,15,
  16.17,20,21,22,24,29*,
  32,37,39,41*,42,45,
  46*,47,49,50,51*,53,
  59*,61,62*,64,65,66,
  67*,68,69,71,73,75,77,
  78,79,81,82*,85
Cambridge 21,27*,46,51
Dorchester 78
Gardiner 33
Harvard 9
Haverhill 5
Marblehead 15,58,68,79
Milton 51
Nantucket 5,13,20,24,32,
  40,77,84,87*
Needham 44
New Bedford 66
Newbury 15
Newbury Port 8,18,75
Penobscot 83
Reading 8
Rochester 46
Roxbury 9,19,25,41,71
Salem 23,58,59,75
Springfield 64,68
Stockbridge 54*
Westfield 59
Williamstown 53
Worcester 13,60

Michigan

Bellevue 35
Cambridge 72
Ann Arbor 45
Detroit 2,74,77,82,83
Ionia Co. 61
Sharon Richfield 70
Stafford 71

Mississippi

Claiborne Co. 66
Middleton 17
Natchez 56
Washington 29
Yazoo Valley 26

Missouri

Clark Co. 13
Columbus 70
Commerce 22*
Mayoville 82
Pleasant Hill 61
Rolls Co. 66
St. Louis 2,3,5,20,62

New Hampshire 48

Concord 49
Exeter 61
Nashua 62
Portsmouth 9,24,33,49,
  84

New Jersey 17,25,42,44,
  59,74,75,78

Allentown 16
Bedminster 17
Belleville 25
Bordentown 28
Bound Brook 44
Burlington 10,73
Camden 18,37
Camptown 74
Chatham 16
Edgerston 68
Gloucester Co. 38
Hanover 16
Hoboken 60
Hunterdon Co. 78
Jersey City 82
Keyport 74
Moorestown 34
Morris 24
Mount Holly 23
Newark 6,7,9,31,32,43,
  54*,55,56,59,72,77,
  83,86
New Barbadoes 11
New Brunswick 29*,67
New Providence 18
Orange 22
Patterson 57
Perth Amboy 6,78
Soder Hill 77
Somerset Co. 80
South Amboy 46
Spottswood 38
Sussex 4
Sussex Co. 9
Trenton 40

New York

(References to New York
City and State excluded)

Albany 9,17,19,25,29,34,
  36,42,74,78,85
Amonia 4
Athol 16
Auburn 54
Aurora 65
Bath 49
Bathurst 78
Bennington 29
Benton 75
Brooklyn 7,14,20,33,38,
  50,53,60,67,69,73,74,
  75,78,79
Buffalo 13,18*,19,34,45,
  54,55,74,78
Canton 75
Castleton 56
Charlton 4
Cicero Corners 70
Clermont 52
Constantia 7
Cornwall 83
Dexter 3
Eagle 30
Flatbush 56
Flushing 65
Fredonia 8
Freedom 88
Greece 55

New York (cont'd)

Greenbush 19
Harlem 58,80
Hector 86
Hempstead 51,52
Henrietta 74
Hudson 52*,54
Hyde Park 63
Ithaca 6,57*
Laminburgh 12,86
Lebanon 53
Lee 4
Lockport 36
Long Island 14,55
Lyndon 49
Lyons 38
Lysander 7
Manlius 6
Mill Farm 76
Mount Pleasant 5*,63,75,
  76,82
Naval Yard 8
Newburgh 2,50*
New Palz 52
New Rochelle 40
New Town 56,64,80
Ogdensburgh 59
Ossigon 29
Oswegatchie 81
Oswego 17
Oyster Bay 77
Palermo 28
Peekshill 82
Pelham 31
Philipstown 61
Poughkeepsie 39,75
Putneyvill 5
Queensbury 36
Queens Co. 23
Red Hook Township 22
Richmond 10
Rochester 4,26,43,62*,66
Rondout 32
Salina 25
Saratoga Springs 15,35
Saugerties 4,47,55
Schenectady 47,52
Sing Sing 81
Skaneateles 25,28
Southampton 60
Southfield 4
Springfield 14
Stafford 63
Staten Island 2,18,39,40,
  59,70,81
Sullivan 70
Syracuse 53
Thompson 15
Troy 30
Upper Canada 34
Utica 44,63,66,74
Vernon 14
Wards Island 65
Warren Herkimer
Washington Co. 60
Waterloo 7
Watervliet 35
Wawarsing 45
Westchester 29,33,83,85
Whitehall 6
White Plains 48
Whitesborough 74
Williamsburgh 24,67,69

New York (cont'd)

Williamson 5
Williams Town 7
Yonkers 69

North Carolina 8,36,49,
                      75

Craven Co. 1
Cumberland Co. 48
Horse Shoe Swamp 50
Orange Co. 76*
Pringo 8,20
Raleigh 49
Wilmington 9,16,25,39

Ohio 2,63,70

Amherst Plato 11
Bethlehem 6
Cheviot 49
Cincinnati 5,9,10*, 11*,
   12,14,19,28,37,42,43,
   51,52,57,61,63,79,84,
Cleveland 54,67,83,84
Delaware 81
Elyria 45
Fearing 12
GreenTownship 31
Hamilton 42
Hamilton Co. 18*
Knox Co. 68
Lagan Co. 71
Limaville 61
Madison Township 66
Marietta 22,68
Massillon 15
Mount Vernon 54
Newark 67
Oberlin 66
Ohio City 10
Perry Co. 18
Royalton 65
Sharon 46
Springfield 25
Steilcoom 36
Steubenville 86
Talmadge 55
Toledo 13
Zanesville 33,54

Oregon

Fort Vancouver 30,64,77,

Pennsylvania 1,33,35,41,
                      77

Allen Town 11
Bensalem 29
Berwick 44
Big Beaver 71
Bradford Township 18
Brandy Wine 14
Canonsburgh 69
Ceres Town 73
Chester 65,84
Clearfield Co. 18
Coolspring 15
Delaware 14
Delaware Co. 1,2,85

Pennsylvania (cont'd)

Easter 3
Easton 71
Fernton 60
Frankford 10
Germanstown 79
Harrisburg 33
Haverford Township 85
Holmesburg 18,53*,81
Huntingdon Co. 18
Kingston 41
Lancaster City 69
Lancaster Co. 27,31
Le Raysville 33
Mansfield 79
Martinsbury 12
Mead Township 32
Middletown 35
New London 41
Oxford Township 58
Penn Township 17,36
Philadelphia 3*,6*,7*,8*,
   9,10,12*,13*,14,16,17*,
   18*,19,20,21*,23*,24,
   25,26*,27,28*,29*,30*,
   31,32,33*,34*,35,36*,
   38,39,40*,41,42*,43*,
   44*,45,46,48,50,51,
   52*,54,55,56,57,58*,
   59*,60,62*,63*,64,65*,
   66*,67,69*,72*,73,75,
   76*,79*,80,81*,82*,
   83*,85,86*
Philadelphia Co. 38,80
Pittsburgh 4,14,32,51*,
   73,83,85
Point Township 37
Providence 1,76
Ridley 1,2
Roxborough 76
St. Clair 44
Scranton 67
Somerset 86
Southwark 71
Washington 6*
York Town 20

Rhode Island 24,48

Cranston 1
Kings Town 31
New Bedford 55
Newport 2,23,26,39,46,
   73,87
Providence 1,47,84
Warwick 33

South Carolina 5*,10,14,
   15,18,28,51,52,60,61,
   72*

Charleston 4*,5,6,8*,9*,
   13,14*,16*,19,21,23,
   25,27*,28*,29*,31,32*,
   33,34,36,38*,40,41,42,
   43,44*,45*,47*,48*,50*,
   52*,53*,55,57,60*,61,
   62*,63*,64,65*,67*,68*,
   71*,72*,73*,76,78,80,
   81*, 84,85,87
George Town 2,43*,56,84
Goose Creek 38.
Granville Court House 46

South Carolina (cont'd)

Jacksonborough 78
Pendeton 74
Prince William 39
Rocky Branch 13
Saluda Mills 1
Spatenburgh 81
Waccamaw 29
Wasamtam 87

Tennessee

Gibson Co. 47
Memphis 19
Nashville 44*,86
Warren Co. 51

Texas 2,12,38,77

Anahuac 47
Columbia 16
Columbus 68
Crocketts 34
Galveston 3,37,58,82
Houston 29,51
Kimbles Bend 18
Nacogdoches 42
Port Caddo 11

Vermont 16

Barnet 70
Brandon 16
Ferrisburgh 32

Virginia 7,12,29,46,
   58*,65

Alexandria 21,86
Barboursville 69
Bath Town 61
Berkeley Co. 16
Brook 13
Cabell Co. 6
Culpeper Co. 47
Fairfax 13*,14,39,66
Frederick Co. 11
Fredericksburg 5
Goochland Co. 31,52,60
Hampton 30
Leeds 15
Lyonsburg 10
Madison Co. 41
Makefield 47
Middlesex 23
Mount Sinai 80
Norfolk 11,13,21,22,24,
   32,45,46,69,72,84
Petersburgh 5,18,26
Portsmouth 46
Richmond 7,8,10,11,27*,
   30*,36,44,46,48,54,61,
   67,73,88
Staunton 75
Union 60
Westover 11*
Whuling 15
Williamsburg 4,13,59,67,
   72

99

Washington

Columbia 42

Wisconsin

Berry 2
Dane Co. 2
Iowa Co. 56
Milwaukee 21,38,53
Palmyra 24
Potosi 73
Racine 32
Sugar Castle 27
Turtle 51

Unidentified

Clydeside 48
Newgarden 62
Savinilla 27

CANADA

Charlotte 66
Chippawa 56
Coteau du Lac 46
Grenville's Camp 26
Halifax 19,52,73,82
Hamilton 74
London 25
Montreal 8,19
New Brunswick 47,67
Newfoundland 59
Paris 25
Picton 37
Quebec 6,56
Red River Settlement 78
Rockland 37
Sheffield 34*
Shelburne 10,57,59,71
Sydney 37
Toronto 42,79

WEST INDIES

Bahamas 22,71
Barbados 25,59
Bermuda 56,75
Cuba 58,61,66,68
Demarara 63,83
Grenada 62
Jamaica 2,10,11,15,22,
  39,40,54,84
Martinique 62
St. Bartholomew Is. 49
St. Christopher's 43

WEST INDIES (cont'd)

St. Croix 36,57,80,82
St. Domingo 38,57,85,86
St. Martin 75
St. Thomas 2
Trinidad 44,49

SOUTH AMERICA

Argentine 47
Chile 60
Guyana 12,63
Mexico 5*,21,22,34,87
Peru 60,68

ENGLAND AND WALES

Bedfordshire

Bedford 73

Berkshire

Beckett 63
Hungerford 9
Newbury 36

Brecknockshire

Moor Park 62

Buckinghamshire

High Wycombe 44
Millend Farm 36
Saunderton 65
Wolverton 5

Cambridgeshire

Cambridge 51
Whittlesey 72
Wimblington 35

Cheshire

Altrincham 87
Chester 61,76
Hyde 14

Cornwall

Camborne 37
Launceston 12
Looe 32
Phillack 53

Cumberland

Maryport 69
Wetheral 31
Whitehaven 11,24*,62

Derbyshire

Chesterfield 12
Derby 39
Letchurch Lodge 54
Muggington 29

Devonshire

Barnstaple 71
Crediton 78
Davenport 56
Exeter 32,35,37,75
Holsworthy 23
Little Hampstone 56*
Martinhoe 31
Plymouth 42
Rawleigh 29
St. Thomas Apostle 26
South Brent 19
Tawstock 66
Thorncombe 33
Totnes 27

Dorset

Chideoak 41
Lyme Regis 29
Poole 33,85
Puddletown 81
Weymouth 31
Wyke Regis 43

Durham

Gateshead 75
Sedgefield 77*
Stockton upon Tees 1

Essex

Adwell 83
Colchester 56
Grays 44
Ilford 53
Layton 9,45
Loughton 1
Plaistow 34
Thorpe le Soken 55

Flint

St. Asaph 42

Glamorgan

Newton Nottage 10

Gloucestershire

Alverton 85
Blakeney 84
Bourton on the Water 10, 27
Bristol 8,13,17,18,19,24, 28,29*,33,38,40,42,46, 65,67,68
Buckland 45
Hartpury 61
Minchinhampton 83
Newnham 69
Stoke Bishop 83
Strensham 34
Stroud Water 53
Tewkesbury 51
Uley 50

Hampshire

Alton 32
Eling 77
Gosport 79
Headley Park 56
Midland Cottage 76
Petersfield 60
Portsea 79,82
Titchfield 74

Herefordshire

Bromyard 51
Galway 54
Hereford 58,73
Leominster 62
Ross 68

Hertfordshire

Baldock 84
Hemel Hempstead 74
Hertford 2
Marden 27
Ware 37

Jersey 45,66

Kent

Brenchley 78
Canterbury 16
Chatham 8
Dover 60
Folkestone 16
Frendisbury 52
Greenwich 15,36
Maidstone 1,12
Margate 39
Milton 70
Sevenoaks 74
Sheerness 1
Woolwich 15,28,37,42,73

Lancashire

Butterworth 26
Everton 12

Lancashire (cont'd)

Liverpool 12,13,19,20,27, 45,48,53,55,56,68,73, 85
Manchester 24,72
Salford 67

Leicestershire

Leicester 14
Market Harborough 33
Nailstone 44
Sapcote 72
Saxby 4

Lincolnshire

Boston 3
Clay Bridge 64
Holbeach 5
Lutton
Stamford 29

London & Middlesex
7,19,32,50,59,71,76, 77*,82,85

Adelphi 15
Aldermanbury 36,56
Aldersgate Street 23,85
Austin Friars 5
Barnards Inn 59
Bedford Square 46
Bethnal Green 42
Bloomsbury Square 53
Bow 65
Brentford 53
Brompton 73
Camden Town 28
Cavendish Square 18,29
Charing Cross 12
Cheapside 65
Chelsea 19,85
Clements Inn 78
Colman Street 7
Connaught Square 78
Copthall Court 88
Crutched Friars 44
Dalston 6
Doctors Commons 26
Edmonton 56
Exeter Change 38
Fenchurch Buildings 4
Fetter Lane 59
Finsbury Square 85
Finsbury Terrace 11
Fitzroy Square 13
Fulham 17
Golden Square 60
Gower Street 73
Grays Inn Road 35
Grosvenor Square 26,59
Hackney 28,35
Hammersmith 3,48,71,72
Hampstead 58
Hampton Court 69
Hatton Garden 49
Haymarket 9
Highgate 32,73
Holborn 65

London & Middlesex (cont'd)

Holborn Hill 26
Homerton 71
Houndsditch 55
Hounslow 80
Hoxton 14,44,49
Islington 28,32
Kentish Town 59
Kingsland Road 26
Knightsbridge 5
Leadenhall Street 34
Leicester Square 69
Limehouse 55
Lothbury 8
Manchester Square 21
Mark Lane 34
Middle Temple 38
Minories 54
Moorfields 34
New Broad Street 23
New Road 66,81
New Synagogue 34
Old Broad Street 45
Old Street Road 70
Oxford Street 30,78
Park Lane 17
Pentonville 3
Piccadilly 14
Pimlico 88
Poplar 45,60
Portland Place 3,41
Portland Street 5
Portland Town 5
Portman Square 36,58,84
Red Cross Street 54
Red Lion Square 21
Regent Street 72
Russell Square 54
St. Andrew Undershaft 28
St.Botolph Aldgate 41
St.Botolph Bishopsgate 19
St.Clement Danes 62
St.George Martyr 88
St.James's Street 1
St.Martin in Fields 8,31
St.Marylebone 59,67
St.Pancras 53,60
St.Sepulchre 16
St.Thomas Apostle 70
Shadwell 52
Shoreditch 40
Snow Hill 79
Somers Town 7
Stamford Hill 70
Stanmore 59
Staple Inn 67
Stock Exchange 46
Strand 59,61,66,69,76,81
Throgmorton Street 42
Tottenham Court Road 42, 44,76
Twickenham 37
Upper Thames Street 33
Wapping 5,14,46,61,77
Westminster 15,21,36,82

Monmouth

Dolgelly 42
Llanfihangel Crucorney 83
Newport 20
Pontypool 66
Trelleck Grange 46

Norfolk

Diss 2
Bradfield 2
Norwich 20
Yarmouth 57

Northamptonshire

Northampton 84

Northumberland

Newcastle upon Tyne 40,
83
North Shields 69
Swansfield 32

Nottinghamshire

Clayworth 46
Coddington 41
Nottingham 83

Oxfordshire

Chipping Norton 64
Eynsham 12
Goring 49
Witney 43

Pembrokeshire

Robleston Farm 87

Radnorshire

Newbridge 78

Shropshire

Bridgenorth 75
Brosely 6
Coalbrook Dale 32
Higley 26
Ludlow 51
Shrewsbury 79

Somerset

Bath 13,25,26,27,39,66,
79,86
Bridgwater 35
Cadbury Castle 56
Catcott 24
Crewkerne 9
Flax Bourton 34
Freshford 62
Haselbury Plucknett 64
Huish Champflower 84
Hutton 30
Laverton 38
Minehead 77
Pill 70
Shepton Mallet 68
Taunton 19,51
Weston super Mare 76

Staffordshire

Handsworth 79
Stafford 34
Tipton 37
Tutbury 4
Uttoxeter 2

Suffolk

Bungay 30
Hitcham 69
Lakenheath 15
Lavenham 83
Lowestoft 71,86
Wetherden 41

Surrey

Bermondsey 7,10,23,52
Blackfriars Road 27
Brixton 15
Camberwell 17
Carshalton 4,24
Chelsham 39
Christ Church 17
Clapham 79
Croydon 38,80
Esher 45
Lambeth 14,24,58,78*,82
Lingfield 49,74
Peckham 73
Rotherhithe 9,23,79
Southwark 38,57,85
Stockwell 40
Streatham 31,39
Wandsworth 2,47
Westminster Road 70

Sussex

Brighton 20,68
Buxted 76
Hastings 37
Rye 77
Wadhurst 74

Warwickshire

Birmingham 5,11,22*,33,
46,58,60,64,69,81
Filloughley 22
Halford 81
Kington 83
Rugby 82

Wiltshire

Bishopstone 62
Box 18
Bradford 55
Corsham 42
Devizes 39
Heddington 18
Leend 70
Sutton Veney 47

Worcestershire

Bromsgrove 18,67
Bushley 47
Ditchford 84
Dudley 17,48
Kidderminster 81
Old Swinford 38
Princeton 9
Stourbridge 87

Yorkshire

Beverley 21
Birstal 45
Brotherton 53
Hamborough 74
Leeds 24,80,81
Rotherham 68,80
Saddleworth 45
Scarborough 66
Sheffield 17,31,80
Wakefield 20*
Whitby 71
Woodlands 83

SCOTLAND

Aberdeen 48
Balintrade 14
Berwick on Tweed 25,78
Blairskinnock 43
Dumfries 38
Dundee 29
Edinburgh 5,7,8,25,57,
59,75
Glasgow 43
Greenock 59,86
Inverness 49
Kelso 59
Kirkmabreck 22
Leith 73
Montrose 76
Orkneys 77
Paisley 62
Penningham 22
Roughwood 70
Stirling 74
Uist 49

IRELAND

Bandon 33
Belfast 73
Cork 20
Dalkey 44
Donegal 17
Dublin 34,57
Dungarvan 4
High Park 44
Killala 68
Levington Park 44
Londonderry 1
Maguires Bridge 51
Pontaferry 12
Prosperous 16
Sligo 19,71
Youghall 63

OTHER COUNTRIES

Australia 51,58
Austria 21,73
Cape of Good Hope 19
Cape Verde 54*
China 67
France 22,26,32,46,47*,
  57,71,73*,84,86
Germany 6,61,69,84
Goree 65
Holland 21,76,80
India 10,11,41,58,59,75
Italy 4
Russia 29
Sicily 39
Spain 16
Surinam 24
Switzerland 14,23,56

SHIPS

Agenoria 71
Ajax 26
Andromache 35
Arctic 17
Bolivar 35
Britannica 40
Brook Watson 87
Caesar 87
Carolina 30
Caroline 61
Ceres 78
Charles Bartlett 10,23,
  28,35,53,70,78
City of Glasgow 83
Colonel Thompson 47
Columbia 30
Dick 58
Drake 70
Ellen 71
Europa 70
Factor 16
Goliath 23
Great Western 60
Greenock 16
Harriot 30
Helen 12
Herald 26
Indian 84
Industry 73
Jane 55
Jarrow 55
J.W.Paine 70
Kitty 9
Laurel 59
Leviathan 83
Lily 71
Massasoit 71
Morayshire 45
Nottingham 18
Orinoco 69
Oscela 60
Osprey 33
Pacific 84
Palmyra 8
Panama 12
Penelope 13
President 61
Revenue 26
Roebuck 12
Sampson 45
Sarah Barnes 16
Sarah Sands 35
Sisters 13
Three Brothers 42
Two Friends 70
William and Elizabeth 71
Worcester 15